HANDS ACROSS THE ? SEA

H A N D S
A C R O S S
T H E ? S E A

U.S.–Japan Relations, 1961–1981

Timothy P. Maga

Ohio University Press
Athens

Ohio University Press, Athens, Ohio 45701
© 1997 by Timothy P. Maga
Printed in the United States of America
All rights reserved

Ohio University Press books are printed on acid-free paper ⊗ ™

01 00 99 98 97   5 4 3 2 1

Library of Congress Cataloging-in-Publication Data
Maga, Timothy P., 1952–
    Hands across the sea? : U.S.-Japan relations, 1961–1981 / by
Timothy P. Maga.
        p.   cm.
    Includes bibliographical references (p.   ) and index.
    ISBN 0-8214-1210-8 (alk. paper)
        1. United States—Relations—Japan. 2. Japan—Relations—United
States. 3. United States—Foreign relations—1945–1989. I. Title.
E183.8J3M28   1997
    303.48'273052—dc21
                                                                97-25016
                                                                    CIP

Contents

Preface

HE IS CALLED *henna gaijin* (strange foreigner), but this 1990s immigrant to Japan welcomes the label. Speaking flawless Japanese, he has become a folk hero and overnight fascination to much of his adopted nation. He wears kimono at home, prefers traditional Japanese cooking, and is in love with the beauty and gentleness of Japanese culture. Lecturing the government about its unfortunate attraction to corruption, international bullying, and selfishness, this young man, known simply as Mizkoff, has dedicated his life to *nippon no kokoro* (the search for the Japanese spirit).

A creation of cartoonist Michio Hashimoto and editor Takashi Nagasaki at Big Comic Original Corporation, Mizkoff is a comic-book character. In contrast to the American literary scene, "Mizkoff" is a compliment to political commentary rather than an insult. The comic book plays a more important and respected role in Japanese life than in the United States. Mizkoff is the ultimate Japanologist, and Japan lost its soul to him during the heyday of the Japanese "economic miracle" of the 1960s and 1970s. From the tea ceremony to family values, the "real Japan," he believes, was sacrificed on an altar of greed and shameless ambition. From his two dozen or so pages every month, Mizkoff reminds his millions of readers that Japan has surrendered too much of its quiet culture to dreams of superpower wealth and influence. Growing unemployment and declining GNP or not, no one, he concludes, should bemoan the recent passing of Japan's mighty "bubble economy." Perhaps now, as the country struggles into the twenty-first century, Japan can recapture its honorable, peaceful past.

As a foreign observer and comic-book legend, Mizkoff is the perfect social commentator in a society that often views such analyses with suspicion. Although he glamorizes and waxes poetic about the beauty of "real" Japanese life, Mizkoff implies that the economic successes of Japanese governments, ranging from Hayato Ikeda in the early 1960s through Masayoshi Ohira in the late 1970s, did more harm than good. And many believe him. Since much of Japan's success during the critical twenty-year period of the sixties and seventies was intimately connected to the U.S.-Japan trade relationship, that relationship is held suspect here as well.

In the mid-1990s, the debate over opening the Japanese market to U.S. economic inroads grew as intense as the argument in the sixties and seventies to keep it closed. There would have been no time, space, or tolerance for Mizkoff nostalgia and soul-searching during the boom years of the 1960s and 1970s. Dreams of superpower status were in; reflections on culture were not. Between 1961 and 1981, the economic roles of Japan and the United States reversed. Whereas the United States entered the 1960s as the world's most unassailable economic and military power, it would face military defeat in the Asian Third World and a myriad of economic difficulties in fewer than twenty years. In many respects, especially in the Pacific itself, Japan soon filled America's superpower void. Although it reached economic superpower status during this period, Japan struggled over what that meant. To some Japanese governments, it meant an aggressive posture against Washington's economic demands, as well as a display of new political self-determination, such as in the debate over the future of Okinawa and the Ryukyu Islands. To other Japanese governments, superpower status meant caution. The alternative might mean American revenge; that is, the loss of Japan's great influence in the U.S. consumer economy and/or the end of its treaty-guaranteed defense by the U.S. military. Indeed, the very nature of the post–World War II U.S.-Japan military alliance continued to be questioned, particularly in the face of America's stumbling in Vietnam.

At the same time, Washington politicians learned to deal with the "New Japan." It was a trying experience, and America's struggling Japan policy symbolized it. In a speech reminiscent of John Kennedy's call for a New Frontier of unlimited U.S. power, commitment, and "vigor," Prime Minister Ikeda coined the term *New Japan* in early 1961. Through boundless energy and determination, Japan, Ikeda promised, would be a great world power by 1970. What that might mean to the U.S.-Japan relationship was unclear to Ikeda at the time. It was even more unclear to Washington.

In the 1960s, Japan was "Defeated Japan" to the John Kennedy and Lyndon Johnson administrations; that is, yesterday's hated enemy. Both Kennedy and Johnson could claim some interest and even expertise in the field of U.S.-Japan relations, but they rarely viewed Japan beyond its military worth to the Cold War. If they did, they were often mistaken in their assumptions. Cultural misunderstanding would trouble the Tokyo-Washington relationship throughout the Vietnam War years.

Reflective by nature, Jimmy Carter would be the first U.S. president to consider Japan's new importance, both to the world economy and in the light of America's new struggles within it. Besieged by pressing foreign-policy crises and a growing conservative backlash at home, Carter continued the intricate "fence mending" detente policy with Japan begun by a man he denounced in public speeches, Henry Kissinger, the secretary of state for Presidents Richard Nixon and Gerald Ford. With Kissinger's guidance, Nixon and Ford had attempted to defuse years of U.S.-Japan economic and defense policy tensions through high-profile negotiations. Their successes varied widely, and their primary interests also remained wedded to larger Cold War concerns. Calling for "new directions," Carter tried to "make a difference" in the realm of more innovative and cooperative policies that might benefit the U.S., Japan, international energy policy, and human rights. Nevertheless, the general effort to construct and enforce a working post-Vietnam foreign policy, coupled with his own fight for political survival, kept Carter away from seeing "new directions" become new policy.

By the late 1970s, many Americans, including the president of the United States, recognized that U.S. power now had limits. Whereas the Japanese toyed with the new possibility of their unlimited economic reach, Americans contemplated the meaning of Vietnam and how their nation should proceed. Without question, by 1981 the United States and Japan had witnessed a sea change in their view of each other's value and contribution to the global community. There could be no turning back, although the United States would welcome a little nostalgia through the election of Ronald Reagan. The new president preferred expressions of America's Cold War greatness to Carter's ideas of American goodness. But, even in his 1980 campaign, the tough-talking Reagan did not deny or challenge the changes in the world economy and the new influence of Japan. Japan would not experience similar conflicts of purpose and direction until the 1990s and the unforeseen collapse of the "bubble economy." The Mizkoff phenomenon even came to represent that national confusion.

In a different time, the reversal of the fortunes of the United States and Japan, and the resulting high tension because of it, might have sparked a horrible war. It is a testament to Tokyo and Washington's commitment to a continuing dialogue that war, and even the collapse of diplomatic relations, was easily avoided during the 1960s and 1970s. This book analyzes this peaceful development, the struggle to maintain it, and what proper, workable U.S.-Japan relations meant to two very different and clashing cultures.

Hands across the Sea? is the product of primary research efforts, ranging from work in presidential libraries across the United States to oral interviews with former policymakers on both sides of the Pacific. I hope that the many archivists and colleagues who assisted in this project will accept my general thanks. I was especially honored by the time and dedication offered by Edmund Muskie, former secretary of state and senator, Kiichi Miyazawa, former finance minister, foreign minister, and prime minister, and Walt Rostow, former National Security Council adviser and veteran diplomat. Their comments were most valuable. I would also like to thank the center of my universe, my wife, Patsy, for her continuing patience and aid in yet another book project. And a warm debt of gratitude is offered to Mark McGuire, formerly of Emory University, for his brilliant, analytical mind, good humor, and fine support of this project.

Tim Maga
Bradley University

HANDS
ACROSS
THE ? SEA

1

Partners in Misunderstanding

The New Frontier Meets the New Japan, 1961–1963

The people of Japan are not interested in being sold to the highest bidder. On the contrary, if our aid is given on the assumption that this will buy us friends, if they feel they are being made pawns in the Cold War, if they regard the United States only as a military guardian, a giver of goods or a lender of cash, then no amount of economic aid will strengthen our cause in that area.

Instead, we must return to the generous spirit; stress our positive interest in and moral responsibility for relieving misery and poverty; and acknowledge to ourselves and to the world that communism or no communism, we cannot be an island unto ourselves. We want Japan and America, with common ties and common concerns, to consider each other what they really are: partners in the world community.[1]

SENATOR John F. Kennedy first used the words quoted above in a speech to a sympathetic crowd of Japanese-American supporters in Honolulu during his 1958 lobbying for Hawaii statehood. He would use the speech again during the 1960 presidential race and whenever else it appeared appropriate. Linked to a sincere apology for the internment of Japanese Americans during World War II, Kennedy's speech also endeared him to Tokyo. To young Japanese politicians eager for power, such as Kiichi Miyazawa, Masayoshi Ohira, and even the twenty-year-old Toshiki Kaifu, Kennedy represented youthful good sense and "truly, America's first postwar leader."[2] He welcomed the ambitions of the developing world, they believed, and his peculiarly U.S. interest in Cold War victory could be maneuvered to benefit "Japanese destiny." The elder deans of the Liberal Democratic Party (LDP), Japan's ruling political machine, soon agreed. Marking the end of the post-Occupation period in American-Japanese relations, President John Kennedy's "New Frontier" policies and Prime Minister Hayato Ikeda's "New Japan" policies would also establish the modern Tokyo-Washington dialogue.

Symbolized by wide cultural differences, disagreements over anti-communist commitments, the place of conventional and nuclear forces within those commitments, and the proper direction of the world economy, U.S.-Japanese relations in the 1960s and 1970s might have been labeled miserable and unfortunate. Yet, both Japanese and American politicians and businessmen, influenced by the ugly memory of World War II and challenged by the fast-moving global political-economic changes of the time, usually described their relations as positive and healthy. By the end of the Cold War, the political communities on both sides of the Pacific wondered if this unique, enduring relationship had been worth the trouble. America's new post–Cold War politicians especially proved the point.

"The Cold War is over, and Japan won. There can be no disputing this truth," declared Paul Tsongas, the former senator, to a February 1992 outdoor rally of shivering New Hampshire business students. Preoccupied with ideologically confronting the Soviet Union since the end of World War II, America had ignored "dollar diplomacy," Tsongas explained, and this had led to Japan's 1960s and 1970s economic coup over U.S. business acumen at home and abroad. Speaking at New Hampshire's Daniel Webster College, Tsongas, for a short time the Democratic Party frontrunner in the early primaries for the 1992 presidential campaign, said that it was the business graduates' responsibility to rescue their country from its status of vassal state to Japan. Although decrying "Japan bashing," the former Massachusetts senator insisted that the U.S. government's support for still-competitive industries, and for worker-retraining programs in dying industries, was more productive than 1920s-style protectionism. Tsongas noted that the fellow Massachusetts politician who lured him into public life, John Kennedy, would have "asked us to sacrifice and learn to compete." Echoing Kennedy's 1960 campaign theme, Tsongas asked his audience to avoid simple answers to complex problems, and together innovative Americans would make their country "great again."[3]

Tsongas, "the thinking voter's candidate," went on to win the primary in New Hampshire. Suffering badly from the early-1990s recession, New Hampshire would otherwise have been seeking the fast, simple remedies that Tsongas scorned. The appeal to Kennedyesque intellectualism and reason aided his efforts, suggesting that the charismatic Cape Cod–born Irish American had been reincarnated in this shy, Lowell-born Greek American. It also suggested that Kennedy had been somehow above the economic foreign-policy decisions of the early 1960s. Seeing the voter appeal of both the "Japan issue" and John Kennedy comparisons, Bill Clinton, another seeker of the Democratic Party nomination, soon adopted Tsongas-like tactics as his own, going on to head the Democratic Party ticket and win the 1992 general election. Even Clinton's Republican opponent, President George Bush, who early in the 1992 campaign had labeled both Clinton and Tsongas "dangerous disruptions" in American-Japanese relations, eventually promised "to do something about the Japan thing. Just like JFK would have done."[4]

Using the exaggerated image of a martyred president to benefit a political career is nothing new in U.S. politics. The resulting distortion of the historical record is nothing new either. In this case, the exaggerations were wild, for Kennedy had gone out of his way to open the American market to Japanese penetration. He took pride in the endeavor, despised any gesture that inhibited Japanese economic inroads, and involved himself in any effort to make Japanese entry easier in the future.

Expounding on the comments he had made in 1958 in Hawaii, the young president, three years later, proclaimed the key to healthy U.S.-Japanese relations involved a policy of American generosity toward Japan's export-economy dreams.[5] That policy would also assure U.S. defense interests in the Pacific, he said, thereby linking trade policy and raw Cold War priorities for the next twenty years.

Whereas Tsongas, Clinton, Bush, and the 1990s political call to "make America great again"—picking up on Kennedy's campaign logo—suggested urgent necessity, for Kennedy the words had been more slogan than anything else. In 1960, the U.S. military stood undefeated in war, enjoying dozens of undisputed basing privileges around the world. The phrase "sound as a dollar" did not produce snickering, and the American consumer's wage and buying power outpaced those in all other nations. Promising victory in the Cold War, and man on the moon by 1970, Kennedy vowed to maintain a "can-do" spirit of activism in his administration.[6]

Everything was possible with determination and vigor. Peace Corps volunteers could break down the appeal of communism, and destroy the 1950s "Ugly American" image in villages across the Third World. U.S. Special Forces could turn the guerrilla tactics of communist insurgents against those same insurgents, promising a new expertise in extinguishing brush-fire wars. Endless analytical reports, midnight debates, and intellectual jousting between White House, cabinet, and staff would result in the finest, most enforceable policies since the brain-trust days of Franklin Roosevelt's early New Deal. All of this, wedded to a strict adherence to executive privilege, promised a new definition in effective government. It also represented the youthful enthusiasm of the New Frontier and a liberal dose of arrogance.[7] Largely because of this approach, and the high ambitions associated with it, New Frontier triumphs remained frustratingly elusive.[8]

Sweeping away the "tired, old ideas" of the Eisenhower administration was "the first step" in establishing the new era of "can-do" activism. The political beauty of Kennedy's announced "first step" policies was that he did not have to commit himself beyond the changing of certain political directions. Championing a policy to fruition was not required. Hence, he announced in early 1961 that "Republican protectionism" would be eliminated in the "first step" to meet the economic expansionist plans of the "New Japan."[9] The announcement produced more questions than answers, and it soon became apparent to Kennedy that protectionism, as well as hatred for both "Old" and "New" Japan, transcended party lines.

As he did in most matters of policymaking, on Japan policy Kennedy surrounded himself with "the brightest and the best." His

Japanese-studies team included Harvard University's renowned Japan specialist Edwin O. Reischauer, as ambassador to Japan, and Boston University's up-and-coming younger rival to Reischauer's full access to the Kennedy Oval Office, the special assistant to the undersecretary of state, James Thomson. Although Reischauer and Thomson would fire off endless advisory and "educational" memos on Japanese life and letters to Kennedy, the president reserved the right to align his Japan decisions with stronger Cold War and domestic political considerations. This approach kept Japan on the fringes of the great U.S. versus USSR confrontation; however, Kennedy was troubled by the fact that the fringe could also determine the outcome of that confrontation.[10] It was a curious dilemma. Hence, he insisted on an enormous amount of data from his experts on Japanese goals and ambitions. Yet, there is little evidence to suggest that he ever attempted to understand those same, complex Japanese policies, much less fully appreciate their significance. Kennedy's bottom line, thanks to his campaign and inaugural promises, always stressed Cold War victory. Although a healthy Japan policy was required to reach that goal, it did not mean that the president had to answer Japanese demands upon him. Or did it?

Within Kennedy's assessment of Japan (political conditions, defense outlook, and economic plans), there was a considerable amount of knowledge and a considerable amount of misunderstanding. Given the very different cultures involved, this situation was not unusual. But, the stakes were high, and the political survival of his presidency, Kennedy believed, hinged on new, innovative ways to win the Cold War, and quickly. The clock was ticking. Brilliant analytical mind or not, Kennedy shared the "tired, old" Eisenhower's doubts that Japan was a strong ally in the anti-communist crusade.

From the American point of view, Japan's postwar anti-communism was most confusing. Except for a brief interval in 1947, Japan's postwar governments had been conservative ones since the end of World War II. Any changes in Japanese administration generally occurred when a prime minister lost the support of the majority of his own party, rather than through action by the opposition. The conservative anti-communists had maintained a broad base of popular support, but were particularly strong among businessmen and in the rural areas. This conservative outlook, James Thomson once explained to Kennedy, was entirely due to the U.S. military occupation of Japan from 1945 to 1952. The Douglas MacArthur–led Occupation government had sponsored land-reform measures that led to stability in agricultural policy, winning the conservative allegiance of Japanese farmers. Other reforms stressing government-business cooperation, industrialization, even (in U.S. terms) pre–Progressive Era approaches to business, and the elimination of medieval traditions in business practice also took root in the Occupation period. The political impact of this revolution, and in both urban and rural Japan, meant consistent two-thirds votes for coalitions of conservative candidates throughout the 1950s. In 1955, the LDP was formed when rival factions within socialist and conservative groupings united. When Kennedy took power, the LDP held 296 of 467 seats in the Lower House of the Japanese Diet and 142 of 250 seats in the Upper House. Promising a closer economic relationship with the United States in the late 1950s, the LDP issued the usual pro-U.S., anti-communist statements of an American ally in that era. On the other hand, the key to continuing these statements now depended on the creation of a new U.S.-Japan economic relationship.[11]

Despite his campaign denunciations of the aging "Eisenhower crowd," and despite his inner circle of Japan watchers, Kennedy's first presidential briefing on the LDP and U.S.-Japan relations came from John Foster Dulles. As an elderly, arch–cold warrior, whom Kennedy had criticized for "not understanding the ambitions of the Third World," Dulles was an unlikely character to advise the new Kennedy White House on Japan matters. But, the young president requested the meeting, and he welcomed the wisdom of this former career diplomat.

Dulles, the secretary of state throughout most of Dwight Eisenhower's two terms in the White House, believed the LDP tempered its solid support for the U.S.-led view of global anti-communism for "selfish" domestic reasons. Those "selfish" reasons included lingering animosities from World War II, concern over the purpose of forty thousand U.S. troops still stationed in Japan, an especially strong disgust over the continuing U.S. military occupation of the Ryukyu Islands, and frustration with the reckless political rhetoric of U.S.

politicians who threatened the use of nuclear force in the U.S.-USSR confrontation.

Anti-U.S. sentiment was not unheard of in the Free World, and Dulles advised the incoming Kennedy administration to cater to the conservative business tastes of Japan's ruling elite. That meant "pointing Japan towards Southeast Asia." Dulles, who had helped negotiate the peace between Japan and the United States after World War II, believed that Japan's business community was dreaming, and wildly, when it planned for an export economy of automobiles and electronic products to the U.S. consumer market. At best, Dulles thought, the American consumer would take many years to accept any significant product from yesterday's hated enemy. Realistically, if Japan desired any profit from an export economy, it should be directed toward the former French colonies of Southeast Asia and other developing nations in the Pacific region. The profit would be meager, he predicted, because many of these countries had a poor economic infrastructure and required development assistance themselves. Most of them had also been brutally occupied by the Japanese Imperial Army during World War II, and had even less reason to be cooperative with Japanese planners than they had with the Americans. Consequently, Dulles advised Kennedy to ignore Japan's complaints over economics, political matters, military priorities, or any issue of U.S.-Japan relations. Japan's opinion lacked international clout, he said, and an ambitious new presidential administration should not be influenced by it.

Unimportant or not, Japan still required "guidance," Dulles noted. Maintaining U.S. military basing privileges across Japan—and without Tokyo's harassment—represented, to Dulles, the heart of Washington's Japan connection. An effective policy that assured a quiet, cooperative Japan would be "up to the new White House." According to Dulles, Japan was a "stationary aircraft carrier" on the Pacific front of the Cold War. Its strategic role in any future battle with the Soviets or the Chinese was obvious. He therefore had little use for any Japanese rapprochement with communist China or the Soviet Union. He also thought the Japanese would never attempt a full rapprochement, if America stood firm against them. Any threat on the part of the Japanese to conclude sweeping trade agreements with communist China or the Soviet Union, Dulles advised, would be "politically motivated and unlikely to succeed." The incompatibility of the communist world and capitalist Japan, he reasoned, made any Japanese economic initiative toward the communists a difficult prospect. If U.S. opposition alone proved inadequate, certainly a coalition of Free World allies would humble Japan into accepting a strict embargo on Chinese or Soviet deals.[12]

Like Japan itself, Dulles was a puzzle to Kennedy. He "has an amazing knack," the president told Thomson, "of doing the wrong thing the right way."[13] On the one hand, Kennedy preferred to give the benefit of the doubt to Japan, regarding Dulles's advice symbolic of the type of callous, "Ugly American" policy that the entire developing world had come to reject. Yet, Dulles's Cold War commitment remained a matter of great respect within Kennedy's inner circle, whether they despised his denigration of Third World ambitions or not. Kennedy also believed that Japan had the clout and the economic might to woo the Chinese or the Soviets into a special trade agreement. The presence of U.S. troops would not halt it, and anti-Americanism would not go away because Japanese politics was becoming more conservative. Although he prided himself in recognizing the perils of allied solidarity in global anti-communism, Kennedy still had little use for important allies, such as Japan, who sought to abandon U.S. guidance in the Cold War.[14] In contrast to Dulles, Kennedy took anti-American opinion in the developing world seriously, always wondering if the next step would then be pro-communist behavior. The trick was translating at least some of these views and concerns into a working policy. Dulles was dead right on at least one point. An innovative Japan policy was truly "up to the new White House."

When Kennedy took office, both he and his Japan advisers painted Japan as a portrait of confusion, waffling between wild-eyed economic dreams and anti-American outbursts. It was an unkind portrait, still influenced by a vision of wartorn Japan. In reality, the Japanese government knew exactly what it was doing, planned accordingly, and welcomed a vigorous, determined new "man of the sixties" as their national leader, Hayato Ikeda. Nicknamed the "JFK of Japan" by the *Washington Post*, Ikeda quipped that JFK was the "Ikeda of America." During his whirlwind years as prime minister, Ikeda faced, or faced down depending on the point-of-view, two presidents of similar determination and vigor (JFK and LBJ). Also surrounding himself with "the brightest and the best," Ikeda, like Kennedy, used 1970 as a target date for the final accomplishment of great tasks. "My country shall rise to the call of world power by then," he predicted, "and by any means necessary."[15]

Ikeda's "any means necessary" comment troubled Kennedy, but the U.S. president was eager to move forward with a new American-Japan relationship.[16] Indeed, Ikeda would be the first foreign leader to visit the White House following the Kennedy inaugural, and it was not a social call. Insisting that all protectionist legislation against Japanese goods would be lifted shortly, Kennedy's generosity toward Japan's interest in penetrating the American market served as the foundation for that new relationship.

Ikeda's LDP government was only six months old when Kennedy took the oath of office. Kiichi Miyazawa, a member of the House of Councillors and future foreign minister and prime minister, wrote Ikeda's "announcement of a grand vision for the 1960s," the speech that served as his American-like inaugural address. The Ikeda announcement stressed a plan to double Japan's national income by 1970 and through a policy of exports to the United States. Totaling $3 billion per year by 1969, these exports would force the United States to rethink its continued vision of world economic dominance and to accept, instead, an economic partnership with Japan.

In the early 1960s, Miyazawa's concerns were reminiscent of the U.S. Progressive economist and politician Brooks Adams. At the turn of the century, when the United States opposed the strong economic position of Great Britain, Adams had predicted "stagnation and collapse" would result if a market for American exports were not found. British economic dominance equalled the worst kind of "selfishness." Miyazawa, in turn, assaulted the "economic selfishness" of U.S. policy.[17]

Ikeda and Miyazawa had reason to express themselves in strong terms. Japan's rate of economic growth in the postwar years had been phenomenal, averaging more than 9 percent a year in real terms. It ranked fourth in the world in production of crude steel (surpassing Britain), fourth in electric energy production, first in shipbuilding and in fishing, and fifth as a maritime nation. It even led the world as an exporter of textile products. And the rate of savings in Japan (about 30 percent of its GNP) was also the highest in the world. The economic boom reached such proportions by January 1961 that the Japanese government was required to initiate measures to dampen it in order to relieve strains in the economy. In spite of Ikeda's measures, industrial production still rose 22 percent, reaching a peak nearly double the 1958 level and to a level 32 percent higher than in 1955. Employment increased and unemployment declined, the Tokyo press hailing Japan as the Pacific's new "industrial giant."[18]

Although an amazingly fast-moving success story, Japanese economic development still paled in contrast to American economic might. Its $48 billion GNP might have been impressive, but the Japanese economy was still rated by the United Nations at one-tenth the size of that of the United States. Ikeda planned to double that GNP by 1970, but catering to the U.S. consumer remained the only key to success. The 1950s record of U.S.-Japan trade pointed the way.

By 1961, the United States supplied more than 35 percent of Japan's imports and purchased almost 25 percent of Japan's exports. Japan ranked second only to Canada as a market for United States exports, and from 1957 to 1961, America had sold the Japanese $117 billion more merchandise than it had imported from them. When Kennedy took office, U.S. exports to Japan exceeded $1.7 billion with imports from Japan valued at about $1 billion. When Reischauer presented Kennedy with these figures, the president was amazed. Despite having served on the U.S. Senate Subcommittee for Asian/Pacific Relations for several years, he had no idea Japan's "economic forecast was so forward looking." The U.S.-Japan trade relationship was "beneficial," he concluded, "both to the U.S. economy and balance of payments generally and to a number of important U.S. industries."[19]

These "benefits" would not come easy. While refusing to endorse the Miyazawa thesis of impending Japanese economic stagnation, Kennedy did see dangers in the lack of a focused Japanese export policy. One of his strongest concerns remained, like Dulles's, in the area of allied solidarity against communist China and other communist nations. With the timetable for Cold War victory set, Kennedy found most annoying the growing Japanese trade relationship with communist bloc countries. Japan's purchases from the Sino-Soviet nations increased from $125 million in 1960 to $214 million in 1961, a rise of 71 percent. Japanese exports to those same countries also increased from $73 million to $102 million, a rise of 39 percent. Japan's trade with the Soviet Union dominated the commercial ties to the communists, but all of the bloc countries enjoyed higher levels of trade with Japan in the opening weeks of the Ikeda government alone.[20]

In total, the Japan–communist bloc trade relationship amounted to only 3 percent of Tokyo's entire international trade network. Ikeda made it clear to Kennedy that this rising trend would never include "strategic materials" to the communists; however, that was not good enough for the American president.[21] The Japanese prime minister struck a blow for Japanese "sovereignty" with his bold, new approach, but the 3 percent relationship had the potential of derailing the much larger trade relationship Ikeda desired with the United States. Allied "nonrecognition" of China was "nonnegotiable," Kennedy quipped, and ties with other, older communist nations would be viewed with suspicion unless those ties were "influenced" by the White House.[22]

Since 1949, and the success of the communist revolution in China, U.S. presidents had insisted on allied nonrecognition of the world's largest nation. This demand was easier said than done. Led by Australian Prime Minister Robert Menzies, America's Asian/Pacific allies were already snubbing the White House demand when Kennedy took office. It was a mild affair. Menzies' government approved educational exchange programs with China as well as visits by labor activists and interested businessmen. The Australians were reluctant to dispatch trade delegations to the United States, thereby angering Washington. But, Menzies made great political mileage at home over sidestepping nonrecognition, and even rescued his long-lasting conservative government through this "standing-up to the Americans" issue. Ikeda happily followed Menzies' lead, but wanted real economic results in addition to the domestic political benefits.[23]

To Kennedy, this was nothing less than a Pacific revolution. From the Wisconsin primary in April 1960 to a speech before the Foreign Policy Association in New York during the general election, Kennedy had promised to keep the allies in line on the issue of China nonrecognition. It was an important part of winning the Cold War, and no nation, he implied, should be permitted to stand in the way of that destiny. China, he said, "symbolized" the evil of communism more than any other country. Its regime, he believed, always at odds with the Soviets over the proper path to successful communism, seemed likely to totter and collapse if isolated by the world community.[24] This was wishful thinking more than policy.

In the Soviet Union and its satellites, the issues were more complex. The Soviets' industrial-based communism appeared more secure than China's agrarian-based communism. Not only was the Communist Party well-established and in charge of Soviet economic development, but Kennedy's key adviser on Soviet affairs, Dr. Walt Rostow, claimed that the Soviets had the capability to overtake U.S. industrial output, flourish as a society, and make a mockery of U.S. capitalism. Rostow had published on the topic as a professor at MIT. Kennedy admired his work and had brought him onto his "brightest and best" team largely because of his ability to analyze Soviet-related economic matters. In any event, Kennedy reasoned, the Soviets certainly did not need any economic help from America's allies to achieve their domestic goals.[25] Stopping those allies was another matter.

Should opening the U.S. market to full Japanese economic penetration be contingent upon the American right to guide Japan on the non-recognition issue and all other communist-relations issues? Kennedy considered a positive answer to the question; however, the Third World reaction might be devastating. For years, Kennedy railed against the Eisenhower administration's lack of concern over the everyday needs of Third World residents. Winning the Cold War, he had stressed, depended on their allegiance. The United States needed to accent its democratic tradition on the march to Cold War victory, he said. It was not enough to be against communism. America had to be "for" something.[26]

These types of comments and concerns won Kennedy praise from foreign-policy analysts and even votes from the general electorate. Bullying Japan, therefore, might even invite domestic political opposition. Resurrecting World War II–founded animosities through any anti-Japan measure was also intellectually distasteful to Kennedy, and the wrong direction for his administration.

As was always the case in the Kennedy White House, a variety of policy options were analyzed, discussed, and examined again. Kennedy once admitted that he enjoyed the discovery of many options and variables, but hated making policy from them. His Japan policy symbolized this dilemma. As early as April 1961, Kennedy thought he had found an answer to winning Japan's full allegiance in the American-led cause of Cold War victory. From China nonrecognition to U.S.-Japan trade matters to further security for the large U.S. military presence in Japan, Kennedy's answer came in the form of a proposed new United Nations–styled international organization for the Asian/Pacific region. To be called the New Pacific Community, this organization, headquartered in Australia, was expected to direct Asian/Pacific economic development for non-communist nations and do it more efficiently than any existing international arrangements. Although presented to the world as an innovative, coordinated, and independently-run organization especially concerned with infrastructure development, the New Pacific Community would be quietly financed and directed through American efforts. It would have the large benefit of redirecting Asian/Pacific investment, totally isolating communist nations such as China and North Korea, and moving the United States closer to its 1970 goal of Cold War victory.[27]

Secretary of State Dean Rusk, who had spent several years in the State Department as a senior policymaker in Far Eastern affairs, helped construct this proposal. He took a personal interest in it. Although concerned that some might perceive the New Pacific Community to be an "American front organization," Rusk believed that "Ugly American" complaints would be overshadowed by economic success. In the case of the Japanese, the Ikeda government would be permitted to penetrate the American market as it saw fit. But the United States would not be Japan's only salvation. The New Pacific Community could manufacture a variety of lucrative trade relationships over the years with other Pacific Rim member nations.

To Rusk, the most pleasant benefits of the New Pacific Community ranged from silencing Australian critics (thanks to their country's headquarters role in the organization) to the fall of communist China. Although details of its precise responsibilities were sketchy in 1961, the proposed organization was warmly endorsed by Kennedy. He informed both Ikeda and Menzies personally about the plan, urging them to work with his administration in building the New Pacific Community. Ikeda's reaction was disbelief. The United States was avoiding the "reality" of U.S.-Japan relations, he noted, in its pursuit of this cleverly disguised effort to mask American Cold War objectives in the Pacific. Menzies was more critical.[28]

Truly seeing the anti-American issue as a means to remain in power, Menzies attacked the Rusk-Kennedy proposal as raw imperialism and an insult to Australian sovereignty. Australia, he said, would never host an American imperial policy on its soil. In private conversations with Kennedy as the months went by, Menzies would apologize for his tenor and tone, noting that he wished he had the polite, gentlemanly manners of a Hayato Ikeda. As the Pacific's most significant democracy after the United States, Australia, Menzies stressed, would remain host to U.S. military bases and support the general thrust of American anti-communism.[29] It would not become a junior partner to the New Pacific Community plan. Although always under assault by a resurgent Labor Party, the conservative Menzies remained in power and became one of the longest-reigning prime ministers in Australian history.

Snubbed by the two Pacific leaders he wanted most to impress, Kennedy refused to give up on the New Pacific Community proposal throughout his administration. His father, Kennedy once joked with Ikeda, taught him "never to shrink in the face of adversity."[30] Whenever U.S.-Japan relations became bogged down over matters of military priority or trade policy, Kennedy would always remind Ikeda that a better arena for ironing out differences had already been proposed. Ikeda never reversed his position, and the New Pacific Community became a primary example of one of Kennedy's self-proclaimed "noble ideas" that never became policy.

Whereas Kennedy saw economic generosity as a lever to keep Japan a happy participant in American-led efforts to win the Cold War, Ikeda saw defense-related matters as a means to assure that generosity. It was a delicate game to Ikeda, whereas Kennedy was never sure if a game was being played at all. When Kennedy took office, the American-Japan defense relationship was supposed to have been solved, if not written in stone. In 1960, the U.S. and Japanese governments signed the Treaty of Mutual Cooperation and Security. The treaty provided for the stationing of U.S. troops in Japan in order to maintain security "in" Japan as well as the Asian/Pacific neighborhood. Yet, the issue of U.S.-provided security "in" or "around" Japan remained interpretive.[31]

According to article 9 of the 1947 Japanese constitution, "land, sea, and air forces as well as other war potential, will never be maintained." As early as 1950, during the dark days of the Korean War, this position had been modified by the establishment of the National Police Reserve. Even before the end of the Occupation in 1952, steps had been taken to create a self-defense force out of the National Police Reserve. A post-Occupation National Defense Agency was established to accomplish the task, and a unanimous 1959 decision of the Japanese supreme court confirmed that article 9 did not negate Japan's right to defend itself. Nevertheless, the United States would continue to carry the brunt of the security obligation, for other sections of the Japanese constitution, combined with a postwar attraction to pacifism, made it legally and politically impossible to finance the creation of an effective national defense infrastructure.

Both the far Right and far Left in Japan's political spectrum had opposed the 1960 defense treaty with the Americans. Anti-treaty demonstrations, nicknamed "demos" by the Japanese, were common in front of U.S. military bases and in city centers during the treaty-ratification process. But even the Japanese wondered if these demonstrations were more rooted in lingering World War II animosities than anything else. Generally, the Japanese political community welcomed the idea of an American-provided defense guaranteed by treaty. This development assured that the constitution would not have to be modified again to cover defense obligations, and, more to the point, government revenues could be better used to assist business in the effort to improve upon the export economy.[32]

To Ikeda's friend Kiichi Miyazawa, the treaty was a godsend. As the prime minister's chief financial adviser and the press-dubbed "guiding force" in Japanese economic affairs, Miyazawa welcomed the new era of American-Japanese relations. Combined with the election of John Kennedy, the treaty represented great possibilities to Miyazawa. Japan was now free to concentrate fully on the building of a "miracle economy." America suddenly represented opportunity rather than obstruction to Japanese goals. While Kennedy hoped to maneuver Japan into the New Pacific Community and other matters of Cold

War solidarity, Miyazawa hoped to maneuver the United States into Japan's own economic ambitions. It would be a test of skill, and it is this opportunity that most appealed to Miyazawa.[33]

Although forty-two years old, or one year younger than Kennedy when the latter entered the White House, Miyazawa had already spent nearly twenty years working on Japanese finance policy. Fluent in English, he often acted as interpreter for Ikeda, a former finance minister himself, and Miyazawa's mentor. Forever specializing in U.S.-Japan trade relations, Miyazawa believed in a get-tough policy toward Washington. As deputy chief of the LDP's Finance Division, Miyazawa also assured his colleagues that the Americans would respect only a determined Japan in the 1960s. Washington's political/economic backlashes against Tokyo would, he said, be few. Home defense issues, the future of the Ryukyus, and opposition to U.S. nuclear policy must be separated from Japanese export-policy planning, he stressed, or that planning, and the nation's economic future, would be seriously harmed.[34] Nevertheless, Miyazawa was not averse to a little gamesmanship, if necessary, over these issues in order to achieve that successful export policy. Stressing the same type of get-tough policy thirty years later, Miyazawa used his expertise in U.S. trade relations to win the prime ministership of Japan for the LDP.

Miyazawa's grandfather, Heikichi Ogawa, a minister of justice in the 1920s, and his father, Yutaka Miyazawa, a six-term member of the Diet, were both known for a certain belligerent political style. Kiichi Miyazawa, convinced that Japan needed to break away from the MacArthur era, from a reconstructionist mentality, and from submission to U.S. whims, believed that Japan could truly exert its independent postwar status by economic means. A belligerent stance was overdue. The 1960 Tokyo "demos" suggested to Miyazawa that Japan was an "irresponsible ally." The postwar Japanese interest in pacifism was unrealistic, given the proximity of the Soviet Union and the existence of U.S. bases in Japan. The Americans had little respect for anti-treaty sentiment, said Miyazawa. An aggressive economic policy, stressing exports to the United States, would win America's respect, as well as great monetary reward for Japan.

Although Ikeda welcomed Miyazawa-style pressures on the Americans, he also worried that Japanese complaints about Kennedy's attraction to "massive retaliation" (in other words, nuclear combined with conventional-force solutions to Cold War dilemmas) might derail economic inroads at the Washington end.[35] In a move that confused the Japanese, but was meant to calm American doubts about a friendly Japan, Ikeda announced to the Diet that he even preferred "new eating habits for a New Japan"; i.e., meat over fish and wheat over rice. Ostensibly, a taller, huskier generation, based on an American superman or New Frontiersman model, would result from this new regimen. This was labeled "good for Japan." An outraged Japanese public, fearful of Ikeda's culture-killing ambitions, forced apologetic retractions from the prime minister. In any event, the episode had the desired effect in Washington during the initial Ikeda-Kennedy relationship. The Japanese, Kennedy believed, were becoming "more like us."[36] The old enemy, which had in a sense provided him with the PT-109 image of courage and with the resulting electoral benefit, was indeed becoming the new, trustworthy Japan.

That did not mean certain strains in the U.S.-Japan relationship could be discarded and forgotten. Especially complicating the development of a new, friendly economic relationship, the Ryukyu Islands issue refused to go away. Flexing their post-treaty muscle, both young activists and aging anti-Americanists in the LDP insisted that the continuing American administration of the Ryukyu Islands be made the dominant issue in 1960s Tokyo-Washington relations. Miyazawa disagreed strongly, fearing that an angry and annoyed United States would refuse Japanese inroads to the U.S. consumer market. Although more politically cautious than the outspoken Miyazawa, Ikeda shared similar concerns;[37] it was a question of time and place, and Japanese protest of U.S. rule over the Ryukyus constituted the worst possible time. Ikeda had little personal interest in the focus of the protest.

Yet, LDP Diet members and many LDP supporters, energized by the 1950s debate over the American bases issue, saw great unifying value in anti-American causes. The messy matter of hauling down the Stars and Stripes in the Ryukyus in favor of the Rising Sun promised an ugly confrontation with Washington. It also promised, to some, continuing LDP rule. But did the LDP really care about the residents of the Ryukyus and their desires for the future? The islanders would soon be trapped in a political struggle between Washington and

Tokyo, where, ironically, the Kennedy administration cared more about their civil rights/civil liberties than their Japanese protectors from "American imperialism."

As part of his effort to remove "Ugly American" approaches to U.S. foreign policy, Kennedy promised early in his administration that U.S. sovereignty over the Ryukyu Islands would disappear in the 1960s. It was only a matter of finding the proper arrangement. Hitting upon the American president's open timetable, Japanese politicians urged a sooner rather than later end to the U.S. occupation. Insisting that the American presence in the Ryukyus equaled the continuation of the U.S. occupation policy over "all" of Japan was a stretch of the political imagination for Washington, but a real issue in Tokyo. Ikeda, under Miyazawa's insistence, offered apologies to Kennedy for the issue's growing popularity, but it soon became apparent to the White House that something might have to be done quickly to answer the complaint.[38]

The Ryukyus, at a distance of less than one thousand miles south of Tokyo, played host to one of America's most significant overseas military infrastructures. Okinawa, the largest of the Ryukyu Islands, was home to Kadena Air Base, the U.S. Marine bases of Camps Foster and Butler, the U.S. Army's Torii Station, and the Navy's White Beach facility. Labeled by the Pentagon as America's "most important link in Pacific defense," the Okinawa bases remained vital to Kennedy's Cold War victory priorities. Particularly proving their value as staging areas during the Korean War, the Okinawa bases played primary roles in all the projected military crises in the Pacific region.[39]

As always, Kennedy loved contingency planning, and, therefore, asked the Pentagon to assess the possibility of moving the Okinawa bases to another Pacific location. The Pentagon's survey of the dollars and cents implications of the issue was enough for Kennedy. Indeed, the cost of moving Kadena Air Base to Anderson Air Base on the U.S. Territory of Guam was conservatively estimated at $1 billion.[40] The bases were staying put, but American sovereignty over the everyday political and economic life of the Ryukyus might fade into history.

Given the angry argument in Tokyo, Kennedy wondered if the Japanese might ever see the difference between America's raw defense interests in the islands versus lack of interest in the area's political future. It would be a delicate negotiation effort, forever threatening the larger Tokyo-Washington dialogue. True to character, Kennedy himself had doubts over whether a straight dichotomy could be drawn between U.S. defense and political interests in the Ryukyus. To both Kennedy and particularly Ikeda's LDP, a resolution to the problem meant truly relegating World War II to the past and the beginning of the New Frontier–New Japan relationship.[41] The symbolism, as always, was more important to Japan than America, but the visionary Kennedy, at least, understood the issue.

The World War II battle for Okinawa, then a Japanese prefecture and even then the most impressive island in the Ryukyu chain, cost nearly thirteen thousand American lives in 1945. This bloody siege offered the American military a bitter taste of what warfare in Japan proper might be like. Largely thanks to the atomic attacks on Hiroshima and Nagasaki, the projected one million American losses in an invasion of Japan were spared. Consequently, Okinawa and its sister islands took on a certain "last stand," heroic image for many Japanese. It also stood as a symbol of the brave American commitment to crush Japanese militarism. World War II ended with these images and symbols clearly in place.[42] During the next several years, President Harry Truman kept American troop strength in the Ryukyus at high and expensive levels. The fear of resurgent Japanese militarism was given as the reason for this decision, but it also involved the basic point that the United States had defeated Japan on the Japanese soil of the Ryukyus.

By the time of the Korean War, justification for the American military occupation of the islands adjusted to the Truman administration's Cold War concerns. Japan was no longer a threat; however, Japan could fall to communism due to pressures from Mao's newly established communist China or from the budding communist movement within Japan. America's new mission in the Ryukyus was to safeguard Japan and contain communism. Indeed, Okinawa was closer to major Chinese urban centers, such as Shanghai, than to Nagasaki or, especially, Tokyo. Given the twenty-five-minute flying time between Okinawa and mainland China, Okinawa's position as a forward outpost of the Cold War was assured by the Truman and Eisenhower administrations.[43]

American Occupation authorities called Okinawa the Rock. Before World War II, many career U.S. military officers considered Guam, several hundred miles to the south in the Mariana Islands, the least desirable assignment in the Pacific. Remoteness, poverty, and typhoons were just a few of the problems that the U.S. military had endured on Guam, also nicknamed the Rock. Equally as remote, poor, and in the path of "typhoon alley," Okinawa inherited the honors, while Guam, in 1950, became a civilian-administered Territory of the United States.[44]

Writing in 1966, a renowned Japanese-studies specialist, Professor Lawrence Olson, observed that the United States never had any intention of colonizing the Ryukyu Islands. "Despite the visionaries," he concluded, "who saw the islands as an entrepot for Western Pacific trade or even as a Pacific U.N. headquarters—a kind of international Canberra—most responsible Americans had no such fantastic illusions."[45] Olson's "visionaries" were U.S. military officers of the 1950s. Some of them hoped that the rugged terrain of Okinawa could be "modernized" in an American image, but most of these hopes were confined to officers' club discussions and inter–Defense Department memos. Kennedy's vision for Okinawa and the Ryukyus obviously rejected "permanent military dominance" over local affairs.[46] Since Truman and Eisenhower made no move to create a "permanent" administration, Kennedy inherited a certain reluctance on the part of Washington-based officials to repeat, somehow, the territorial relationship that existed between Guam and the United States.

The Ryukyus, of course, did not enjoy the long-lasting relationship with the United States that typified the history of Guam. The latter was even brutally occupied by both the Japanese army and navy during World War II, winning, especially for the effective anti-Japanese resistance on the island, a warm, heroic image in the American public mind.[47] Meanwhile, the U.S. leadership molded the postwar Ryukyus into what many islanders soon came to regard as the "best" of America's democratic tradition.[48]

In the peace treaty with Japan, the United States acquired complete responsibility for the administration, legislation, and jurisdiction of the Ryukyu Islands. Nearly all of that responsibility, including budgetary matters, stressed Okinawa. The treaty placed the people of the

Ryukyus in the position of being residents without a country. They were citizens of neither Japan nor the United States. To prevent any hostility over this arrangement, the Defense Department created the Government of the Ryukyu Islands (GRI). A hybrid version of the advisory, pseudolegislative Guam Congress of the prewar years, the GRI was organized with legislative, judicial, and executive branches. The chief executive of the GRI was appointed by the high commissioner, the ranking officer of the United States Army. Meanwhile, the twenty-nine-member GRI legislature was elected by the people.

Funds for the administration of the islands were provided by the American government acting through the United States Civil Administration of the Ryukyu Islands (USCAR). USCAR "supervised" the GRI, and its ruling body consisted of active-duty military officers, as well as retired military men and expatriate civilian Far East hands. Enjoying a life of power and prestige that might elude them at home, the latter group of USCAR officialdom remained the most energetic and influential in local policymaking.[49]

In 1961, at the height of the LDP and Socialist Party–supported street demonstrations in Tokyo over "Reversion Now" (i.e., the reversion of U.S. sovereignty over the Ryukyus to Japan), Prime Minister Ikeda made a swing tour of Okinawa and neighboring islands. He found more suspicion and fear upon his arrival than support. Evidence of the American postwar economic boom was everywhere, especially on Okinawa. Be it a billboard for "the beer that made Milwaukee famous," the superhighway from Naha, Okinawa's major urban center, to Kadena Air Base, or the left-hand-drive American luxury cars on that highway, it was clear that the United States had already influenced island life. Indeed, there were questions about what this influence meant for Ryukyuan culture, and local businessmen and farmers feared that the insatiable U.S. military demand for more and more land for runways, training grounds, and other facilities might soon lead to the death of the sugarcane industry, commercial fishing, and a general way of life.[50] But was "reversion" the answer?

Ikeda found race, not reversion, to be the major concern in the islands. The shorter, stockier, and darker Ryukyuan, in contrast to the Japanese "mainlander," worried that the lack of civil rights/civil liberties protection in Japanese law guaranteed "second-class citizenship" for all Ryukyuans. The islanders claimed, and quite accurately, that it was virtually impossible for even the most educated and talented in their midst to find adequate employment in Japan. The reason was pure racism, they said, also noting that Kennedy's proposed "revolution" in civil rights in the United States was especially intriguing to them. Staying with America, especially given the Cold War–guaranteed jobs on the U.S. military bases, further guaranteed that race would not get in the way of social and economic mobility.[51]

American "brutality," Ikeda discovered, was truly hard to find. Nevertheless, he went through the motions, explaining, in a certain politically correct format, that the Ryukyuans were in bondage to American military enterprises and cut off from their Japanese "roots."[52] The key to surviving this mess was twofold. First, Ikeda and Miyazawa had to convince Kennedy that they enjoyed the strong political support to remain in power no matter what happened in the Ryukyuan debate. Second, the Ryukyuan issue had to be demoted from a major to minor issue. The alternative, both Ikeda and Miyazawa feared, meant losing the "economic miracle" forever.[53]

Unwittingly, the U.S. president rescued Ikeda and Miyazawa from their political misery. In the spring of 1961, Kennedy appointed a number of former assistant secretaries of state and defense going back to FDR and a host of academic experts—as well as Ambassador Reischauer and James Thomson—to the Task Force Ryukyus. This new, high-profile group was expected to come up with the right working panacea to the Ryukyus issue and "the resulting collapse in Japan-U.S. relations." On the very day of the task force's creation, Kennedy ordered USCAR to haul down the U.S. flag on all off-military base public buildings and hoist the Rising Sun. He also reinstated the observance of Japanese holidays throughout the Ryukyus and even encouraged patriotic, pro-Japanese parades on those dates. These types of actions were particularly designed for the Japanese and Ryukyuan press in a deliberate effort to influence public opinion before Ikeda arrived for a special June 1961 visit to Washington.[54] They were moderately successful.

Ikeda welcomed Kennedy's move. It symbolized, he told the Tokyo press, the Americans' desire to overcome the past and recognize the New Japan. He hoped, like Kennedy, that the Ryukyuan controversy was subsiding; however, the Diet mandated him to keep it at the top of his state-visit agenda. Kennedy, tired of the matter, and, perhaps, a little angry, insisted that the Ryukyus would not be on his agenda at all. Enough was enough, but his new task force disagreed.[55] Through their pressure, the president issued an official Ryukyus statement timed for Ikeda's arrival. The statement promised a special economic-aid package for the islands, and Kennedy also urged Ikeda to match it with one of his own. The military bases, and their growth, remained priorities outside of local or Japanese influence.[56] Although this statement read like America's final word, it was meant to be consistent with the Kennedy administration's commitment to civil rights/civil liberties at home and abroad, Cold War defense policy, the ever-present New Pacific Community organization dream, and, simply, a better U.S.-Japan dialogue.

In short, Kennedy awaited the real final word from his Task Force Ryukyus. Ikeda's visit came ill-timed in that regard. While Kennedy and Ikeda exchanged bows and handshakes on world television, the Socialist Party in the Diet called for a new working alliance between themselves and the LDP on the Ryukyus issue. They found an eager audience, although strong Ikeda supporters worried that any new Socialist-LDP alliance might harm larger economic goals. Kennedy hit upon that concern, noting that his administration respected the Japanese desire for economic growth. As the Diet called for more demonstrations against American "oppression," Kennedy offered more economic concessions. All Nippon Airways (ANA), for instance, became the first Japanese air carrier to be granted U.S. permission for daily flights to Naha. The White House made the announcement with great fanfare, proclaiming that jet-age Tokyo-Naha connections would lead to a new era of Japanese-Ryukyuan-American "communication and development."[57]

Ikeda was glad that Kennedy recognized the importance of the Ryukyus issue, but the piece-by-piece concessions fooled no one. A new policy was required, not cleverly timed press releases. Somewhat in the realm of the bizarre, the Ikeda-Kennedy meeting of June 1961 kept the Ryukyus topic outside of the official summit room. The Big Picture matters of new economic connections and Cold War solidarity dominated the discussions. Yet, success remained elusive as long as the Ryukyuan matter remained unresolved and separated from the primary agenda.[58] While friendly U.S.-Japan relations hung in the balance, the "Reversion Now" demonstrations grew more angry and the anti-American rhetoric of the Diet grew more belligerent. The New Japan–New Frontier relationship might never be, and Ikeda, more than Kennedy, realized that that was happening.

When will reversion come? Ikeda received no answer to this question throughout the remaining months of 1961. Finally, just days before Christmas 1961, the Task Force Ryukyus offered its report to Kennedy. Clever, cagey, and concise, the report represented America's best foot forward, and the task force believed it was a big enough step to silence all Japanese critics. Chaired by White House troubleshooter Carl Kaysen, the task force offered the usual, decade-long New Frontier formula for success, also recommending several options to quiet immediate Japanese concerns. Kaysen's group worked from the basic premise that the U.S. military bases posed, as Kennedy believed, "special consideration" in all reversion discussions. If Japan and the Ryukyus failed to recognize those "considerations," there was nothing Washington could do.

The task force agreed that the entire U.S.-Japan relationship now hung in the balance. Hence, a certain "dramatic answer" was required of the Kennedy administration. They suggested a "massive" economic-aid package that would, in a sense, have the same impact as a "massive retaliation" effort of the U.S. military. Kaysen, who prided himself as another one of Kennedy's "brightest and best," tailored his document to resemble Kennedy's public image of action and youthful enthusiasm. "Massive retaliation" was a favorite expression of the president's, implying full commitment, vigor, and inevitable success. Recommending against an economic-aid plan lasting several years, such as the Marshall Plan for Europe of more than a decade earlier, the task force called for one, and only one, budget for Ryukyuan development. The Diet would be in sole charge of its administration, although the GRI and the White House would have "advisory" roles on how precisely it should be spent. This would set up a cooperative relationship between Japan, the Ryukyus, and the United States that might impact other areas of U.S.-Japan concern as well as assure the democratic interests of the Ryukyuan islanders. Assuring the full economic development of the islands would be considered part of the reversion process, and USCAR would disband after the plan was successfully underway.

Kaysen also recommended that Kennedy announce to the world how America felt about the growth of anti-American sentiment in Japan over the Ryukyus matter. The Ikeda regime was in deep political trouble over reversion, and Kaysen suggested that the fall of Ikeda meant the rise of radicalism in Japan. America's support for new economic ties with Japan should constitute that announcement, Kaysen noted, rather than denouncing Ikeda's critics. Meanwhile, Washington would back away from "insisting" on full civil rights/civil liberties for Ryukyuan islanders following reversion. Instead, Kennedy now "recommended" it with the warning that any departure from civil rights/civil liberties guaranteed little headway in the war of words against communist tyranny.

Kaysen, Reischauer, Thomson, and the other task force members tried to understand the Japanese complaint over the American presence in the Ryukyus. If a true appreciation for Japanese concerns was reached, then the tasks of U.S.-Japan relations might be easier in the future. Cultural misunderstanding threatened the very heart of that relationship, the task force admitted, and Kennedy would have no problem agreeing with them.

According to the task force, the central problem in U.S.-Japan relations in the new post–Mutual Security Treaty era remained defense-related. This time the focus was on U.S. military bases in the Ryukyus, and not mainland Japan. Since the United States considered Okinawa one of its most important links to successful Asian/Pacific defense, then the Japanese, Kaysen concluded, saw this defense linked to future wars against fellow Asians. Hence, that important link, to the Japanese, was rooted in American racism. Furthermore, these possible wars would be conducted from Japanese soil and the scene of Japan's "last stand" of World War II. The symbolism was too much for many Japanese. Finally, there was the fear that Kadena Air Base already maintained a stockpile of nuclear weapons to wage these wars. This sadly reminded the Japanese of U.S. nuclear attacks on Hiroshima and Nagasaki. Such a stockpile did not exist in the early 1960s, although Kennedy would have had no problem secretly arranging one if necessary. All of these issues, whether real or imagined, were matters, the task force concluded, that the Kennedy administration would have to respect and accept. Answering these concerns was something else.[58]

The key to success, the task force always reasoned, was more and more money. Be it the "largest peacetime economic aid package for a Far Eastern country in American history," or a special lease, at deliberately inflated prices, for the U.S. military's use of Okinawan land, the task force slyly suggested that "money talks." The latter constituted their final word on the reversion process. For instance, Washington paid virtually nothing for the Okinawan bases. No one was even sure how the token annual fee of $6 million had been set in stone. In contrast to their significance, the Okinawan bases were quite a bargain. "Cheap" rents for basing privileges were considered in the realm of $10 million per year (Libya) or even $20 to $40 million per year (Morocco). A moderate-to-expensive but fair rent was deemed $150 million per year (Spain). Kaysen recommended the Spanish model for Okinawa, with payments made to a Tokyo-Naha consortium. The money would almost certainly be used for economic infrastructure projects, either in the Ryukyus or on the Japanese mainland, and, therefore, served as a supplement to the straightforward economic-aid plan.

Kennedy welcomed Kaysen's hard work, but found an instant flaw in the effort. Little had been said about Miyako, Ishigaki, Iriomoto, and even smaller Ryukyu islands. The charge of neglect had already been leveled against the Kennedy White House by the Diet. All that the United States cared about, the Japanese complaint noted, was the fate of the American bases on Okinawa. Kennedy answered the complaint by ordering Kaysen to tour every Ryukyuan island—and with the world press in tow. Every charge of neglect, Kennedy said, would be answered.[60] Expense was no object.

To Ikeda, the task force's biggest problem was its lack of a firm date for the final Ryukyus reversion. The Big Money plans were welcomed by most Japanese, but Kennedy could have eased Ikeda's trials in the Diet by setting a specific reversion date. That date was not, on the other hand, in Kennedy's interest. If the U.S. Congress was to be lobbied on behalf of lowering protectionist barriers against Japanese products, and generally encouraged to accept a new, working relationship with a resurgent Japan, Kennedy needed a healthy dialogue with his conservative Congress as well. Although his Democratic Party enjoyed slim majorities in both the Senate and the House, the tenor of the early 1960s Congress remained suspicious of Kennedy's call for rapid change. The Congress, Kennedy believed, would frown on giveaways to America's old World War II enemy, and the last thing he wanted was the Ryukyus to become an issue in American politics. Consequently, he preferred to ease the tension with Japan, throw money at the Ryukyus, speak glowingly of a new era for American-Japanese friendship, and get on with the larger security and economic matters at hand.[61]

Defusing the Ryukyus issue in Japan was the first step in the procedure, and, given the very visible work of the Task Force Ryukyus, Japanese public opinion began to turn toward working with the Americans rather than slandering them. By 1962, a new political correctness had been established in Tokyo. Both Kennedy and Ikeda's rhetoric of cooperation began to take hold, as the Japanese press came to the realization that much could be lost if the Ryukyus debate continued. Timetable or no timetable, reversion was now seen as inevitable before the end of the decade. It was time, as Kennedy and Ikeda had long pointed out, to move forward.

From the Japanese point of view, the Ryukyus issue had brought about a certain American respect for issues of Japanese pride and sovereignty. Equal treatment, and an American view that welcomed Japan as a brother nation and not the defeated enemy, was an important first step in the coming New Japan–New Frontier relationship. Ikeda said that "America's respect" had been won over the Ryukyus discussions, and much of the LDP electorate believed him.[62]

From the American view, this early phase of the Ryukyus issue had been a waste of time that, ironically, had threatened the future of Cold War security arrangements in the Pacific. In the heyday of the Cold War, Washington easily considered any disturbance in allied relations as a threat to America's march to victory over communism. The Ryukyus issue proved the point. Kennedy was happy to move on; however, finding the right policies would be much more difficult than promising them. Although frustrating to him, the Ryukyus issue did not pollute his view of U.S.-Japan relations. Winning the "hearts and minds" of the Japanese to America's Cold War victory priorities could be achieved, Kennedy still believed, through special economic arrangements.[63] Outside of Ryukyus-related matters, Japan did not need economic infrastructure assistance from the United States. It did need U.S. generosity to its export economy plans. That generosity would be a beacon to a variety of nations around the world who hoped, someday, to follow the Japanese into the American market. The promise of wealth, the Kennedy administration assumed, was a powerful lure away from the attractions of communism. Given that fact, America's Cold War victory was indeed a matter of time, and the U.S.-Japan trade relationship would symbolize the value of capitalism to the entire Free World. Always impressed by their own invention of symbols, the Kennedy team was determined to succeed with their Japan policy.

Especially concerned about America's interest in world peace versus the desire for Cold War victory, the Japanese remained suspicious of Kennedy's intentions. With the Ryukyus issue fading from the headlines, Kennedy took the offensive on behalf of "the American image in Japan." In an interview with NHK television of Japan, and an even more candid interview with Tokyo's *Mainichi Shimbun* newspaper, Kennedy vowed to reduce U.S. military posturing throughout the world, and especially in Japan. Tokyo, he asserted prophetically, was "destined to rule" the economic world of the Asian/Pacific region. A relationship that stressed U.S.-Japan cooperation in the early 1960s would have "great benefits" for both nations when the Cold War had "withered" in the late 1960s. Although devoid of specifics, the Kennedy interviews were a rousing success in Japan, winning him the desired "peacemaker" reputation in public opinion. Ikeda, at first, regarded Kennedy's splash in the Japanese press as a coup for charm and persuasion. The real Kennedy, he worried, remained a passionate cold warrior.[64] Meanwhile, was the much discussed new era of economic relations truly possible?

In 1954, Prime Minister Shigeru Yoshida had proposed a special economic summit with the Eisenhower administration, but Secretary of State Dulles rejected the idea on the grounds of its irrelevance to Cold War priorities. Yoshida's successor, Nobosuke Kishi, asked again in 1957, but met the same response. At a time when the future of America's defense structure in Japan appeared uncertain, Eisenhower and Dulles found Japan's "sideshow interest" in economics annoying.[65] Kennedy's praise for Ikeda's ambitious "export economy" vision constituted a shift in U.S. policy.

While the Ryukyus issue paralyzed U.S.-Japan trade talks, Kennedy had already established a new trade status for Europe. The results of his work were eventually approved by Congress in 1962 as the Trade Expansion Act (TEA). Kennedy recognized the new industrial might of postwar Europe, declared the Marshall Plan period of U.S. paternalism toward the Europeans officially over, and suggested that an Atlantic free-trade zone might be imminent. Promising to promote the U.S. dollar in Europe, ensure the free flow of U.S. agricultural products there, assist the position of U.S. companies already there, and deaden anti-American sentiment that could harm U.S. military basing privileges, the TEA was declared "one of the greatest economic advances of the century" by the Kennedy White House itself.[66]

The TEA said nothing about Japan, and that bothered Ikeda. Whether rooted in U.S. self-interest or not, the TEA also opened up the market to European trading partners to a degree unseen before. Meanwhile, the Organization for Economic Cooperation and Development (OECD) would discuss and debate the mechanics of European export policy with American representatives. Coordinating economic policies so as to benefit both Europe and the United States constituted the promise of the TEA approach and of OECD specifics. Japan's only role in this endeavor involved a seat on the Development Assistance Committee of the OECD. Ikeda considered this a deliberate effort to prohibit Japanese economic growth, and to keep his nation forever tied to a Third World future. He wanted full recognition of Japan's potential and real position in the world economy.[67] Only Kennedy had the power to break down Europe's fear of Japanese economic penetration; only Kennedy had the power to assault U.S. domestic protectionism. Ikeda was ready to accept the latter as the great new beginning for Japan. He could worry about European protectionism, and Kennedy's toleration of it, later.

Despite the American president's commitment to analytical decision making, the Kennedy view of Japan remained rooted in yesterday's reality. Japanese industry meant trinkets and toys, or family-owned factories with antiquated machinery linked to an overdose of hard labor. As in the case of the disastrous Bay of Pigs invasion, in which Fidel Castro was expected to surrender at the very sight of U.S.-trained Cuban exile invaders, Kennedy's analytical powers were lacking at times. Scoffing at Japan's growing economic might constituted one of those times.[68] Japan's fast-approaching superpower status was all too clear.

It would take Kennedy more than a year to accept this turn of events, but Japanese success still hinged on the American market. Was it truly in America's interest to be generous toward Japanese economic growth? In 1962, Kennedy admitted to his cabinet that he was concerned about the impact of a generous Japan policy on domestic industry. On the other hand, he mused, it would take time for Japan to become destructive. Economic indicators or not, Japan was still a struggling nation to Kennedy. The bottom-line concern, therefore, remained what might happen if the United States did not respond to Ikeda's plans, and whether a slow-moving or even negative response would compromise U.S. success in the Cold War.[69]

The attempt to find the "right key" in winning the Cold War was always associated with the politics of desperation. Given Cold War tensions, the Kennedy team saw even strong capitalist nations such as Japan prepared to embrace communism under the "right" circumstances. As the Cold War heated up during the Cuban missile crisis, Kennedy grew close to both the staunch cold warriors in his administration, as well as those looking for a quick peace. In the former category, this meant an even chummier relationship with Walt Rostow. In 1962, Rostow's opinion of Japan was at an all-time low. Japan, he concluded, was tottering in the Cold War, largely because of its lack of democratic traditions and its attraction toward authoritarian economic decisions. Crystal ball in hand, Rostow saw Japan as a strong Soviet ally by the end of the decade "unless America did something soon."[70]

That "something" was influenced by an unusual Soviet appeal. In November 1962, just days after the Cuban missile crisis, A. I. Mikoyan, the Soviet deputy premier, met Kennedy at the White House. A die-hard anti-Stalinist and old friend of Soviet Premier Khrushchev,

Mikoyan stressed Soviet plans to remove long-range bombers from Cuba. Kennedy criticized his slow-moving agenda. Nevertheless, a post–missile crisis calm prevailed, and Mikoyan took advantage of the situation. Insisting that the time was right to demonstrate the new peaceful dialogue between Washington and Moscow, Mikoyan asked for a capitalist-style free-trade agreement. Talking about a "new world" of economic cooperation, he said that it was time for the United States to illustrate its global economic responsibility by helping to guide the economic future of the Eastern Bloc. Whereas Stalin had once refused U.S. aid via the Marshall Plan, Khrushchev, Mikoyan pointed out, now encouraged economic ties in the spirit of "coexistence." "Like Japan," Mikoyan concluded, the Soviet Union had great economic potential. The United States, as it had once done in Japan, could trigger that economic boom. Echoing early-twentieth-century U.S. Progressives, as the Japanese had done, Mikoyan reminded Kennedy that no nation should be permitted to "stagnate in its own progress."[71]

This sudden Soviet interest in American-style capitalism remained way ahead of New Frontier timetables. It therefore posed a problem. The American people were not ready to support Japan as a strong economic ally, much less support their country's main sparring partner in the Cold War. Kennedy told Mikoyan that a true Cold War thaw would be required before trade negotiations could begin. That would take several years, he said. Mikoyan expressed his disappointment, mentioning that the Soviets would soon be encouraging close economic ties with "other nations." Although Mikoyan did not name the "other nations," Kennedy assumed that Japan was at the top of the list.[72] The deputy premier had already made reference to it earlier.

Would USSR overtures toward Japan influence a leftward swing in Japanese politics in the 1960s? Would it influence Japanese efforts to break the allied nonrecognition policy toward communist China? The Kennedy cabinet agreed that the Cold War in the Pacific was changing rapidly, and perhaps faster than American political opinion could accept. Only the United States could be the Good Neighbor to Japan if the Cold War was to be won on America's terms, or so the Kennedy team concluded.[73]

Mikoyan's overtures to Kennedy would be kept secret for nearly a generation, as would the president's reaction to them. The Kennedy administration responded directly to Mikoyan's challenge with reference to Japan. The United States was now dedicated to halting a Soviet-Japanese rapprochement.[74] Wooing a Japan that did not have to be wooed over to the American market became a priority policy. Fighting for political survival at home after their perceived surrender to Kennedy over the removal of Cuban missiles, Khrushchev and Mikoyan were left to their dreams of a new economic world order. Kennedy, however, left nothing to chance.

Convinced that Japan would embrace a new authoritarianism, either from the Right or from the Left, if the United States ignored its needs, the Kennedy cabinet worked hard to meet Ikeda's and Miyazawa's economic agenda. The Japanese Communist Party, Kennedy believed, was especially eager for the opportunity to seize power. The United States was not going to provide it.[75]

The Japanese Communist Party—a legal entity in Japan since 1945 —in the 1960s held only three seats in the Lower House and four in the Upper House. Although its membership was fewer than ninety thousand, Kennedy saw its influence in front organizations such as student groups and the labor movement.[76] Ironically, one of those student groups calling for an immediate and full opening of the U.S. market to Japan was run by Toshiki Kaifu. Labeled a leftist radical by the Kennedy administration, Kaifu was destined to become the conservative LDP prime minister of Japan in the late 1980s.[77]

The Kennedy administration still ridiculed its Republican predecessors for viewing communism as a great monolith. That view divorced U.S. policymaking from analysis and logical policy, preventing nation-by-nation considerations and assessments of political groups within those nations. The "Ugly American" image had also grown out of this reality, providing the Third World view of American arrogance and deceit. Kennedy, however—the ridicule notwithstanding—saw anyone in Japan outside of the prime minister's office as ready to join a communist-led anti-American cause at a moment's notice.[78] Part of the problem involved lingering memories of the Pearl Harbor "sneak attack" and anti–Mutual Security Treaty riots. Some of it involved the U.S. ambassador, Edwin Reischauer, and his warnings against lingering Japanese authoritarianism. It also involved "regionalization"—

considering Japan vulnerable to communist attractions, just like other Far Eastern states such as South Vietnam or Laos. In late 1961, for instance, Kennedy ordered the U.S. military base commanders in Japan to report on "communist insurgent group activity" near their bases and the military requirements needed to thwart them.[79] There was no communist plot afoot, and never had been.

Politically, Kennedy saw the divisions within the Socialist opposition to Ikeda's government as easy fodder for communist exploitation. In 1960, the Democratic Socialist Party, under the charismatic leadership of Suehiro Nishio, had seceded from the Japan Socialist Party. Disappointed at the extremism characteristic of the Japan Socialist Party, and particularly over the retention of the concept of class warfare, the Democratic Socialists attempted to form themselves into a moderate party similar to Britain's Labour Party. Plagued by organizational weakness, the Democratic Socialists held only seventeen seats in the Lower House and eleven seats in the Upper House during the Kennedy presidency. Kennedy expected clever communist organizers to reverse the Democratic Socialists' fortunes. ZENRO, the All-Japan Trade Union Congress, consisting of 1.1 million members, represented the backbone of the Democratic Socialists. Most of its members worked in the textile industry, and they demanded more of the American market for their labors.

SOHYO, the General Council of Trade Unions of Japan, enjoyed 3.9 million members. Filled with public service workers, SOHYO supported the "destiny" of Japan's "rightful place within the American market" as a matter of principle. They preferred the Japan Socialist Party to the LDP.

To Kennedy, the choices were obvious: (1) engineer success for Ikeda's and Miyazawa's cause and thereby strengthen conservative anti-communist forces in Japan; or (2), deal with a determined and angry Left.[80] Time was running out. Even ultraconservative Japanese bankers were turning to an "Eastern alternative": endless Japanese government trade missions to Moscow in order to begin the new Japan-USSR economic partnership. One banker reminded Kennedy that the United States paid "more attention to India and Africa than Japan." America had "seen Japan," he concluded, "primarily in the light of its own strategy—as a permanent U.S. military base and as a potential military ally. Americans tend to forget that Japan is also a great power, an ancient culture, and a prime symbol of economic development to hundreds of millions of non-Europeans."[81] Another banker suggested that an open U.S. market would not only demonstrate America's Good Neighbor leadership in the Cold War, but also serve as a denunciation of anti-Asian racism. "The individual American," he explained, "who shows an interest in Japan—her history, her economy, her arts, her universities, her religion—may do more to tie us to the Free World than all the policies of your government."[82]

Such comments fitted nicely into Kennedy's anti–Ugly American approach; the Japanese, however, played an anti–Ugly Japan game as well. Negating the belligerent World War II image and substituting that of the reliable ally with great economic worth to the world remained a basic theme of Japanese foreign policy. Ikeda even said that the main reason for Japan welcoming more imports from the United States than from any other nation was the need to prove Japan's worthiness as a reliable economic partner. The days of defeated, struggling Japan were over.[83]

To the Ikeda government, the greatest threat to full penetration of the U.S. market remained, of course, American attraction toward protectionism. In order to avoid any injury to U.S. industries that might justify restrictive American measures against imports from Japan, Tokyo had adopted voluntary controls on a number of commodities exported to the United States. These controls related to quality, quantity, and price. In imposing them, the Japanese objectives included the orderly development of a significant share of the American market. Ikeda's voluntary controls covered textiles, wool suits, hardwood, plywood, transistor radios, chinaware, sewing machines, woodscrews, flatware, and tuna fish.[84]

The Americans were expected to return this generosity in kind. Revered in Japanese public opinion as Edokkotaishi (in English, Tokyo-born ambassador), Reischauer ensured a warm Tokyo-Washington dialogue on these economic issues. Always making it clear that he was "at home" in Japan, Reischauer had an academic background that made him invaluable in political and defense issues. Yet in practical terms, Reischauer's role as point man for anti–Ugly American efforts remained of limited value. Kennedy, at home, had to do the work.

Breaking down protectionist sentiment in Congress would constitute that work. It also ensured success for the executive branch–negotiated TEA, as well as Japan's complete entry into it and the OECD as a fully recognized and encouraged trading partner of the United States.

Removing protectionist barriers would not be an easy task. Even denouncing anti-Japanese protectionism as an encouragement to Japanese communists would not do the trick. Representatives John Baldwin and Leo W. O'Brien said they would "do anything to protect the industry of today and tomorrow" from "another" Japanese assault. Both men were members of Kennedy's Democratic Party, the party that reversed the Smoot-Hawley tariff and other protectionist measures during the early 1930s; Baldwin's and O'Brien's legislation would thus be rooted more in nationalist, anti-Japanese fervor than in Democratic Party tradition.

Baldwin proposed legislation that required a modification of executive order 10582, forbidding the U.S. government to purchase any Japanese product for any of its agencies, including the military. Kennedy pointed out that the Buy America Act already prohibited the government from purchasing foreign products unless the prices for domestic goods were "unreasonable." Executive order 10582 was a procurement measure, largely devoted to modernizing government offices with the latest and best equipment. Kennedy saw the Baldwin bill as not only an open door to the new protectionist era, but also an attack on executive order privilege. In a special 1961 message to Congress, Kennedy lashed out at the Baldwin bill and protectionism in general. "A return to protectionism," he insisted, "is not a solution. Such a course could result in retaliation abroad with serious consequences for U.S. exports and our trade balance."[85]

Kennedy later accused Baldwin of injuring American-Japanese diplomacy, harming executive-legislative relations, and dividing Democrats. He asked him to drop the cause. The congressman obliged, but his bill was quickly replaced by an even-more-obvious anti-Japanese measure. Representative O'Brien, an old Kennedy supporter and ally in most areas of legislation, sponsored a bill to observe December 7 each year as "the day that will live in infamy." The bill suggested that a national holiday was required to honor the American dead of the recent Pacific War, mentioning that the president himself had almost been killed in that conflict. Furthermore, the bill implied that the Japanese had not yet repented of the Pearl Harbor attack and other World War II actions. Anti-American sentiment in Japan was used as a fine testament to the fact. Kindness to Japan's export economy, the bill proclaimed, must not be forthcoming.

Since the president's accusations against Baldwin had not halted the flow of anti-Japanese measures from Capitol Hill, his rhetoric became stronger. Kennedy announced that he would never support anti-Japanese protection. He reserved a special rebuke for O'Brien: "I suppose that all of us feel the same about December 7, 1941. However, we are now trying to IMPROVE Japanese-American relationships, and I doubt that calling the Japanese names each year is calculated to achieve that purpose."[86] Although the O'Brien bill failed, the vote was close. Kennedy now had the upper hand in the protectionist debate.

The time was right for both Kennedy and Ikeda to make significant "first steps" in their respective "new beginnings" policies. On the trade issue, this meant the creation of the Joint United States–Japan Committee on Trade and Economic Affairs. By means of this action, Kennedy indicated that Japan was significant enough to merit "special considerations" beyond existing trade accords with Europe. The committee also promised to be the vehicle for preventing a Japanese swing to the left over economic issues, or so Kennedy reasoned. To Ikeda it meant the realization of the export-economy dream, and Miyazawa urged vigilance in the committee's work to ensure that significant results, and not just well-intentioned political rhetoric, came out of committee discussions.[87]

Even well into 1962, the mission of the U.S. delegation on the trade committee was unclear. The State Department informed Kennedy that the committee's "agenda and the specific papers to be discussed are far less important than the fact that the discussions take place." Reischauer said to three U.S. members of the committee in October 1961 that "America now had a unique opportunity to improve our bilateral relations with Japan and to influence as well the entire course of Japanese domestic and foreign policy."[88] Japan was being "maneuvered" away from any leftward attractions. Trade had become "the right key."

Nevertheless, old U.S. industries fearing a new Japanese assault on their sector of the domestic market continued to oppose this "right key." The textile and lumber industries, and workers' associations within both of them, assailed Kennedy for his generosity to Japan. They led the fight to meetings of the halt trade committee.[89] Ironically, this leadership was based more on fears of future Japanese inroads than on current Japanese successes. America's tariff schedules for textiles and lumber benefited domestic producers, and U.S. government figures proved it. In 1956, Japan supplied 76 percent of all cotton-textile imports to the United States. By 1962 that percentage had dropped to less than 19 percent. Similar figures existed for the lumber industry. The reason was entirely rooted in U.S. tariff policy, and the Japanese representatives at the trade committee meetings of 1962 were adamant: they demanded an open share of the market. The Japanese press, and new demonstrations sponsored by Japanese socialists, some LDP factions, and others supported their trade delegation's argument.[90]

Kennedy's answer was a new round of negotiations, with the purpose of finding some sort of agreement. That agreement was reached on February 1, 1963, establishing a scaled-down and complicated tariff structure that, from the U.S. point of view, benefited Japan.[91] Ikeda and Miyazawa praised yet another symbol of "new beginnings," but suggested that the best symbol would be a Kennedy visit to Japan.[92] It would be the first visit of a U.S. president to Japan, although others had been asked and declined. The World War II past could be truly buried through this gesture, and a clear statement against protectionism made at the same time.

On October 23, 1963, Kennedy agreed to make the long journey to Tokyo. Ambassador Reischauer expected him to arrive on January 28, 1964. The theme of the trip would be "Pacific Partnership." "In exchange for a Japanese commitment to greatly increased foreign assistance and collaboration with the U.S.," Kennedy reasoned, "we will offer new modes of consultation and collaboration with Japan in matters of trade."[93] In all probability, those "new modes" simply involved a healthier dialogue in trade discussions.

Kennedy, of course, never made it to Japan. His November 1963 visit to Dallas would be his last journey. Secretary of State Rusk followed through with the "Pacific Partnership" mission on behalf of the new Johnson administration. Arriving as planned on January 28, 1964, Rusk delivered the speech that Kennedy would have made. It was a rhetorical tour de force, calling for linkage of the American and Japanese economies and for the formal burial of ugly World War II memories. Anti-communist solidarity required it. "I foresee, said Rusk, "that 1964 will bring to all of us living in this world marketplace a greater awareness of the interdependence of creditor and debtor, the interdependence of manufacturer and farmer, and the interest, common to all, in setting and attempting to achieve high goals of employment, economic activity, growth, and the end of U.S. Protectionism."[94]

For Kennedy, removing barriers to Japanese economic penetration into the American market had remained essential to continued Japanese support for U.S. anti-communist goals. Trade became "the right key" to "maneuver" Tokyo. The alternative was a left-leaning Japan, and resulting Far East embarrassments to U.S. Cold War leadership. Kennedy probably went to his grave convinced that his Japan policy had been successful.

To Ikeda, a progressive trade policy required American generosity. It also remained in Ikeda's interest to remind the United States of its free-trade commitments and imply cautiously that a leftist, anti-U.S. Japan might develop without a healthy trade agreement. Indeed, the question of who was "maneuvering" whom could be raised here. Ikeda's "right key" was the U.S. obsession with anti-communism and Kennedy's stated goal of triumph in the Cold War by 1970. The Japanese prime minister won an open door for his country's full entry into the American market. Despite a record of rapid growth, however, Japanese industries were still hard-pressed to capture a significant market share in the 1960s. Ikeda's prediction of winning that market was a decade premature.

Did Kennedy the maneuverer know that he was being outmaneuvered? Perhaps. From Kennedy's point of view, it would make little difference. Regardless of the amazing figures and graphs that indicated the rising economic power of Japan, the Kennedy White House saw only a struggling Third World nation, tempted like so many others, albeit minimally, by leftist attractions and anti-American politics. The anger of various domestic producers at the potential influx of Japanese products was considered within the realm of size and scale. The

U.S. economy was booming in the early 1960s. The anger of a limited sector of the American economy was a small price to pay for Japan's happy solidarity in the Kennedy-led march to Cold War victory.

Kennedy would have been astounded at Paul Tsongas's "Japan won the Cold War" remark. His "can-do" generation foresaw the rise of the Third World, but saw it as a rise defined within U.S. policy objectives. Japan had little interest in following those objectives to the letter. Reserving the right to manufacture their own national self-interest, the Japanese forged ahead with economic foreign-policy priorities while America stressed its ideological contest with communism.

Kennedy's proposed announcement for January 1964, indicating "the end of protectionism," told Japan what it hoped to hear. The announcement was based on wishful thinking, but it was never based on realistic policymaking. "America First" sentiments were rooted in political tradition. They would not disappear in the face of the New Frontier. Meanwhile, the Kennedy team believed that their handling of the Ryukyus issue, a rallying cry for Japanese anti-American nationalists, had been masterful. The heyday of Japanese anti-Americanism was over, they concluded, and U.S. defense interests in Japan were deemed secure. Once again, wishful thinking overtook reality. In the Cold War, Lyndon Johnson soon pointed out, "nothing is secure."

The New Frontier–New Japan relationship set the tenor and tone of U.S.-Japan relations for the next twenty years. Despite conflicting national goals and priorities, that tenor and tone established a cooperative framework that is even more important today than it was in the days of Kennedy's "profiles in courage" and Ikeda's "new beginnings."

2

Challenged by Affluence

The Great Society and
Great Japan, 1964–1969

Our two countries are challenged by our affluence, and our problems are largely the problems of prosperity, of growth, and of national progress. In our crowded, restless world, nations can no longer go their separate ways. We all walk a common road when we pursue our peoples' aspirations for happier, healthier, richer, and fuller lives. If America and Japan can continue to focus on each other's Greatness, on our future as friends, we will herald the day when all men can lay aside the weapons of war, when we can together take up the tools to fashion the better world of which we dream.[1]

AT TIMES, Lyndon Johnson welcomed his public image of the rough-and-tumble Texan, the gentleman rancher and hard-nosed wheeler-dealer. It meant that he was never really expected to wax poetic on delicate political matters, or comment analytically on, for instance, the complicated relationship between Japan and the United States. But although he had little use for John Kennedy's patrician manners and Harvard intellectualism, President Johnson could be as cerebral and as perceptive as Jack Kennedy (or any Kennedy, for that matter). This "good side" of him, he fretted, was not often seen or understood by either Congress or the voters. In contrast to the charisma of his beloved and martyred predecessor, Johnson would not be as fortunate in the realm of image making. Hence, the former vice president's intelligent observations sometimes went unnoticed by the press, such as in the case of his comments (quoted at the opening of this chapter) to a group of visiting Japanese governors at the White House during May 1967. But Johnson understood the dilemmas of U.S.-Japan relations better than most policymakers of his day. When he wanted them to be, his powers of analysis and even Kennedyesque eloquence were superb.[2]

As so many have written, John Kennedy's world of elegance and grace was a hard act for Johnson to follow. In policy matters, he vowed to succeed where the Kennedy cabinet only promised, dreamed, and dreamed again. Johnson preferred action. Franklin Roosevelt was this veteran pol's "political papa"; a man of means whose enthusiasm for government service rivaled only his own. In Roosevelt's New Deal image, Johnson hoped to teach the nation that there was a time for vision and the right moment for practical achievement. The time for accomplishment was now, and in U.S.-Japan relations that meant a new working relationship between the two nations.[3] Given the continuing Cold War, that type of personal ambition, instead of being labeled arrogant, imperial, or politically incorrect, was more or less expected.

Johnson's experience in the area of U.S.-Japan relations was impressive, and he would remind Prime Minister Ikeda of that fact following the Kennedy assassination.[4] Holding the joint roles of chairman of the Senate Subcommittee on Appropriations and Senate majority leader in the late 1950s, Johnson had taken personal interest in the manufacturing of the mutual security treaty with Japan. Favoring a strong, bipartisan approach to Cold War priorities in the Pacific and elsewhere, Johnson held numerous closed and public hearings on U.S.-Japan relations in 1960 alone. Insisting that the Eisenhower administration should be worried about dissension behind the front lines of the Cold War, Senator Johnson favored a generous economic foreign policy with Japan long before John Kennedy ever considered the matter. A happier trade relationship for the Japanese was more than just a way of "shutting the hell up our good neighbors in Tokyo." It also involved, he said convincingly, "doing the right thing."[5]

Although as majority leader Johnson insisted on maintaining the integrity of U.S. forces stationed in Japan, he advocated a more active role in Japanese defense by the Japanese themselves. This was years ahead of its political time as well. But although in his view a significant Japanese fighting force should be standing side by side with U.S. troops throughout the Asian/Pacific neighborhood, this never meant that Japan would have a serious say in how military affairs in that neighborhood would be conducted. Nor would Japanese forces be allowed to engage in any military adventurism on their own. Such an event would resurrect ugly memories of World War II, and Washington might be blamed by its Pacific allies for unleashing Japan. To Johnson, the Japanese would be a support force, if ever needed, to U.S. military operations. At the least, a strong American and Japanese military, he once mused, would make communist expansionists think twice.[6]

Also urging his colleagues to abandon World War II animosities against an old enemy and, instead, welcome it as a full and distinguished trading partner, Johnson proclaimed that there was no place for hatred and bigotry in foreign-policy making. "Making-up with Germany," he noted, seemed so "easy" for the U.S. government. How long, he asked, would Washington ask for retribution over Pearl Harbor? "Until we've lost the Cold War? We have lost considerable face in the Orient already, where face counts most," he told the Senate shortly before he joined John Kennedy on the Democratic ticket as candidate for vice president. "The first lesson [in dealing with Japan]," he said, "spoke of mutual respect," a shared "love" of capitalism, and the need for a "strident defense."[7]

"Like Americans," Johnson noted, the Japanese "love things that work." He might have better said "Like Lyndon Johnson," for this Texas deal-maker often saw Japanese interests through his personal view of a forever wheeling-and-dealing world. He never took the time, whether as senator, vice president, or president, to study the recent history of Japanese-American relations or examine the uniqueness of Japanese culture. According to Walt Rostow, President Johnson's key National Security Council adviser on U.S.-Japan relations and other Asian/Pacific matters, his boss rarely gave himself the time to study any issue of importance in Japanese affairs. In contrast to the Kennedy cabinet, where midnight discussions on the intricacies of U.S.-Japan relations were not uncommon, Johnson stated his conclusions within a few, fast-moving sentences. Be it during a helicopter ride from Camp David to the White House, a quick stroll to a waiting limousine at the Austin, Texas airport, or chatting with NSC advisers while greeting Bob Hope at the White House, Johnson crammed his Japanese policy decisions into time also taken up with other affairs of state.

In contrast to other presidential administrations, both before and after his own, Johnson's seemingly impromptu approach to policymaking could imply a certain disregard for the significance of U.S.-Japanese relations. But, even thirty years after the fact, Walt Rostow disagreed. Johnson, he remembered, knew exactly what he was doing, enjoyed an amazing talent for quickly examining the facts and drawing conclusions from them, and provided a clear, coherent course for Washington's relationship with Tokyo. It was also a "helluva lot of fun," Rostow recalled, and Kiichi Miyazawa, former finance minister, trade minister, foreign minister, and prime minister, agreed. To Miyazawa, Johnson, "like John Wayne, was the quintessential American." The Japanese people, Miyazawa noted, knew exactly where Johnson stood on the issues, and "we welcomed the candor."[9]

"They want it all. Just like we do," Johnson once said of the Japanese. Sometimes, his crass view of Japanese and American interests would be right on the mark. Sometimes not. But whatever the Japanese "wanted" was always put in the perspective of America's superpower status. Like Kennedy before him, Johnson believed in an America that was "not first when, first if, first but. But first, period."[10] Continuing to lead an unassailable economy and military, Johnson never gave up on the plan to expand Kennedy's New Frontier from the realm of vision to a New Deal–like success story of working policy.

To Prime Minister Hayato Ikeda, this image of New Deal–style activism was just his cup of tea: Johnson's effort to create a generous Great Society meant that Japanese business might be able to penetrate the U.S. market much quicker; more to the point, given the growing importance of U.S. military bases in Japan to the rearguard effort of the Vietnam War, Japan would have an excellent bargaining position with the Americans on a variety of issues ranging from the future of the Ryukyu Islands to trade and nuclear policies.[11] Was Johnson, proud of his poker-playing skills, ready to deal?

When dealing with Washington, the Japanese always connected

defense and economic interests within one policymaking effort. Kennedy had often misunderstood those connections. As president, Johnson saw and respected Japan's endeavor to wheel and deal with his administration. Nevertheless, American self-interest prohibited him from offering Japan any real success. He also tried to keep separate economic and defense/political discussions moving at the same time, even though he knew that the Japanese saw little distinction. The point remained that his government saw distinctions, and U.S.-Japan negotiations, especially those on U.S. soil, would be conducted with American interests in mind more than any other.[12] The tenor and tone of Johnson-era relations with Japan changed from the inquiring, accommodating rhetoric of Camelot to the political hardball of Texas.

It would be a supreme irony. The man who understood and respected the wheeling-dealing nature of Japanese politics would be the same man who had little use for it in the U.S.-Japan relationship. If anything, the economic connection between the two countries was better clarified during the mid-to-late 1960s than at any time before. Johnson insisted on focused, disciplined economic discussions, whereby U.S. trade negotiators set the agenda instead of leaving it to the Japanese.

Those positions were made obvious during the divisive trade discussions that were held during Johnson's time in office. Some of these trade issues, so well-defined by the Joint United States–Japan Committee on Trade and Economic Affairs in 1965, were the same issues that would divide the two countries a generation later. For instance, the Johnson administration hoped to obtain the removal of Japan's residual import controls as well as the amelioration of certain domestic legislation that was administered in a manner tending to limit U.S. products more severely than the same products from other sources. The import controls were not authorized under Japan's GATT obligations. Furthermore, according to Kennedy's Trade Expansion Act (TEA), the United States could not negotiate on these illegal restrictions as nontariff barriers. The Johnson White House expressed its "concern" over it all, complaining that Japan might continue to exploit the situation.[13]

Since 1960, Japan had removed well over 2,000 commodities from restrictive import licensing, and the United States had benefited from increased exports to Japan of many of the liberalized items. The residual controls consisted of 123 items subject to import-quota allocation. The quotas did not prohibit trade, but did restrict it. Although U.S. trade in so-called restricted items was more than $400 million, the freeing of a number of items for which the United States might enjoy a significant market share in Japan would also have a significant impact on all U.S. exports. This was especially relevant to the agricultural sector, because Japanese consumers had indicated a strong interest (even stronger than the U.S. domestic market itself) for American fruit, vegetables, and meat. Johnson personally initiated bilateral talks, fully expecting results, and soon.[14] But a U.S. coup remained elusive, as it would be for Johnson's successors.

The Japanese excise taxes on the few U.S. automobiles that entered the country, as well as on bourbon whiskey, were especially annoying to the White House. Claiming that many U.S. automobiles were "unsafe" and that U.S. whiskey was "unsanitary," the Japanese kept these overly competitive products on the restricted list. Those few restricted items that managed to slip through did so courtesy of an "advance import deposit." Johnson regarded the latter as blackmail, noting that allies did not treat allies by exacting economic penalties. The Japanese government had no comment outside of its demand for "compensation" if, somehow, they were "humbled" into accepting America's wishes. Indeed, the rhetoric had changed from the Kennedy days, and compromises were few. Yet Johnson told his State and Commerce Departments not to worry. Tougher negotiations would yield the desired results, he predicted.[15]

The impact of Japanese imports on the dying U.S. wool industry was another touchy subject. Kennedy, Johnson believed, had been too generous to the Japanese on the issue, for the United States won nothing in return. Johnson, if not more of a free trader than Kennedy, was at least his predecessor's equal, but that offered little solace to the U.S. wool industry. In 1965, Johnson proposed a Wool Summit, whereby the Japanese would swear to restrict wool-fabric imports for the rest of the decade. The summit did indeed take place, but the Japanese did not swear their allegiance to U.S. trade interests. Held in the U.S. ambassador's residence in Tokyo, the Wool Summit turned out to be an exercise in Japanese manners and politeness. Heaping praise on the American president and people, the Japanese government offered many glowing testaments to the postwar Washington-Tokyo dialogue. But they refused to discuss the wool issue.[16]

Although annoyed with these refusals, Johnson never retreated. Future discussions on wool would be labeled partially successful if the Japanese delegation stayed in the same room with the Americans.[17] But if Washington was beginning to find the Japanese annoying and insulting, Tokyo had already made similar, yet stronger conclusions with regard to the Americans. Throughout the 1960s, the United States remained Japan's largest market, and Japan remained concerned that the aggregation of various measures that it viewed restrictive and protectionist would continue to impede the future growth of Japan's exports to the United States. In spite of attacks by both Kennedy and Johnson on protectionist Democrats in a Democratic-controlled and free-trader Congress, there were still Democrats who proposed restrictive import legislation. The situation made Japanese business and government especially nervous, for they believed that the president, commander in chief, and, technically, the leader of the Democratic Party, should control Democratic Party members.[18] Meanwhile, there was still a Buy-American policy in federal and state procurement, antidumping investigations, and, of course, the U.S. insistence on export restraints concerning wool.

The Johnson administration responded by pointing out the spectacular growth in Japan's exports to the United States throughout the first half of the 1960s ($700 million). This was during a period when the alleged impediments had been in effect. Japan's export controls generally had the impact of forestalling the imposition of import restrictions and had provided for orderly but significant growth. A comparison between the moderate export expansion in items subject to U.S. import restraint, such as stainless-steel flatware, and the substantial increases in items subject only to Japanese export control, such as chinaware, ceramic tiles, or wool fabrics, demonstrated why Japan preferred its export controls to U.S. import restrictions. Or so the Johnson team concluded.[19]

Washington's "escape clauses" also annoyed the Japanese. These were imposed as "exceptions" to America's general trade policy, and the Diet wanted the Americans to eliminate this "unfair procedure" sooner rather than later. The White House claimed that "unfair" or not, these "procedures" were rarely used, and were, of course, "under review." For example, in view of the partial recovery of the U.S. stainless-steel flatware industry in the mid-1960s, the Commerce and State Departments cooperated in a comprehensive review of U.S. trade policy in that area. Cleverly written, the final 1965 review left the decision to continue protectionist practice to the Oval Office itself. In response, Johnson ordered a top-to-bottom review of all "escape clause" protectionist policies. In late 1967, those U.S. industries under protection had to prove to the Tariff Commission that protection was still necessary. Customs valuations were also put under review, and Johnson hoped it would all lead to a summit to discuss getting rid of tariff barriers. He was wrong. The summit would never take place, but, in difficult, low-key discussions with the Japanese, antidumping regulations were amended in January 1965 to take account of "both foreign and domestic interests." The rest, Johnson explained in a secret memo to the Japanese government, was up to the U.S. Congress. Meanwhile, he promised to help "his friends in Congress make up their minds."[20]

Issuing executive branch condemnations of congressional action to restrict imports, bureaucrats from the Commerce Department, State Department, and the NSC offered testimony in Congress against proposed "anti-Japanese legislation." They also urged the repeal of older measures. It was the Johnson team's best offensive against protectionism, but Buy-American requirements, for instance, remained in place due to "balance of payments necessity." Learning the hard way that it was difficult for Americans to reach a certain consensus over economic foreign-policy issues, Johnson continued to speak out against protectionism. Pointing a finger at the guilt was never a simple matter. Whereas Washington renounced making any industrial policy as undue government interference in the free flow of the economy, state governors enacted legislation that limited trade with Japan at the nonfederal level. Johnson explained to the Japanese government that protectionism involving states rights "raised serious Constitutional problems," but that his government never condoned discriminatory action by states. But the Diet complained that the Johnson administration had let the situation "get out of hand."[21]

As early as 1965, Johnson suggested that the shouting match

between the United States and Japan could be quieted if his administration worked harder to assault protectionism and if Japan opened to direct U.S. investment. Ikeda claimed that he had done more than Johnson suggested, but the Americans had good reason to dispute the claim. On July 1, 1963, the Ikeda government had announced that the rigorous criteria that ruled over potential American investors in Japan was soon to be "liberalized." More than two years later, there was no obvious evidence to prove "liberalization" had ever taken place. The Diet refused to release any information on the subject, yet insisted that "liberalization" needed more time to work. With no data outside of contradictory press reports, and a frustrated U.S. business community claiming "liberalization equals incarceration," Johnson decided to enforce a little-known postwar treaty, the U.S.-Japan Treaty of Friendship, Commerce and Navigation (FCN). The treaty permitted the U.S. federal government to represent the concerns of potential investors in Japan on a case-by-case basis. With thousands of cases to champion, the United States could overwhelm Japan with legal challenges. The latter would be a very public spectacle, and, Johnson hoped, rather embarrassing to Japan's self-image of the cooperative, happy democracy with world-power ambitions. The onus would be on Japan to abandon restrictions and welcome the investors. The misery would be Japan's, not America's.[22]

Johnson did not consider the fact that U.S. businesses might not want to be pawns in the larger story of U.S.-Japan relations. According to the clauses of the FCN, the White House would have to prove that U.S. businesses had been materially injured by Japan's refusal to permit investment. This would not be easy. Given the Japanese government's intimate connection to Japanese business, many U.S. businesses were reluctant to participate in a Johnson-led campaign that might prohibit the Japanese market from them for years to come.[23] Even if Johnson won every case, there was concern that the resulting climate of ill will that might be directed from Japanese government/ business toward U.S. business would still make any future investment procedure difficult indeed.

Facing the retreat of U.S. business, the Johnson administration backed away from its promised battle with Japan. Instead, it drafted a simple complaint to Tokyo and hoped for happier results in other areas of the U.S.-Japan relationship: "The United States calls attention to Japan the unfavorable public image which is being carried within the United States as well as in other developed countries as a result of Japan's continued restrictions on private capital flows. The United States requests that Japan review its policies with respect to direct investment inflows and outflows, with a view toward constructive liberalization steps."[24]

Takeo Miki, the director of MITI in the mid-1960s, had little interest in responding to these "American charges." Favoring a hard line against Johnson's hardball politics, Miki dreamed of his own prime ministership someday. Standing tall against U.S. posturing would benefit his career. Only in his fifties, Miki represented the future of the Liberal Democratic Party, or so he hoped. Etsusaburo Shiina, the Japanese foreign minister, disagreed. Shiina had helped negotiate the mutual security treaty with the Americans, and had been Ikeda's first MITI director. Aged and in ill health, Shiina opposed antagonizing the Americans on economic issues, and he thought Miki was something of the Lyndon Johnson in the LDP; in short, he found Miki overly belligerent and inflexible. That did not mean Shiina favored an economy open to American investment and trade. He just found the new anti-American rhetoric distasteful and ungentlemanly.[25]

The split in the Japanese cabinet over the proper policy toward the United States put the Japanese ambassador to the United States, Ryuji Takeuchi, in a precarious position. Johnson believed that one of the major reasons for the growing tension between Japan and the United States involved American ignorance of the full Japanese view. One way to solve the problem involved frequent contact with the Japanese ambassador. Consequently, more so than in any other postwar administration, the Japanese ambassador was often called to the White House. Quite fluent in English and known for his wicked sense of humor, of the members of the foreign diplomatic corps, Takeuchi was one of the U.S. president's favorites. When Japanese diplomatic relations were established with Washington in 1952, Takeuchi had been the first chargé d'affaires of the new Japanese embassy. He was also one of the founding fathers of MITI, a former vice minister for foreign affairs and a strong admirer of America's consumer culture. Bucking the image of the stereotypical workaholic and humorless

Tokyo bureaucrat, Takeuchi once noted that a good diplomat should bring "life experience and verve" to his assignment, rather than "parchment from Harvard and Tokyo University." This backhanded insult of both Edwin Reischauer and much of the Diet did not go unnoticed by Johnson. He welcomed the opportunity to deal with someone, like himself, "who calls it like he sees it."[26]

But did Takeuchi represent Takeuchi or the Japanese government? There were times when this was not easily answered. Johnson nevertheless continued to enjoy Takeuchi's company. Whereas the official Tokyo position suggested a Japanese economy always on the verge of takeoff, but needing great care and security lest that takeoff fail, Takeuchi presented a Japan whose economic world clout was well-established and growing.[27] Washington's think-tank studies of the Japanese economy also reflected this confusion. Hence, it was not unusual for Johnson to hear several different versions of the Japanese "economic miracle." Whether influenced by Takeuchi, the pressures of the war in Vietnam, the need to better coordinate America's Asian/ Pacific economic policies, or all of these matters, Johnson considered Japan an ally whose role in the world was already too meager for its economic standing. Easing Japan into that global role, and for the betterment of U.S. policy as well, would become a frustrating task for Johnson.[28]

In reality, the Japanese economy was neither flawless nor failing in the mid-to-late-1960s. The early New Japan policies were proceeding according to plan, but it remained to be seen how unpredicted events, such as America's struggle in Vietnam, would influence Japan's steady rise to economic power. Fiscal policy remained cautious. In June 1965, the Japanese government reduced the Bank of Japan's basic discount rate to the lowest level since 1951. Deflation was avoided, and the Japanese government's new discount-rate policy prevented a large number of business failures as well as sharp declines in the securities market. By using both monetary policies and accelerating public-works programs, the Japanese government stimulated consumer demand. Growth had brought its problems to Japan, and it was this issue that illustrated the fact that the Japanese economy was not the "miracle" some politicians proclaimed.

The extremely rapid growth of the Japanese economy had led to serious structural imbalances that had been only partly corrected by the time Johnson came to power. Many firms had expanded productive facilities without adequate attention to sound financial management or future demand conditions.[29] Japan's GNP growth rate during 1965, for instance, was 7.5 percent. By U.S. standards, this was hardly a recession or cause for alarm. Yet the Japanese press and some politicians suggested that the era of growth was coming to an end; hard times were ahead. Or so they predicted.[30]

Compared with the 10.5 percent GNP growth rate for 1964, the 7.5 percent figure was a disappointment, but hardly the end of the world. By crying over these figures, the Johnson White House concluded, Japan was attempting to avoid the economic responsibilities of a soon-to-be world power. Johnson recommended that the Japanese government take "corrective measures" to prevent further declines in industrial production. On the other hand, he also insisted that Tokyo act more like the world power and less like the defeated nation of World War II.[31]

Takeuchi made it clear to Johnson that his government did not have the confidence of the "sound American dollar." He predicted that the Diet's full attentions would be placed on domestic economic "recovery" for the next few years. This influenced the entire U.S.-Japan economic relationship, for there would be no Japanese softening of the hard line against liberalizing import policy, no listening to U.S. complaints over textile issues, and no consideration of Johnson's personal requests for Japanese aid to developing Asian/Pacific countries. Considering the Japanese government's own GNP growth figures, this response remained most frustrating to Johnson.[32] Nevertheless, Tokyo's position on its allegedly bad economy also remained unchanged throughout the remaining years of the 1960s.

Fighting frustration with irony, Johnson informed Takeuchi that the Japanese government might make up for its bowing out of significant economic-cooperation measures with the United States by reconsidering its trade relationship with the communist bloc. The revenue Japan earned through its economic connections with the communists could be used to help the United States better develop non-communist Third World countries in the Asian/Pacific region. This revolving door of money might illustrate Japan's continued commitment against communist expansionism and restore a healthier Washington-Tokyo dialogue at the same time. Both Johnson and Takeuchi enjoyed the irony of it all, but in reality the president was not so concerned about the precise financial source of a Japanese aid plan to the Asian/Pacific Third World.[33]

During the mid-to-late 1960s, the Japanese government continued, on the one hand, to cooperate with the United States in limiting its trade in strategic material with communist nations (including Cuba). On the other hand, it developed a brisk trading relationship in nonstrategic material. America's Western European allies had trailblazed the way in making economic connections with the communists, providing long-term credits to the USSR and Eastern Europe. The Japanese deplored a credit race, but they worried that Western European inroads with the communists might lead to a successful penetration of communist China. The latter, they believed, should be Japan's destiny. Meanwhile, Japan led America's allies as the number one trading partner of Fidel Castro's Cuba. Indeed, the Japanese had become the world's largest purchaser of Cuban sugar, and one of Cuba's leading suppliers. Johnson protested this development, but Takeuchi insisted that sugar imports were in private hands and not licensed by the government.[34] The Japanese importers followed "commercial considerations," he said.

Johnson warned his Japanese friend that Washington could no longer tolerate maverick nations on the outskirts of the Free World's march to Cold War victory. In fact, Johnson's warning was a stern one. The trading of insults was not unusual between Takeuchi and Johnson; however, this time, the president's hard line was difficult to brush aside. It also represented irreversible U.S. policy.

> We oppose the extension of long-term credits to the Bloc, believing a credit race would seriously injure free world interests. We will continue to press for agreed rules. On Cuban sugar trade, the Government of Japan can help by encouraging refiners to purchase as much sugar as possible from free-world suppliers, thereby depriving the Castro regime of support and helping free-world exporters in a time of excess supplies and depressed prices.[35]

Busy cultivating their growing trade relationship with the United

States during the Kennedy era, the Japanese had hoped the procedure would continue smoothly under Johnson. But, as they quickly discovered, Johnson could be as unpredictable as they themselves were. Trading procedure, and particularly trading in blocs, remained a particularly touchy subject in Tokyo. Championed by Australia and Nigeria in international forums ranging from the United Nations to the OECD, the idea of preferential trading blocs was taking hold in a number of the countries that faced rapid economic growth. To Japan, a being limited to a single trading bloc promised to deprive them of a healthy consumer market for their heavily consumer-oriented export economy. Diet members spoke out loud and clear against the very concept, while Washington chose not to offer an official position. The Japanese government assumed that the Americans were opposed to trading blocs and favored free trade with free countries. This was true, but Johnson's comments on the trading-blocs idea were always lukewarm in the presence of Japanese government officials. His approach implied to the Japanese that he would denounce the blocs if Tokyo broke down its own barriers to trade. That was exactly the impression Johnson wanted to leave; however, the State Department disagreed with him.[36]

Secretary of State Rusk worried that Johnson, always so unpredictable in contrast to Kennedy, could add more tension to the U.S.-Japanese relationship than necessary. Rusk was particularly interested in wooing Japan into a financial-contributions policy toward Southeast Asia infrastructure development. Certainly, it would demonstrate anti-communist solidarity as the Vietnam War continued to escalate. But it might influence political developments in the region as well. Johnson shared similar ambitions, but Rusk always warned the president that Washington's Japan policy was the product of a variety of economic, political, and defense-related priorities. A failure in one area could trigger a general failure of the entire policy. Viewing the Japanese as shaky, confused allies in the Cold War, Rusk, like Johnson, hoped to avoid embarrassing problems behind the front line of the Vietnam War. But he worried more than the president did.[37]

Whereas Johnson preferred an activist Japan on "all fronts"—moral, diplomatic, political, economic, and even military (if necessary) in the continuing Vietnam War—Rusk stressed the "possible fronts." Beginning in the summer of 1965, Rusk pressed the Japanese to join a proposed U.S.-led Southeast Asia Development Program. Put forward in the meetings of the Joint United States–Japan Committee on Trade and Economic Affairs, this aid scheme was considered a means of victory over communism throughout Southeast Asia. As a sort of Marshall Plan with international participation, this massive infrastructure-assistance effort was expected to deaden the appeal of communism village by village. More to the point, it would, in Johnson's own terms, "do the job" in contrast to the limited operations of the Peace Corps and other assistance plans. Continuing to enjoy the ironic twists, Johnson planned to ask North Vietnam's Ho Chi Minh to join in this economic excitement. Perhaps, finally realizing his nation's isolation and banishment from rapid economic development, Ho might become part of this cooperative Pacific community; the Vietnam War would soon be history. This, of course, was all wishful thinking, and Rusk, apparently, preferred dreaming out loud. He said Japanese participation in the new program was the key to a successful U.S.-led appeal to Ho.[38]

To Kiichi Miyazawa, the new director of Japan's Economic Planning Agency, Rusk's Southeast Asia Development Program smacked of the defunct New Pacific Community proposal. Japan was no one's junior partner, the always-tough-minded Miyazawa believed. Nevertheless, Rusk's latest anti-communist dream intrigued him. Miyazawa admitted to his pro-Washington colleagues that Japan could gain from some Southeast Asian role with the Americans, as long as Rusk's program promised results and as long as the Americans did not make requests that compromised Japan's constitutional commitment to peace and anti-interventionism. Miyazawa favored an official announcement that Japan "was about to join" Rusk's program, a move to be followed by a period of "watching and waiting" while the Americans took the first steps.[39]

Takeo Fukuda, the finance minister, and Foreign Minister Shiina worried that a "wait and see" policy might annoy the Americans and backfire against Japan's U.S.-centered export policy. But Miyazawa's point that the Rusk proposal was a rehash of New Pacific Community dreaming was well taken, and no one in the Diet wished to exhaust Japanese economic resources in an American-led effort to throw money at Southeast Asia. So the Japanese government offered its "moral" support to Washington's efforts while it "studied further economic action."[40]

Given the glowing rhetoric that was included in Tokyo's endorsement of the Southeast Asia Development Program, Rusk assumed that active Japanese participation was forthcoming. Japan, he believed, was making up for its lack of support for Kennedy's New Pacific Community organization. As the months went by, Rusk complained that the Japanese government was too slow-moving in dedicating a percentage of its GNP to infrastructure projects in South Vietnam and Laos. Miyazawa insisted that his government favored "hard loans" and "tied aid" to Southeast Asian countries, and that breaking down this fiscally conservative decision would take time. Miyazawa's agency held jurisdiction over any Southeast Asian economic involvement for Japan, and he claimed that his country's economic resources were not as great as the Americans assumed.[41]

In reality, Washington's assessment of Japan's great economic success was quite accurate. Rusk demanded that Japan renounce its Third World mentality, become "more flexible," and join the ranks of "donor aid nations without strings attached." Receiving no reply on this issue from Tokyo, an angry Rusk cabled the Japanese government noting that the stabilization of Southeast Asia should be a Japanese matter of concern. "Expanded trade and economic opportunity," he warned, "can only be achieved in the future by making aid available on a flexible basis now."[42]

Rusk proposed a conference on the Vietnam/Laos aid issue alone, suggesting, like the good diplomat, that his angry comments did not mean to threaten Japanese trade with the United States. The Washington-Tokyo dialogue remained a healthy one, he said.[43] Without question, in contrast to the trade, nuclear, and Ryukyus policy matters that often dominated Japanese politics, the Americans continued to see communist expansionism as the only issue that should dominate any democratic nation's politics. Explaining the continuing evil of communism to the Japanese was most annoying to the Johnson administration. But, in a special conference of the Joint United States–Japan Committee on Trade and Economic Affairs, Rusk provided five points to the Japanese government concerning why they should be actively and immediately involved in a massive economic plan for Southeast Asia.

First, the "Free World's economic front" in Southeast Asia was meant to "rescue," rather than simply aid, the economies there. Hence, there was a certain urgency to the matter. During the opening months of this "economic offensive" in Southeast Asia, the region's inhabitants would become "more deeply opposed to Chinese expansion in that area," or so Rusk promised. Japan would have the opportunity to help "build" this new bastion of anti-communism. The secretary of state chose his words deliberately, contrasting the new, "concerned" Japanese citizen to the older, World War II–era Japan of "destructive power" fame. He urged the Japanese to accept their destiny as an influential peacemaker.

Second, Japan's participation would lead to a sharing role with the United States in "fostering regional cooperation." Rusk meant that Japan could reap some economic profit in the near future from Vietnamese and Laotian consumers. But Miyazawa and his colleagues concluded that some sort of military consortium was under consideration by the Americans. Rusk's lack of clarity here would provide the Japanese a later escape clause from the entire proposal.

Third, the complete effort was meant to "sway" Ho Chi Minh away from his Chinese and Soviet ties—to lure him into the "peaceful economic development of Southeast Asia" and to help him define "national liberation" in terms of a better life for the North Vietnamese people. Japan would win global recognition for its participation in this peaceful persuasion, Rusk insisted. From the U.S. viewpoint, that benefit alone was worth full Japanese participation.

Fourth, although Rusk had had doubts on the matter, he urged the Japanese to take advantage of their trade relationship with the Soviet Union and urge the latter to invest with Japan in Southeast Asia. This Soviet involvement, Rusk assumed, would follow the initial success of his aid program. Early involvement might stimulate a nonaligned position from the targeted countries, whereby, in a fit of nationalism, Southeast Asians would reject the involvement of the two superpowers, the United States and the Soviet Union, in their respective economies. Japan would serve as mediator here; however, the Americans were quite vague over Tokyo's precise role in winning Soviet support.

Finally, Japan's economic assistance would assure a certain harmony among Asian/Pacific peoples, burying old World War II–era animosities, promoting lasting peace, and eliminating the threat of communist insurgency. Indeed, the U.S. secretary of state had great faith in the power of the dollar, yen, and other currencies, for "this was not the early 1960s," Rusk told his Japanese audience. The United States had no intention of putting back together the poorly received New Pacific Community organization. There were no threats to sovereignty, no calls for military retaliation against Ho Chi Minh, and no suggestion that aid participation should harm the donor nation's domestic economy. It was, he said, the new direction of anti-communism in the Asian/Pacific region. It pointed the way to the 1970s and beyond. Japan, Rusk concluded, should be part of this new era of global economic responsibility.[44]

The secretary of state's thesis in this top-secret conference assumed that his country's growing military presence in South Vietnam was irrelevant to the tasks at hand. American military power was invincible and the U.S. dollar, acting in full coordination with the ever-rising Japanese yen, could work miracles in Southeast Asia. Meanwhile, Miyazawa, Shiina, Fukuda, and other senior Japanese government officials at this summer 1965 conference did not have a crystal ball. They did not foresee the reversal of U.S. military fortunes in Vietnam. But they did see Vietnam in a more complex light than big aid plans.[45]

Part of that complexity involved Ho Chi Minh. Ho had little interest in being maneuvered by Washington, Moscow, Beijing, or any foreign capital. Interested in victory for his cause, and not international aid plans, Ho, nevertheless, remained a mysterious figure to his Western opponents.[46] To the Japanese, communist or not, Ho was a determined opponent to Western culture and influence.[47] At least in the realm of propaganda, Ho's "Vietnam for the Vietnamese" cause was similar to Japan's World War II cry of "Asia for Asians." Although the Japanese government would later claim that they understood North Vietnam's military ambitions better than Washington, there was no indication during and after the Southeast Asian Development Program conference that the Japanese had any first-hand knowledge of those ambitions or that they had any interest in the U.S. agenda at the development-program conference itself. Reluctant to engage in any policy that might threaten hard-fought gains in world trade and the resulting good economic fortune at home, the Japanese government was not interested in a Southeast Asia crusade.[48] That lack of adventurous spirit would be left for the Americans to figure out, because Tokyo never offered a formal rejection of Rusk's aid plan. Preferring to stall for time, and hoping that wartime developments would overshadow Rusk's plans, the Japanese expressed a token interest in Southeast Asian interventionism.

Speaking on behalf of the Japanese government, Miyazawa favored a limited agricultural role for his country in Southeast Asia. In fact, he called for the establishment of an "agricultural development fund." Its purpose would be to reduce the Southeast Asian nations' need for food imports and to spur economic development in general. If implemented properly, Rusk thought the fund proposal was a decent one. Forever pressing Miyazawa for details, Rusk would never get a deadline from the Japanese on the precise date for implementation. He was also unsure how the fund was expected to work. From Rusk's point of view, Miyazawa's measure seemed to suggest that Japan also wanted to move Southeast Asia away from successful rice production and exports. A booming rice economy in Southeast Asia, unless influenced by Japan, was not in Tokyo's interest. Building the region into a potential major competitor for Japanese economic interests, agricultural or not, was also a contradiction in Japanese policy. Miyazawa never admitted this point of view to Rusk, although the frustrated secretary of state attempted to discuss the issue with Miyazawa throughout the remaining years of the Johnson administration.[49]

While refusing to answer the Americans straightforwardly on the Rusk initiatives, Foreign Minister Shiina offered his own no-nonsense policy for peace in Vietnam. Shiina proposed to meet with the Soviet leadership, volunteering Japan's "good offices" as a go-between for peace. Meeting in Tokyo with the Soviets and the North Vietnamese on one side of the peace table and the Americans and the South Vietnamese on the other, the Japanese government planned to broker a peace before the end of 1966. Expecting the full discussion to last one year, Shiina explained that any reason for delay would be entirely America's fault. The United States, he said, maintained a "holy war spirit." Trying to win the Cold War, Shiina argued, had led Washington to further the nuclear arms race and wage a "dirty war in Southeast Asia." Indeed, upon learning that North Vietnam might place downed U.S. bomber pilots on trial for war crimes, Shiina compared that possibility with the postwar trials of alleged Japanese war criminals by the Americans after World War II. Most of America's complaint against Japan's World War II leadership had been misplaced, he said, and the trials were a mistake.[50]

To Johnson, Shiina's comments were "bizarre" and "uncalled for." They implied that the predicament of the downed U.S. flyers in North Vietnam constituted, somehow, overdue revenge for the so-called unnecessary war-crimes trials of the immediate postwar period. Shiina had nothing more to say on the matter, but other Japanese political and press figures continued to discuss the "war crimes issue" in the remaining months of 1966.

Meanwhile, Andrei Gromyko, the Soviet foreign minister, on the one hand welcomed the Japanese invitation for Vietnam peace talks; on the other, he insisted that the United States would have to make some gesture toward military withdrawal from Vietnam before serious negotiations could begin. In the name of humanity, Gromyko urged the Japanese government to use its powers of persuasion over Washington and initiate the first step toward true Southeast Asian peace. Shiina joked that his powers of persuasion were more imagined than real, but Johnson found little humor in the new Tokyo-Moscow dialogue. Johnson's anger reached a boiling point in the hot summer of 1966.

During late July 1966, Gromyko and Shiina met in Yokohama to discuss a variety of issues ranging from North Pacific fishing rights to nuclear proliferation. But it was their Vietnam discussion that troubled the U.S. president. Shortly before Gromyko left Japan, Shiina and the Soviet foreign minister held a joint news conference. The two diplomats presented an amiable, if not jolly, demeanor to the world press. Suggesting that they saw eye to eye on matters of nuclear disarmament and Vietnam, Shiina and Gromyko parted the best of friends. Or so it appeared in public. With this situation in mind, Johnson dispatched Assistant Secretary of State William Bundy to Tokyo. As the featured speaker at an academic conference on U.S.-

Japan relations, Bundy had been expected to praise that relationship. Instead, an animated and angry Bundy attacked the Japanese government. Accusing Japan of selfishness, deceit, and worse, Bundy proclaimed that the LDP had departed from its democratic path. Embracing appeasement instead of steadfastness against communist expansionism, the recent Gromyko-Shiina meeting, Bundy said, represented little more than an "Asian Munich." As the democracies learned during Hitler's 1938 conference in Munich over the future of Czechoslovakia, the Japanese government must learn, Bundy concluded, that a peaceful future cannot be built on "surrender to aggression." Speaking on behalf of the U.S. commander in chief, Bundy announced that there would be no U.S. military withdrawal from Vietnam in the near future. There would be no Japanese-brokered peace, and that the Soviets were too interested in their own ruthless agenda to be considered sincere advocates for peace. The Japanese, he noted, were being tricked and played for fools by the Soviets. The American economy had little room for fools.[51]

Bundy's last statement implied that the U.S. market might be closed off to the Japanese "economic miracle" if Tokyo continued to interfere in Vietnam policy. He denied the implication, but it had the desired effect. Shiina insisted that the United States had misinterpreted the meeting with Gromyko, and that U.S. politicians made their conclusions about Japan based on the English-language Japanese press. The latter, he noted, never represented the Japanese government's position in world affairs. Shiina even gave a radio address in which he attacked certain Japanese newspapers and news agencies for providing a false impression of Japanese policy to the Americans. Urging Washington to determine the difference between press reports and Japan's good intentions in international affairs, Shiina insisted that Tokyo was as anti-communist as ever.

The maligned Japanese press did not take Shiina's charges lightly. Finding quotable bureaucrats in Shiina's own Foreign Ministry, the *Mainichi Daily* and *Tokyo Shimbun* attempted to prove that the Japanese government was indeed opposed to American actions in Vietnam and in favor of the Soviet position for immediate U.S. military withdrawal from the war. Akira Sono, longtime foreign-policy making colleague of Shiina and Foreign Ministry liaison to the world press, was one of them. Next to Shiina, he had been the most visible government official in the public fight against the alleged anti-American press. Privately, he was opposed to Japan "always going along with the United States." The war in Vietnam was "racist," he believed, and the Americans had been "war happy" since 1941.

Once his private views were exposed, Sono insisted that his comments were exaggerated by the press and that the whole matter symbolized the press conspiracy that haunted U.S.-Japan relations. His only concern vis-à-vis the Vietnam matter, he admitted, was that the United States did not have the best humanitarian interests of the Vietnamese in mind. Raw anti-communist considerations dominated U.S. policymaking, he said, and the new, peaceful Japan had an obligation to remind Washington of the importance of human rights.[52]

"Misunderstanding" might be the only "cement" in the U.S.-Japan relationship, Bundy lamented in a late-1966 report to Johnson. Whereas in other countries, an anti-Vietnam position could be easily labeled "leftist," easy labels remained elusive when applied to the Japanese scene. No one could ever accuse the conservative Shiina or Sono of leftist agitation. Because of the confused Japanese political spectrum, Bundy predicted that Japan would eventually "come around" to America's point of view on Vietnam. Washington's united, unassailable determination to eliminate communist threats in Southeast Asia was destined to prevail, Bundy said, and Japan, tired of confusion and always ready to work with winners, would become America's strongest Pacific region ally.[53]

Bundy's analysis represented the Johnson administration's best assessment of U.S.-Japan relations at the early height of the Vietnam War. It also staved off Johnson's "the hell with them" attitude toward the Japanese at the time. During the Gromyko-Shiina meeting flap, Johnson noted that it was time to ignore Japan and suffer any consequences. To Johnson, Japan was first and foremost the home of U.S. military-basing privileges relevant to the war in Vietnam. Kadena Air Base on Okinawa in the Ryukyus was already playing a major role in the daily air war over North Vietnam. As in the matter of expanding the war itself in Southeast Asia, Johnson intended to expand rear-area U.S. military privileges in Japan if the war demanded it. If Japan did not want to be considered an enemy of the United States, it would simply have to agree to more conventional U.S. forces, and even ignore the presence of nuclear weapons if need be. The latter, of course, was a slap in the face to the spirit of U.S.-Japan friendship. But that friendship was becoming too difficult to define for Johnson, and the war in Vietnam had to be won.[54]

Bundy urged his boss to let diplomacy take its course. Let Japan reassess its relationship to Washington in light of its economic dreams, he said, and especially in light of the Gromyko-Shiina fallout. A frustrated Johnson agreed, but he began the second half of his term believing that Japan must prove itself a loyal ally in the continuing Cold War.[55]

Although a growing disgust for Japan represented a certain White House view, it did not guide the general thrust of U.S. policy. Bundy, and especially Rostow, hoped to quiet Tokyo, making sure that anti-Vietnam rumblings in Japan did not embarrass the Washington-led anti-communist solidarity in the world. Inheriting the Japanese insistence on Ryukyus reversion from the Kennedy administration, the Johnson team now endured even louder complaints from Tokyo on the issue. Retiring from his post shortly after the Gromyko-Shiina meeting, Ambassador Reischauer had warned the White House that Japan would soon be taking advantage of America's stalemate in Vietnam. The pressure would come in the form of Ryukyus reversion demands rather than from trade matters, he predicted.[56] Trade was too important and sensitive a subject to toy with in the international arena. The Ryukyus constituted a different matter, stressing issues of racial justice, moral leadership, and true Japanese independence from "colonial rule." All of these issues had relevance to America's mission in Vietnam, and the Japanese intended to remind Johnson of that fact. Ending United States sovereignty over the Ryukyus would, in the Japanese sense, purify America's anti-communist mission in the Asian/Pacific region. Urging Johnson to negotiate wisely and avoid emotional reactions to Japanese pressure, Reischauer insisted that the fate of the entire U.S.-Japan relationship was at stake over Washington's response on the reversion issue.[57]

The outgoing ambassador, who left for personal more than political reasons, was quite correct in his prediction of new Japanese pressures. Like Kennedy, Johnson admired Reischauer's credentials and expertise. On the other hand, Johnson found Reischauer's warnings and predictions overly dramatic and spectacular. Drama and spectacle remained well-placed in Kennedy's Camelot, but Camelot died in Dallas. Johnson preferred no-nonsense advice and fast-moving results. Japan, Johnson believed, still lacked the clout and significance to influence the course of the Cold War in Asia. The new ambassador to Japan, U. Alexis Johnson—a Texas businessman and cousin of LBJ's— agreed with the president. But he also went to Tokyo convinced he was about to face a whirlwind of Japanese demands over the Ryukyus.[58] He was not mistaken.

In terms of charisma, lifestyle, and political approach, Ambassador Johnson following Reischauer was much like Lyndon Johnson following Kennedy. Meanwhile, ugly contrasts, not happy comparisons, between Reischauer and the new ambassador were made by the press on both sides of the Pacific. To Ambassador Johnson, Reischauer would indeed be the hard act to follow, but he believed that Reischauer's retirement was long overdue. Reischauer, he concluded, had treated the Japanese like children, talking down to them from the position of his own great intellectual prowess and his country's superpower might. Times had changed, and that reality must be symbolized by a less visible U.S. ambassador who remained respectful of Japan's desire for world economic power. Writing in his diary, he noted: "My own feeling is that relations between our two countries now need to be put on a mature basis of two great countries dealing with each other with a sense of maturity and with a mature fashion. Thus, I look forward to more normal diplomatic practice, more normal diplomacy with them, working through their government."[59]

The new ambassador agreed with Reischauer on the growing significance of the Ryukyus in Japanese politics, but he disagreed on how "real" the issue had become to the Japanese government. Every Japanese politician, from the far Right to the far Left, had to pay lip service to the reversion matter. Wrapped up in nationalism, sovereignty, human rights, anti-Americanism, and history, the Ryukyus debate always pushed the right political buttons in Japan. Because of that fact, Ambassador Johnson reasoned that the Japanese political community was not too anxious to see the debate resolved. It was too valuable to personal political ambition and, therefore, for the moment, more valuable as a debate than a concluded U.S.-Japan agreement.[60] That meant the United States had time to bargain and come up with the best negotiated deal.

Ambassador Johnson's interest in low-profile wheeling and dealing made him the president's best man for the job. Did Japan truly wish to inherit the military responsibilities that might quickly follow reversion? The new ambassador doubted it, and his intuition here was quite right. Foreign Minister Shiina spearheaded the reversion argument personally, insisting on "statements" from Ambassador Johnson that might promise that reversion in the "near future." When pressed by Ambassador Johnson on the issue of why he preferred "statements" over "policy," Shiina was shocked at the very question and had no comment. The new ambassador told the Japanese government that it would have to reach consensus on what to do over the Ryukyus. The time for political slogans was over, and the time for meaningful negotiations had begun. Hence, Ambassador Johnson, fully supported by the White House, blamed Japan for the slow-moving reversion of the Ryukyus to Japan.[61]

Blaming Japan was a clever tactic. It bought time for the Johnson administration to conduct Vietnam air operations from Kadena without worrying about the impact of reversion on them. Ambassador Johnson was also right on the mark in reference to Japanese disunity and confusion over the Ryukyus. The Japanese political community stood united in its attacks on U.S. colonialism, but a specific plan for the reversion period and immediate postreversion period remained far from reality.[62] Japan's anti-American politics, cheered on by Ryukyus reversion activists, would always be a problem, Ambassador Johnson predicted. But it was a tolerable problem.

> When they look at Okinawa with realistic eyes, they recognize that our bases and our military posture down there could possibly again involve them in war, and they shrink back from that. Yet at the same time, they want the administration of Okinawa returned to Japan. My own approach on handling this has been to point out that this is really not an issue between Japan and the United States, it's an issue for Japan itself to resolve. Japan must decide what kind of military presence they want the United States to maintain out here, both from their own immediate standpoint and from the

standpoint of the rest of East Asia. Once they determine that, then we can discuss the question of Okinawa in much more realistic terms.[63]

The last thing President Johnson needed as he began to turn his full administrative attention toward the war in Vietnam was a collapse in the Tokyo-Washington dialogue.[64] Whether the White House wanted to accept the fact or not, Okinawa promised to become a major stumbling block to friendly U.S.-Japan relations. Under article 3 of the peace treaty with Japan, the United States had acquired full powers of administration, legislation, and jurisdiction over the Ryukyu Islands, including Okinawa. America's military bases there had represented the heart of Washington's Asian/Pacific military presence. The treaty had never obliged the United States to return these islands to Japan, but, when the treaty was signed, the U.S. government recognized that Japan retained residual sovereignty over the islands. The United States, especially during the Kennedy administration, had reaffirmed that right of sovereignty. With that fact in mind, both McGeorge Bundy and Walt Rostow warned Johnson that the reversion issue would get worse before it got better.[65]

At least, by 1966 the Johnson White House could claim that it had "heard" the Japanese arguments for reversion. Hence, U.S. policy fell into three categories: (1) reiterating America's intention to return the administration of the islands to Japan; (2) accommodating Japanese interests in establishing a greater degree of identity between Japan proper and the Ryukyus; and (3) accommodating to the maximum extent possible the Ryukyuan desire for a high degree of local autonomy. For a time, the Johnson team thought these assurances and positive comments would placate growing Japanese anger.[66] Part of the reason for this optimism involved the new (since 1964) Japanese prime minister, Eisaku Sato. As one of eight faction leaders within the LDP, Sato represented the most conservative coalition. Labeled "pro-American" because of his staunch anti-communism, pro-Washington position on Vietnam, and vigorous support for the U.S. bases in Japan, Sato's new government, in contrast to Ikeda's, was a breath of fresh air to Lyndon Johnson. But quickly the air turned stale. The LDP had reached its weakest level of public support in its brief history, as

Sato's opposition criticized the "Americanization" of the prime minister's office.[67] To stay in power or make his stay more politically comfortable, Sato would have to embrace a strong "nationalist" position. The Ryukyus issue was most convenient.

Soon after Sato's rise to power, Johnson had assured the new prime minister that Washington would "return the Ryukyu Islands when security interests of the Free World in the Far East will permit the realization of this desire."[68] Sato had welcomed the president's remarks, and many Japanese voters had interpreted this welcome as "weakness." By spring 1966, Johnson's key Japan advisers were predicting a "diplomatic hailstorm" over Okinawa within two years. The resulting shouting match between Tokyo and Washington would have a negative effect on allied relations everywhere, and that would impact the 1968 election at home. A new policy was needed.[69] But would the proud president, tired of Japanese rearguard pressures, have anything to do with it? Bundy and Rostow thought that Johnson would listen to them if things were put in economic terms. The Okinawa issue, they predicted, would soon influence U.S.-Japan and U.S.–Asian/ Pacific trade, hurting domestic and international business. In addition to some regional complaints over the U.S. role in Vietnam, a new Pacific-based trade war, they said, would equal the collapse of American influence "west of Guam." Presenting a deliberately dismal picture, Johnson's Japan experts continued to exaggerate the significance of Okinawa to solicit a presidential response.[70]

Without question, the entire Okinawa matter was a difficult one for Johnson to accept. He preferred the Japanese to "give" their support to the United States, and not the other way around. Thailand, the Philippines, South Korea, and even New Zealand and Australia were "giving" to Johnson's Vietnam War. In an initiative nicknamed the More Flags program, Johnson had been soliciting Asian-region military support for the Vietnam War effort since 1964. His primary interest remained in the area of combat volunteers, and he wanted fifty thousand of them. Those Asian/Pacific troops would not be offered to the United States for free, and Johnson became embroiled in a variety of impromptu-aid plans in exchange for a handful of men. At no time did Johnson contemplate full Asian/Pacific military participation in the making of Vietnam War policy. Yet he still expected the contribution of "some" combat volunteers. What he won amounted to a mercenary force that fought and died in, but had little influence on, the progress of the war.[71]

As far as Japan was concerned, Johnson continued to win an insignificant amount of infrastructure support for modernization projects in South Vietnam's Mekong Delta—and a lot of grief over Okinawa. It came as a surprise. As late as 1965, Johnson thought the Japanese might be persuaded to take a larger role in the Vietnam War. The pacifist Japanese constitution was irrelevant to him. The "right" political leader, if found, would move Japan into the "right" American direction, he believed. Hence, Johnson had included Japan in his long list of potential "more flags."[72] Japan, in this view, never existed as an independent entity with specific needs and wants. It was part of a regional whole that must benefit U.S. security priorities. Yet Johnson knew better: the complexities of Japanese politics would remind him of that fact, and the dream of having Japan as pro-American cheerleader remained short-lived.[73] Reality required the proper addressing of the Ryukyus issue. In any event, a workable reversion policy would have to satisfy both Johnson's desire for a coherent, unpressured, American-led defense strategy for the Pacific and Japan's interests in mutual respect and U.S. "decolonization." McGeorge Bundy wondered if a balance could ever be struck.

> In essence, the desirable trade would be one which restored Japanese civil government in Okinawa while insuring explicit Japanese acceptance of whatever military rights we need there. The trick here is that we need nuclear rights in Okinawa and that it will be hard for the Japanese to grant them explicitly. Perhaps this circle can be squared if we give the Japanese time and if as a government we are ready with our own position ahead of time.[74]

Johnson's brief flirtation with Japan as part of More Flags did not mean he discounted the need for healthy U.S.-Japan relations. He also understood the significance of Japan's interest in Ryukyus reversion. On the other hand, he disliked anti-American politicians in Tokyo setting a U.S. agenda during a time of war.[75] His original response to Bundy and Rostow's Ryukyus effort involved a simple endorsement of special U.S. monetary assistance to Ryukyuan infrastructure projects and more promises of reversion. Johnson had already approved a measure granting $22 million for the payment of 180,000 Okinawan land-rights claims. These claims grew out of seven years of U.S. military occupation (1945–52) and they had been waived by the peace treaty with Japan. Johnson said that this generous payment clearly indicated the "equitable and moral responsibility" of the United States. It was also given with Washington's "continuing concern for administrative authority over this archipelago."[76]

While Johnson and his staff mulled over a better response to the Ryukyus situation, Japanese politics aligned in two powerful camps. In one camp were those left-leaning politicians and reversion activists who favored full detente with the communist world, and who especially admired the independent spirit of Mao's Red China. China's official position on reversion demanded a nuclear-free Okinawa once the Americans began the reversion process. This played into the hands of the strong antinuclear movement in Japan, many of whom took an openly Maoist stance. They opposed reversion unless a nuclear-free agreement was part of the final deal. The other camp worried about a disgusted United States pulling out all-together, leaving the bulk of defense-related matters to Japan. The new Japanese foreign minister, Takeo Miki, had no problem agreeing with the Chinese-supported position and found Sato's pro-American approach most politically incorrect. Johnson commented that Miki, who once helped build the staunchly pro-U.S. bureaucracy of the Foreign Ministry, would do anything to achieve full power himself.[77] To Johnson, the Okinawa issue was tailor-made for "somebody like Miki." The president's assumptions were right on the mark, but this still did not create Washington's new approach to the reversion matter.

Both because of it and in spite of it, Sato remained in power throughout a full year of political confusion on reversion. He had wanted a quiet administration, reaping the profits of the New Japan launched by the frenetic politics of Ikeda and Miyazawa. It was not to be. With Okinawa occupying nearly his entire agenda, Sato traveled to Washington during November 1967. In the recent past, the Kennedy and Johnson administrations had been especially conscious of the Japanese preference for brief, no-nonsense diplomatic discussions, accompanied, ironically, by long, and very formal social gatherings.

This time, Johnson cut the formalities short, and the Sato meeting produced a quick U.S. conclusion on reversion.

With Rostow's and Bundy's close assistance, President Johnson knew his response to Japan even before Sato arrived. That did not mean it was a truly workable one. In Japan, Ambassador Johnson even worried that Sato was no longer in control of his own pro-American instincts. The ambassador remained unsure of the message that the prime minister was taking to Washington. On the very day Sato arrived at the White House, Lyndon Johnson's advisers were at a loss to predict any positive outcome of the meeting. The president was on his own.

Insisting that he was still in control of his own government, Sato presented a moderate position on reversion. Emphasizing the "strong will of the Japanese people" for the return of "administrative rights" in the Ryukyus, Sato noted that an "adequate solution could still be reached based on mutual understanding and trust."[78] The healthy dialogue between Tokyo and Washington was not over, he implied; no one truly expected a firm, immediate agreement to result from his mission. In a "few years," Sato suggested, reversion must be accomplished.

Johnson welcomed the calm, inviting tone of Sato's remarks, proclaiming that he, too, favored reversion. On the other hand, the priorities of U.S. military-basing privileges also assured the security of Japan, as Johnson pointed out. The distinction between administrative and military rights would have to be carefully ironed out. Addressing the issue of U.S. colonial oppression of Ryukyuan islanders, President Johnson reminded Sato that Japan had done little to uplift anyone's civil rights/civil liberties. He asked the Japanese prime minister for a financial commitment from Tokyo, whereby the latter would help the United States raise the public health, welfare, and education of Ryukyuan residents by 1971. In fact, Johnson recommended that Japan take the lead in this endeavor. At the same time, he promised U.S. support in establishing working economic relationships between Ryukyuan and Japanese businesses, but urged Japan to make those initial connections soon.[79] Change, Johnson said, would come quickly to Okinawa, and even the local government would have to reflect that fact; for instance, the Government of the Ryukyu Islands (GRI), so strongly modeled on the constitutions adopted by the various states of the United States, should evolve into a legislature styled more like the Japanese. This latter point was urged by both Johnson and Sato.[80]

All of Johnson's reversion decisions reminded Sato that the United States had been a generous overseer of Ryukyuan affairs; that many local residents had appreciated the effort, and "colonial oppression" had never been an issue there. Sato preferred to keep much of his Johnson meeting confidential, leaking various points made within it to the press at the right political moment. Since the U.S. theme at the meeting was cooperation with Asian/Pacific ambitions, Johnson saw great propaganda value in immediate discussions of such matters with the press; consequently, Johnson's press releases and follow-up news conference stressed great achievement and cooperation. Sato made little comment, noting that three years to reversion was a "long time." He hoped the process would be smooth.[81]

The most difficult discussion within the Sato-Johnson meeting had involved the position of the U.S. bases on Okinawa and whether they must continue to fall under the guidelines of the mutual security treaty after reversion. Sato avoided specifics, insisting that an official Japanese position would emerge during the coming three-year discussion period. He had no further comment on the matter. To Johnson, the issue of the bases was the whole purpose of the meeting. Sato's noncommittal behavior suggested to the entire Johnson team that Japanese politics were even more confused than usual.[82] They worried that Sato might indeed be dead right on at least one issue. It would be a "long" three years.

The first year proved the most difficult, and it had nothing to do with the negotiation process. A remarkable series of crises, some more imagined than real, would plague the general U.S.-Japan relationship going into the U.S. election of 1968. Individually, these crises did not paralyze U.S.-Japan relations; together, they had the potential of disturbing the Washington-Tokyo detente for years to come. One of them involved allegations that there were radiation leaks from the U.S. nuclear-powered submarine *Swordfish*, which prompted a number of antinuclear, anti-American demonstrations outside a U.S. Navy base, Sasebo, near Nagasaki. The Americans denied any nuclear pollution existed.

Another incident involved the reaction of U.S. bases in Japan to North Korea's capturing of the *Pueblo*, a U.S. Navy vessel on an intelligence-gathering mission off the coast of North Korea. Even nuclear-armed B-52 bombers arrived at Kadena Air Base on Okinawa, and other U.S. bases in Japan accelerated training exercises adjacent to heavily populated areas. The carrier *Enterprise*, a symbol of the U.S. Navy's nuclear-powered fleet, made port in Japan as a show of force against North Korea, but some Japanese saw it as a show of force against them, too.

Much of this took place during the period of the Tet offensive, the combined North Vietnamese and Vietcong-guerrillas assault on U.S. and Saigon government positions across South Vietnam. Facing a possible military defeat, Johnson maintained a state of readiness for all U.S. forces in the Pacific region. To the Japanese, this seemed to mean that Japan-stationed U.S. Air Force planes were constantly in the air above them, swooping low over their homes, forever training for war. Something was bound to happen. That something involved the crash of a U.S. F-4 fighter plane into the newly constructed computer center of the University of Kyushu. No one was injured and the two pilots ejected safely. But the aircraft's top-secret black-box recorder had to be retrieved from the destroyed computer center by armed U.S. military personnel.

To many Japanese, the F-4 incident was the last straw. It symbolized America's callous disregard for Japanese safety. The retrieval of the black box symbolized U.S. rejection of Japanese law; armed U.S.forces had no right to "invade" a Japanese computer center. Indeed, in a nation where symbolism continued to hold great political significance, the F-4 crash also suggested the lingering World War II power of the U.S. Air Force. It was U.S. air power that had destroyed so much of the old Japan; now, the new symbols of peaceful, postwar Japan, such as the University of Kyushu computer center, were disturbed by U.S. warplanes again. The latter was the subject of a number of reflective editorials in the Japanese media. President Johnson's only comment on the matter was that he was pleased to learn the two F-4 pilots were safe. Since some Japanese were expecting a presidential apology, Johnson's comments reaffirmed America's arrogant image.[83]

Politically, those dark days of 1968 meant daily demonstrations in front of a number of U.S. military installations, as well as the sudden alignment in the Japanese Diet of left- and right-wing forces who shared strong anti-American sentiments. Prime Minister Sato announced that a nuclear-free Okinawa was now "most likely essential to successful reversion," even though, and only weeks before, he had never personally associated himself with the issue.[84] Meanwhile, racial tensions between Americans and Japanese occupied top media attention in Tokyo. Thousands of U.S. marines in Vietnam, who had helped hold back success for the enemy in the Tet offensive, were either returned home or ordered to Okinawa. On Okinawa, some marines exhibited a strong distaste for their Asian/Pacific environment, triggering a violent crime wave such as the island had not seen before. Local police reports of rapes and beatings of Okinawa residents by these hardened combat veterans dominated the Japanese news, the marines insisting that their victims were "just Gooks anyway."[85]

U.S.-Japan relations had reached yet another low point. At that very moment, President Johnson, having lost the confidence of the American people over the Vietnam War, shocked the world with a March 1968 decision to retire from public life at the end of his term in office. Most likely, U.S.-Japan relations were not on the president's mind when he announced this decision, but Johnson's pending exit from the Washington scene raised a basic question: Could the Washington-Tokyo dialogue be restored?

Johnson's very retirement decision offered hope. In Tokyo, Ambassador Johnson saw importance in the fact that many Japanese interpreted the president's early retirement as an apology to Asian people everywhere for the racist war in Vietnam. It also meant an apology for U.S. arrogance, along with additional apologies for Washington's reckless military and political power. But Lyndon Johnson's political passing also symbolized a new beginning for U.S.-Japan relations. Suddenly, the future seemed much brighter.[86]

Indeed, most likely, Japan's immediate reaction to his retirement remained far from the president's mind during the remaining months of 1968. Ambassador Johnson saw U.S.-Japan relations quickly recovering from the trans-Pacific shouting matches of early 1968; however, he worried that the open Tokyo-Washington dialogue of the mid-

1960s and earlier might remain a relic of the past. The primary tasks of the ending days of the 1960s, Ambassador Johnson advised his boss, involved a final conclusion to the Ryukyus mess and heading off any anti-Japanese-motivated protectionist campaign in the U.S. Congress. Japan, the tired ambassador warned, was on the verge of becoming either an enemy or a friend. For the moment, it was neither.

> Our presence in this country has too long been based upon the Japanese acquiescing in what they thought we wanted here in order to make us happy, rather than valuing our presence for its own sake. Thus I've been trying to get out of this context of our making demands on the Japanese and the Japanese reluctantly acquiescing to them, and get to the point where we can reach common decisions on these things and provide a framework in which our presence here will be better accepted and which will provide a better long-run posture for us here. I think we can make some progress.[87]

A reflective President Johnson agreed with his ambassador, vowing to leave a framework for Ryukyus reversion, and to do it by January 1969, along with a promise to stem any protectionist tide in Congress.[88] These were small goals in contrast to the Johnson White House's previous Great Society schemes, but the events of early 1968 brought with them a heavy dose of reality to the president's Japan policy. The politics of the possible, and with some immediacy, was the new order of the day.

Nevertheless, Ryukyus reversion could not be accomplished overnight, and the Johnson team desired overnight results. In a deliberate effort to distract Japanese attention and pressure away from Okinawa-related matters, the White House negotiated a quick agreement on the reversion of "other Japanese islands" still under U.S. control; namely, the Bonin Islands to the north of the Ryukyus. This was a dramatic and legal follow-up to a 1962 Kennedy administration announcement that the Bonins were "Japanese territory." Johnson's new 1968 view suggested that the Bonins, which included Iwo Jima of World War II legend, were of little significance to U.S. national security. At first, Johnson preferred a reversion package that would include both the Ryukyus and the Bonins, but the political benefit of a special Bonins arrangement made magnificent sense. The key to fast-moving success was no congressional involvement in the affair. Johnson's Bonins decision was accomplished via executive order, for Congress, the president feared, would put up a long fight over the future of Iwo Jima. Indeed, in the final Bonins reversion agreement, the United States would retain isolated, rocky Iwo Jima as a military installation. The Japanese Self-Defense Force, too, would be invited to take advantage of that installation, while the Americans assured the world that Bonins reversion did not mean U.S. retreat in the face of Asian/Pacific political pressure during the Vietnam War. Johnson had anticipated a battle in Congress over the "retreat issue" alone, and wisely avoided it.[89]

The United States had administered the Bonins, like the Ryukyus, under the terms of article 3 of the peace treaty with Japan, while recognizing that Japan had "residual sovereignty" there. Unlike the Ryukyus, the Bonins were the site of small, nonnuclear U.S. military installations. Since the limited nature of U.S. military-basing structure in the Bonins was generally known, it became increasingly difficult for the Japanese public to accept continued U.S. administration. Nicknamed the Good Faith agreement, the Bonins reversion accord was signed in early April 1968. The Japanese saw it as the first step toward Ryukyuan reversion, and they were meant to see it that way.[90] The U.S. military retained its Loran radar stations on Iwo Jima and Marcus Island, the only military facilities in the Bonins that interested the Pentagon. All other military and weather facilities were taken over by the Japanese, whom the Joint Chiefs of Staff expected, in time, to assume antisubmarine warfare and other military responsibilities in the defense of the area. Politically, the Bonins reversion provided for a general waiver of claims against the United States. In the interest of calming any concern from Congress, Johnson asked Sato to agree formally "to preserve the Iwo Jima memorial on Mount Suribachi and that United States personnel may have access thereto." Finally, although the agreement said nothing about serving as precedent for a Ryukyus reversion, the Japanese saw it as the beginning of the end for the "American empire over Japan."[91]

Foreign Minister Miki praised the Americans for their swift action, and urged similar speed over the Ryukyus. But Dr. Morton Halperin, Johnson's director of national security "policy planning" and expert on Okinawa's "military utility," hoped to avoid comparisons between the irrelevant Bonins and the significant Ryukyus. Although favoring Ryukyus reversion, Halperin also worried about the future. U.S. military bases on Okinawa were not only associated with the continuing Vietnam War but linked to nearly all of the Pentagon's military contingency plans for the Western Pacific. Would reversion require Japanese study of America's top-secret military contingencies? This security dilemma was a real one, Halperin insisted, requiring careful study and not quick measures toward reversion. He reported to the president: "Having a well-established base close to potential theaters of operations with unrestricted access adds immeasurably to our over-all capabilities and flexibility, particularly in the early stages of operations. The United States will gain immeasurably in maintaining bases in Okinawa as far ahead into the future as can be foreseen."[92]

Admired by Johnson and his key security advisers for his commitment to detail, Halperin favored a final agreement with Japan whereby Okinawa was subjected to the same restrictions on the use of the bases as applied to U.S. bases in Japan proper.[93] Those restrictions involved a ban on the storage of nuclear weapons, and a ban on direct military operations (except in the defense of Japan and South Korea). Japan, Halperin mused, might prevent the use of bases for other purposes, too, despite Tokyo's treaty commitments. It was unlikely that a veto would be exercised on an Okinawan base, Halperin concluded, but he wondered if the Japanese would now be bold enough to veto U.S. military activities at U.S. military installations throughout Japan.

There was also the issue of great U.S. financial loss from a reversion deal. At a time when the expense of the Vietnam War was questioned by both Congress and the electorate, Johnson did not need further debate over Pacific-based defense budgets. The Joint Chiefs of Staff urged Halperin to investigate the matter and provide the data for an early November 1968 cabinet-level discussion on reversion. Halperin's findings were surprising. Reversion, he discovered, allowed annual reductions of $72 million in the balance of payments and $180 million in budget matters. Reversion did "not represent" a financial loss to the U.S. taxpayer, he concluded, and military budget reductions in the Ryukyus would have "no impact" on the conduct of the Vietnam War. It was welcome news to the Johnson team. With many avenues open to successful reversion, the happy rescue of U.S.-Japan relations suddenly seemed more than possible near the end of Lyndon Johnson's term. Sato, meanwhile, watched and waited for the outcome of the U.S. presidential election. Although he told the press that he was fed up with U.S. stalling on the Ryukyus matter, Sato still hoped for a better deal with the victor of the presidential contest.[94]

With the reversion issue put on hold until after a new U.S. president was inaugurated, neither was there much progress on the economic front. Bilateral discussions, continued throughout much of 1968, reached a dramatic climax shortly before the presidential election. Influenced by the frenetic political developments of that year, the trade talks had been difficult. Expanding and instituting Japanese voluntary controls on ceramic tiles had been the primary as well as symbolic issue for U.S. trade negotiators. The ceramic-tiles debate was stimulated by a coalition of ten U.S. senators who insisted that the U.S. ceramic-tile industry faced serious injury from cheap Japanese imports. They called for a "get tough" policy on Japan.[95]

Sato offered his apologies to U.S. business over any "misunderstanding" arising from ceramic industry issues, and he even presented them with a glowing account of the principles of free trade and U.S.-Japan trade relations. Thrown off guard by Sato's laudatory remarks, the Johnson administration hoped the prime minister's comments meant a working dialogue was about to begin on the problems facing U.S. ceramics and other industries.[96] In reality, it was Sato's final word on trade matters until Richard Nixon became president. Johnson left office with U.S.-Japan relations in a most precarious state.

To a large degree, Johnson's Japan policy had become a prisoner of his Vietnam War commitment. Vietnam strongly influenced the timing and substance of Ryukyus reversion. It influenced the level of commitment to discussion of trade issues. And it accented the old post-World War II view that Japan was little more than the "stationary aircraft carrier" of U.S. military-basing privileges. Tired of their secondary consideration within U.S. policymaking, Japanese politicians reminded Johnson that U.S.-Japan relations were as significant as U.S.–South Vietnam relations. Yet the war-weary Johnson team had little time to ponder what Japan hoped to achieve in the world market. They had even less use for Tokyo's minimal interest in the Vietnam War.

Troubled or not, both Washington and Tokyo realized that their struggling relationship still had value to both of them. Without question, the disagreements over the proper path of Pacific region defense and international trade were especially intense during the Johnson-Sato era. The possibility of diplomatic breakdown remained high. But the general requirements of Cold War cooperation, combined with the benefits, both real and imagined, of trans-Pacific trade, kept the Tokyo-Washington dialogue alive.

The importance of political dialogue even became an issue in the 1968 presidential election. One of Richard Nixon's strongest 1968 campaign slogans urged America to keep "talking, not shouting." Although this slogan involved bridging the domestic generation-gap debate over the necessity of the Vietnam War, it could be further applied to the international scene. The Japanese, for example, lost no time making the connection. Johnson's arrogance was giving way to Nixon's detente.[97] Simplifying U.S. politics was nothing new in official Japanese circles, and the Americans were good at it as well.

After the wild ride of the mid- and late-1960s, both Washington and Tokyo were ready for a quieter, gentler relationship. "Nixon Is the One" proclaimed the 1968 Republican campaign for the White House. Would he be "the One" to turn around the angry Tokyo-Washington dialogue?

3

From Golf-Ball Diplomacy
to the Ford Interlude

U.S.-Japan Detente, 1969–1977

In my opinion, there is a vital need for more active participation in, and contribution to, foreign-policy decisions on the part of Japan as distinguished from the ex post facto acquiescence in decisions that has often been the case in the past. Japan is the major Free World power in Asia; it therefore is in a position to make the major contribution to Free World policy in Asia. [1]

No ONE EVER accused Richard Nixon of great oratory. His lack of rhetorical skill was exposed as "weakness" by John Kennedy in 1960; another example of the "tired men" who ruled the White House. Nixon countered by insisting that his off-the-cuff, sometimes-stumbling speaking style was in the tradition of most Americans. Hence, he was more of the "man of the people" than the elitist, Harvard-educated Kennedy.[2] Whether he was this "man of the people" or not, Nixon did represent expertise in the field of U.S.-Japan relations. That field continued to interest him following his 1960 defeat to Kennedy, and Nixon's above-noted remark was made at that time.

Few Americans, of course, cared about the mechanics of U.S.-Japan relations in the early 1960s.[3] But, long before the New Frontier took control of the White House, Nixon favored the building of a strong U.S.-Japan economic alliance. That made him unique at a time when most American policymakers saw Japan only in its "stationary aircraft carrier" role.

As vice president in both Dwight Eisenhower administrations, Nixon had been part of the decision-making process that brought about policies ranging from the Status of Forces Agreement (SOFA—the pact governing U.S. military conduct in Japan) to the Mutual Security treaty. His support for U.S. Cold War objectives in Japan was unswerving. Yet, as early as 1954, he complained that the United States was not doing enough to recognize Japan's economic potential. He doubted the wisdom of Secretary of State John Foster Dulles's effort to push Japan into an export-import role with struggling Southeast Asia. A healthier economic connection to the United States made better sense. In fact, nearly a decade before John Kennedy began to "consider" the importance of economic diplomacy with Japan, Vice President Nixon pointed out that an active, ambitious Japanese export economy assured the utter defeat of pro-communist sentiment there. A booming economy, Nixon often noted, was the Free World's best argument against communism. With Japan quickly advancing toward that boom, a combined U.S.-Japan economic front would lure the Asian/Pacific Third World away from communist attractions as well. Hence, America had to do everything possible to assist Japan, even if it meant the complete, total, and irreversible opening of the U.S. economy to cheap and competitive Japanese goods. Military pacts and "hearts and minds" policies were important in the march to Cold War victory, Nixon believed, but the economic factor was too often submerged by U.S. policymakers. That was a mistake, he said, promising, someday, to remedy the problem himself.[4]

This type of rhetoric, largely unnoticed in the United States, won Nixon the admiration of Japanese governments ranging from Yoshida's postwar regime to Ikeda's and Sato's "miracle economy."[5] "The real future of freedom in Asia," Nixon explained to the American Chamber of Commerce in Japan (ACCJ) during a 1964 Tokyo visit, "rests squarely on continued and further enhanced Japanese-American economic cooperation."[6] Along with William Rogers, his law partner, former Asian/Pacific affairs advisor during his vice presidency, and future secretary of state, Nixon was a frequent visitor to Japan after the 1960 election and especially after his defeat in the 1962 California governor's race. As a private citizen and New York–headquartered international trade lawyer and Pacific affairs lobbyist, Nixon represented a variety of U.S. corporate clients who already had Japanese operations. He also represented certain California-based companies who hoped to penetrate the Japanese market or do business with the Japanese in the United States. Nixon had no problem championing these corporate interests, but he continued to see U.S.-Japan relations in a broad perspective. Indeed, to his Japanese contacts, Nixon was more than an American political has-been. Few Japanese, including Prime Minister Sato, believed the Nixon political career was over.[7]

Any successful growth of U.S.-Japan economic cooperation, Nixon told his business and government audiences in Japan, depended upon the U.S. Congress's removal of all protectionist legislation. He especially attacked President Johnson's support for an interest-equalization tax. The tax penalized Japanese investment in the United States, and instead of discussing the raw economic consequences of this development, Nixon stressed the Johnson administration's political insult to Japan through this measure, as well as its detrimental effect on Cold War solidarity. He made the same point in front of the U.S. Senate Finance Committee, arguing for a Japanese tax exemption modeled on an earlier exemption provided for Canada. But Nixon's congressional testimony was more appreciated in Japan than on the Democratic Party–controlled Capitol Hill.[8]

The mid-1960s were dark days for the ambitious Nixon. Himself defeated twice for elective office, he saw his party suffer landslide defeats for the White House, Congress, and most governorships during the 1964 election. Even Republican Party stalwarts doubted a Nixon comeback. The Japanese press and government, on the other hand, urged the former vice president to continue his political career and fight the good fight. It was one of the few encouragements he received before the Vietnam War and urban ghetto disturbances reversed the Democratic Party's fortunes. In April 1967, during one of his last visits to Japan before offering his full attentions to the 1968 election, Nixon met with political leaders in both the LDP and the Japan Socialist Party (JSP). Breaking away from his usual discussions of open investment and friendly economic ties, Nixon gave something of the preview of what might become his presidential agenda vis-à-vis Japan.

In the security area, Nixon moved beyond arguments over U.S. troop strength in Japan, stressing the problem of Chinese and Soviet aid to Southeast Asian countries. Explaining that the problem of Chinese-Soviet aid was also Japan's problem, he asked his hosts to stand firm against any growth in communist assistance to the region. The Southeast Asian market, he said, was of increasing relevance to a number of Japanese and American businesses. Consequently, it was in Japan's security as well as economic self-interest to maintain, "alongside Washington," close watch on Southeast Asian developments. Although he also denounced the bloody nature of Mao's ongoing Cultural Revolution in China, Nixon said nothing about continuing the U.S. doctrine of nonrecognition toward Beijing. This did not mean the United States was about to open an embassy there, but the Japanese were intrigued by Nixon's lack of interest in the usual Washington denunciations of China. A Nixon presidency would be good for Japan, the Japanese press mused, and the U.S. ambassador, U. Alexis Johnson, compared this Nixon visit to a presidential-level summit meeting.[9] Nixon was poised for a tough campaign ahead. When it was over, he would be magnificently prepared, in contrast to his predecessors, to lead the U.S.-Japan relationship.

Throughout the 1968 election and the president-elect period, Nixon continued to enjoy the encouragement of the Japanese government. Although the polite democratic tradition of noninterference in foreign elections had been embraced by the postwar Tokyo political Establishment, the preference for a Nixon-led United States was obvious and clear. From former prime ministers to the 1968 Diet, the architects of the New Japan economy saw Ikeda and Miyazawa's dream coming true in the Nixon seventies. Sato officially labeled Nixon a "friend of Japan" who would usher in a new era of economic cooperation, end the Vietnam War, revert Okinawa, and reassess the U.S.–Asian/Pacific relationship from the point of view of "mutual understanding" rather than "continued confrontation."[10]

Yet, at least in the U.S.-Japan relationship, there would be a significant difference between citizen Nixon and President Nixon. Much of Nixon's conclusions on Japan and U.S.-Japan relations were based on non-policy-making considerations, even during his days as vice president. The Japanese expressions of support assumed that Nixon's knowledge of their country would equal a certain hands-on role by the president himself in the crafting of U.S.-Japan security and economic arrangements. This would never be the case.[11] Whether or not it was due to larger Cold War considerations, Vietnamization, the eventual Watergate scandal, or the general priorities of presidential leadership, much of the U.S.-Japan relationship would be designed by the president's foreign-policy team. Nixon was also a different political animal than Lyndon Johnson. He did not consider U.S.-Japan diplomacy an interesting game, in which he needed to be personally involved in every policy twist and turn.[12] Franklin Roosevelt had not been his "political papa," as he told his staff before meeting Prime Minister Kakuei Tanaka in 1973; a movie version of Tokyo-Washington relations might best be titled: *The Burden and the Pain*.[13]

As he did in all other aspects of what was soon known as the Nixon Doctrine, Henry Kissinger, NSC adviser and future secretary of state, provided the foundation for U.S.-Japan affairs. A transplanted Harvard diplomatic historian, Kissinger enjoyed the opportunity of a lifetime. Attracted, like many moderate-conservative academics, to the early 1968 primary campaign of Governor Nelson Rockefeller of New York, Kissinger preferred advising the "education candidate" who welcomed "new ideas." Seen as too "liberal" for Republican voters, Rockefeller was defeated by a Nixon campaign that said little about education, but did promise "fresh ideas" and an unspecified alternative to Cold War extremism. By volunteering the ambitious Kissinger to the successful Nixon campaign, Rockefeller was also offering a foreign-policy expert with clear goals for U.S.-Japan relations.[14] Although, at first, Kissinger claimed to have little enthusiasm for a Nixon appointment, the two men did view foreign affairs in a similar light, and the press praised the new president's decision to bring this honored scholar into the White House.

A complex personality who had little tolerance for those who did not appreciate that complexity, Kissinger, nevertheless, crafted a simple, straightforward, no-nonsense Japan policy in early 1969. It would remain on course for the next several years, and Nixon had no reason to change it. To Kissinger, three problems were inherent within America's postwar approach to Japan. All three of them shared a common factor, and it involved Japan's tottering position as a reliable Cold War ally. In spite of his boss's warm relationship with the Japanese leadership, Kissinger believed that Japan's politeness to Nixon was a smoke screen for a deep-rooted disgust of U.S. power in the Pacific.

Kissinger's first concern involved Washington's insistence on maintaining the status quo relationship with "defeated Japan." This was a serious misinterpretation of Japan's new economic and political clout, he concluded. Taking the military opportunities afforded by Japan for granted, but not considering Japan's own economic interests, could lead the United States to disaster. Kissinger defined that disaster in the form of a frustrated potential world power, Japan, leading a capitalist, anti-American coalition in the Pacific while Washington soldiered on with its struggle against communism. In this thesis, Japan emerged as a "forgotten nation," ignored by America's Vietnam and general Cold War priorities. Offering Japan a generous economic package, including a devaluation of the already inflated dollar, and full access to the U.S. market, was one way to head off this collapse of American Pacific power.

Secondly, although the U.S. government had already gotten used to the idea that Okinawan reversion was inevitable, the "Okinawan issue" was a different matter. Okinawa, Kissinger believed, had become a state of mind in Japanese politics. It symbolized American racism and colonialism, Japan's World War II defeat and MacArthur's postwar Occupation, the continuing war against fellow Asians in Vietnam, and Washington's reluctance to let go of the past. To Kissinger, U.S. military basing privileges were easy to secure in the Ryukyus, aligned with the same privileges enjoyed on the Japanese main islands. The U.S. political role on Okinawa needed not only to end, but to be denounced as an unfortunate experience in U.S.-Japan relations.

Kissinger's third matter of concern involved Pacific region relations within his general thesis of detente. Planning a New Atlantic Charter, whereby America's Cold War allies would be brought together under the umbrella of new strategic and economic accords, Kissinger saw a healthy, pro-American role for Japan if his first two concerns were addressed. Welcomed as a significant world power in this new, watered-down version of Kennedy's New Pacific Community plan, Japan would enjoy special privileges. Together with the United States, for example, Japan could reap the benefits of dramatic and direct investment in China, following the detente-influenced U.S. renunciation of China nonrecognition. America's eventual withdrawal from Vietnam could also mean a happy new era for U.S. world influence, Kissinger hoped, and the New Atlantic Charter symbolized this dream.[15]

All three of Kissinger's concerns suffered from certain contradictions and all three required raw presidential power to succeed.[16] First of all, the Diet was not planning an anti-American coalition in the Pacific. Kissinger, like his predecessors, exaggerated Japanese political banter, and, despite his reputation as the emotionless policymaker, he based his first policy-making assumptions on the emotions involved in Japanese politics.

Secondly, the Okinawan reversion was indeed in reach. Both Nixon and Sato favored an overly interpretive final agreement, whereby both "sides" could claim success if pressed by political critics and the media. On the other hand, Nixon also favored playing the nuclear card for a time, insisting that the status quo defense arrangement on Okinawa was essential to American-led nuclear security in the Pacific region. The stress on regional nuclear security was the key here, largely meant to frighten North Vietnam and North Korea. Once this stress began to annoy Sato and a Japanese government anticipating reversion, Kissinger insisted that the Nixon administration consider the future of U.S.-Japan relations. Again, Nixon had no problem toning down the rhetoric of the Tokyo-Washington shouting match. Hence, reversion would be accomplished under the terms of an accord that made little sense to international lawyers and a critical press, but made perfect political sense to a Japanese and American political community eager for a way out of a long-lasting feud.[17] Indeed, much of the discussion and planning for this event had been accomplished by the Johnson White House. Because of that fact, the passion behind the Okinawan debate, except for the usual anti-American factions, subsided in the Diet. Yet, as long as U.S. troops remained on Okinawa, the issue of the American "right" to be there would also remain in question.[18]

A third contradiction in the Kissinger approach involved his lack of interest in economic diplomacy. Despite a changing world economy and no U.S. policy to meet it, Kissinger believed that the continuing ideological struggle with communism remained Washington's top priority. One of his first actions, both as NSC adviser and then as secretary of state, involved the cutting of economic specialists from his staff. Hence, the stressing of dollar devaluation and New Atlantic Charter benefits for the Japanese were near-irrelevancies in the larger scheme of Kissinger-led U.S. policy. Whereas Kissinger regarded the less-significant dollar, an open U.S. market, and the newer, less-imperial version of the New Pacific Community as the masterful reshuffling of basic U.S. policy themes, the Diet saw dollar devaluation as a matter requiring full Japanese involvement, consultation, and cooperation. They also saw U.S. protectionism as a "growing problem," and the New Atlantic Charter was yet another American attempt to dominate Japan's economic destiny.[19]

Cultural and political misunderstanding still typified U.S.-Japan policy more than the brilliance of its policymakers. Meanwhile, Kissinger was able to translate his concerns into policy because Congress continued to have a minimal role in the process. Congress, with its Democratic majority, was more than aware of the Republican administration's attraction to "executive privilege" government. In the name of both partisanship and constitutional checks and balances, the Congress often delayed Nixon's Japan-policy agenda. Like his hero in presidential politics, Woodrow Wilson, Nixon considered raw presidential power the most efficient form of government. As a wartime commander in chief, he also viewed diplomacy in the light of America's ongoing Vietnam and general Cold War commitments.[20] Consequently, Kissinger's success in Japan policy depended upon Nixon's presidential patronage, and both men enjoyed a grateful press and electorate for their efforts to tone down the Cold War.[21] For Japan, this meant Washington's Cold War strategies were in transition, and the quick resolution of long-standing disputes, such as Okinawa, was part of that transition. In short, U.S. tactics, not policy, had changed, but it was a welcome development from the Japanese point of view.

Perhaps fitting for the changing scene in U.S.-Japan relations was Nixon's gift of personally autographed golf balls to the CEOs of the major Japanese corporations and to key members of the Diet. This 1969 gesture to the world's "golfing capital" did not go unnoticed. Osamu Hirano, of Mitsui Corporation, called it "the most delightful thing" any American had ever done for Mitsui, while former Prime Minister Nobusuke Kishi said that Nixon's "kind greeting" symbolized the "beginning of the end" of tense U.S.-Japan relations.[22] "Golf-ball diplomacy," he observed, meant U.S.-Japan "goodwill." Or did it?

Unfortunately, the president's "goodwill" gesture was accompanied by a darker side to Nixon-era policy making. The golf balls were not the product of impromptu gift-giving, but rather the end-result of a careful personality-by-personality analysis campaign with projected benefits. Prime Minister Sato, for instance, was expected to be most appreciative of the gift, given his "addiction" to golf (he had a sixteen handicap). Once a strong friend of the United States, Sato had become cold toward Washington, and the president's gesture was expected to open him up to a warmer view. Henry Kissinger had nothing to do with the golf-ball study, and he had little use for such stunts. But Nixon enjoyed the task, convinced that his chief foreign-policy maker needed both watching and quiet assistance.

In charge of watching, reviewing, and commenting upon Kissinger's Japan efforts was the former speech writer for Vice President Spiro Agnew, Patrick Buchanan. Along with his aide, Lamar Alexander, Buchanan offered confidential assessments of Kissinger's work to the president, as well as engineering the time-consuming golf-balls campaign. In the postwar history of the U.S.-Japan relationship, no White House official had ever had such a role. Carrying the title of special assistant, and otherwise stressing the communication/media-related concerns of the White House, Buchanan distrusted Kissinger's cavalier attitude toward economic matters, disliked his lack of regard for congressmen (including ones that were pro-Nixon), and saw him as a loose cannon who, someday, might politically injure the president. Loyal to Nixon alone, Buchanan and Alexander represented a shadow government of their own, ready to protect the president from any Kissinger-instigated problems as well as real or imagined press conspiracies. Nixon created their mission and, apparently, always welcomed their work.[23]

In 1969, Kissinger's three-pronged and cerebral approach to Japanese relations seemed most straightforward, implying that Japan policy would soon be a manageable, trouble-free matter. He would not be so fortunate. The trade issue became an unforeseen nightmare for him, largely because he discounted congressional interest in it. In 1970, the chairman of the House Ways and Means Committee, Wilbur Mills, proposed a complex trade bill accenting import quotas on shoes and all textiles. Speaking for the Japanese government, veteran trade negotiator Kiichi Miyazawa threatened to break off discussions with the Americans on "all matters of concern between the two countries" if the Mills bill sailed through Congress. To state it more precisely, the Mills bill moved America from a policy of voluntary restraint (since 1962) on cotton and other textiles to strict control. There would be no escape clause for the Japanese, and higher duties, across the board, were to be placed on their products that "threatened" domestic manufacturers. The bill expected to reduce imports by 40 percent, and admitted that "foreign retaliation was likely."

As the Mills bill made its way through the congressional committee structure during 1970–71, the Japanese-American dialogue remained as tense as ever. Complaining that the Nixon administration was not doing enough to stop the Mills effort, Miyazawa made good on his warning and the Japanese government canceled all of its appointments with U.S. officials in August 1971. This angered Nixon, but the Mills bill already had him mad.[24]

To Nixon, in interesting contrast to his recent predecessors, the most significant aspect of the trade row was its domestic political impact. In 1968, Nixon had defeated his opponent, Vice President Hubert Humphrey, by only a 1 percent margin. Nixon's strongest support came from the once traditionally Democratic middle and lower-middle South; that is, the heart of the U.S. textile industry. In Nixon's mind, Mills's bill was a deliberate effort to win back those traditional Democratic voters and capture an anti-Japanese vote everywhere. Mills had to be stopped. With Nixon's approval, Buchanan gathered "dirt" on Mills, including juicy tales of wild parties, wild women, and booze. Indeed, it would be Mills's politically incorrect personal life that would eventually lead to his downfall as the titan of the House Ways and Means Committee. Consequently, Buchanan did not need to begin his "press offensive" in the Mills "case."

Nixon did release his privately labeled Second Front; namely, Vice President Agnew, Senator Barry Goldwater, and the new Republican Party chairman, Bob Dole. In speeches provided by Buchanan and

other White House staffers, Agnew attacked the "treasonous protectionism" of the Democratic Party. Goldwater compared Mills's bill to
"cowardly isolationism" that only benefited America's communist enemies. Meanwhile, Bob Dole suggested that the Democratic Party had
become a desperate lot, denying their free-trader past and courting
bigotry, emotionalism, and bad fiscal policy.[25] Questioning the patri-
otism and common sense of the Democrats had become a taken-
for-granted political tool of the Nixon White House. Applying this
approach to trade disputes was a natural follow-up to it, but this did
nothing to restore the U.S.-Japan dialogue.

With the White House vigorously attacking an honored Democratic Party warhorse, other Democratic warhorses attacked other as-
pects of Nixon's Japan policy. South Carolina's Senator Ernest "Fritz"
Hollings, a strong Mills bill supporter and member of the Senate
Commerce Committee, assailed Nixon's plan to revert Okinawa.
Citing section 6 of the joint U.S.-Japan plan for Okinawa reversion,
Hollings pointed out that Okinawa could not change political hands
without the necessary legislative support of the U.S. Congress. Backed
by Senator Robert Byrd, a former constitutional lawyer and future
Senate majority leader, Hollings insisted that the Okinawa issue was
now a matter of Senate debate. Nixon saw this as blackmail, reasoning
that the Democrats wanted him to bend on welfare reform and revenue-sharing plans in exchange for their support on Okinawa reversion and free trade with Japan.[26]

There is no evidence to suggest that Japan-related matters were
being used as political leverage on welfare and revenue-sharing legislation. The congressional Democrats were, on the other hand, hoping
to regain policy-making authority after years of watching the White
House conduct a disastrous war in Southeast Asia. Nixon's Japan policy became part of that larger debate over the sharing of powers in the
manufacturing of U.S. foreign policy, and his trade bill, like most
matters of state, resulted in a compromise with the legislative branch.
Meanwhile, Nixon's lawyers argued that section 6 of the Okinawan reversion plan meant that Congress had been "invited" to comment on
the procedure in an "advisory" manner. The involved Senate debate,
therefore, was unnecessary. Such conclusions only intensified the
White House versus Capitol Hill row. Neither side was willing to bend

in this no-win situation, helping to delay final Okinawan reversion for several months and confusing much of the world over who might be in charge of U.S. trade policy.

During this delay and confusion, it became most unclear, again, if the U.S.-Japan dialogue could ever be restored. Genko Uchida, a friend of Prime Minister Sato and a high-ranking MITI official specializing in Japan-Asian/Pacific trade, informed Brian Quickstad, a New York lawyer colleague of President Nixon, that the Japanese government was even planning a new Vietnam policy. With Nixon having stepped-up B-52 bombing raids over North Vietnam, there was concern in Japan over the fate of civilians there. Consequently, the new policy involved infrastructure assistance to North Vietnam and the creation of a special "Peace Corps," funded by both public and private sources, to help in reconstruction. Kissinger saw nothing developing out of this plan, but Nixon aide General Alexander Haig, a Vietnam veteran, disagreed. To Haig, Japan's behavior over the internal U.S. trade policy debate was frustrating and annoying. Now this. Tokyo's "arrogance" had to be stopped. Nixon agreed, prompting a presidential rebuke of Kissinger: "Should we be neutral about Jap assistance to North Vietnam? Not in my book!"[27]

Answering "arrogance" with "arrogance," the State Department issued a stern warning to Japan, noting that the president "did not take kindly" the suggestion of aid to North Vietnam. In response, the Japanese government commented that the whole matter had been a "trial balloon," instigated by left-leaning businessmen and other private interests.[28] Since MITI policymaking often blurred public and private concerns into one decision, it was easy for Sato to blame the private sector and exonerate his government in the North Vietnam matter. Whether his government was testing Nixon's priorities in Asian/Pacific affairs or not, Sato backed away from any Southeast Asian policy that might jeopardize U.S.-Japan relations in the long run.

To some conservative Japanese critics of Sato's government, Tokyo's waffling in the face of American pressure was an insult to Japan's new standing as a major new power in a new decade. To others, Sato had not been outraged enough at Nixon's effort to define Pacific nuclear security in selfish American terms. To many more, Japanese economic diplomacy needed grander focus in an era of American rapprochement with China, dwindling international energy supplies, a struggling U.S. dollar, and American soul-searching over the proper post-Vietnam direction of their economy and foreign policy. Still others were angry at Sato for not "predicting" the new era of China-U.S. accord. After all, he was supposed to be on very friendly terms with Nixon. According to this opinion, Sato had been an overly reliable anti-communist, anti-Maoist ally of the United States in the Pacific. And for what?

Given this turmoil in the LDP, Nixon regarded Sato's resulting fall from grace, and Kakuei Tanaka's rise to power, as "the most significant event" in recent U.S.-Japan relations.[29] As a longtime LDP stalwart, party boss, and former MITI director, Tanaka favored quick results in U.S.-Japan policy. Enjoying the reputation of the gruff, hard-nosed, no-nonsense politician, Tanaka represented the Japanese desire for real success in the U.S.-Japan economic dialogue.[30] He would find a receptive audience in Washington, but not until after a minor scandal.

Already reeling from the Watergate scandal, the White House staff overreacted to press reports that noted that the president had been quite close to the directorship of Japan's Sony Corporation before he became president. The reports implied that Nixon's interest in generously welcoming Japanese electronics imports into the U.S. economy, and his lack of interest in the plight of domestic manufacturers, was somehow rooted in Sony favoritism, pre-presidential deals, and "Tricky Dicky" politics. Ron Ziegler, Nixon's press secretary, was outraged, publicly proclaiming that the reports were representative of the media's anti-Nixon bias. Unsatisfied with a simple denunciation of the press, Al Haig believed that Nixon might be forced to change his Japan policy to win back concerned voters. Anti-Japanese sentiment was growing as fast as was Watergate-induced anti-Nixon sentiment. Together, Haig concluded, both opinions were deadly for the president's political fortunes. Pat Buchanan especially agreed with this assessment, and prepared for a major offensive against the president's press "enemies" in the matter.[31]

As in the Wilbur Mills situation, a great offensive was not necessary. Time healed this latest Nixon crisis. The news story fizzled in light of the Watergate revelations. But the damage had been done. Although there was no evidence to conclude that Nixon made unholy deals with

Sony in the late 1960s, there were those who were convinced it must be true. Meanwhile, Nixon delayed a working summit with Tanaka until the Sony tale disappeared from U.S. political memory. In reality, outside of Washington, D.C. and the political concerns of Nixon watchers and trade specialists, few had ever heard of this new scandal. The White House staff made a great deal out of very little.

Nixon's ballyhooed first meeting with Tanaka was not, in fact, their first meeting. The two had met ten years earlier during Nixon's political wilderness days. The president said he long admired Tanaka's toughness, his up-from-nothing success story, and, especially, his "steadfast determination" to move his country forward as he saw fit.[32] Frankly, Nixon was talking more about himself than Tanaka, although there were similarities in personality. Indeed, both endured charges of unethical political behavior during their public lives. Now, as world leaders, these two "determined" men met in Honolulu to discuss their nations' relationship in the era of detente and economic change.

In Honolulu, Nixon learned that Japan had every intention of defining its 1970s foreign policy with less, rather than more, U.S. influence. That meant Japan–Asian/Pacific relations were supposed to be off-limits to U.S. policy, including Tokyo-Beijing relations. That also meant Nixon was expected to make good on his promise of world leadership in the area of free trade. To Nixon, these "demands" were annoying, but not unexpected.[33] His behavior at this summit accented the point.

Nixon preferred the Honolulu venue over other U.S. locations because of its symbolic political importance; the city had a strong Japanese-American community that was heavily involved in both Democratic and Republican Party politics throughout Hawaii. Nixon belabored this point during his public remarks at the summit. He also put Tanaka through a painfully long ceremony honoring John McCain, a Vietnam War hero and POW (and future Republican senator for Arizona) and other members of McCain's famous military family.

Nixon had been warned by the State Department that Tanaka was not likely to agree to any new suggestions of joint U.S.-Japan security arrangements in the Pacific, and that the only working result of the meeting might be the continuing White House promise of American generosity to Japan's growing export economy. Consequently, there were obvious political dangers for Nixon here, if the electorate was truly paying attention to a U.S.-Japan summit. Kissinger, meanwhile, insisted on "mending fences" with Japan in the interest of post-Vietnam harmony and continuing Cold War solidarity. That would be easier said than done, but the Nixon White House, like those of Kennedy and Johnson, worried about "losing Japan." Complaining about Japan's closed market to U.S. goods, but insisting on cordial Washington-Tokyo relations, was a more difficult contradiction for Nixon to continue than it had been for Kennedy and Johnson. America's Vietnam withdrawal and struggling economy versus Japan's economic growth and optimism illustrated the point. Nevertheless, Nixon, never a charmer, tried his best to "mend fences" with Tanaka in Honolulu.

In his formal welcome to Tanaka, Nixon recalled the Japanese leader's remarks upon assuming the prime ministership. Since Tanaka retained most of the Sato government's policy-making personnel, he had noted that "we are not changing the team, just the pitcher." Nixon took off from there. "I have met other Prime Ministers, and they were some pretty good pitchers," he said, "but Tanaka-san is in their league. He is a big leaguer and has all the pitches. He has a fast ball, a curve, a slider, a knuckler, but no spitball."[34]

Within six months of Tanaka's Honolulu visit, the U.S. dollar would be devalued a further 10 percent. To some Americans, this was a symbol of their country's decline; to others, it was a natural adjustment to the new international economy. To the White House, economic diplomacy remained a frustrating task. W. D. Eberle, the U.S. special trade representative, complained privately that, since 1968, the Japanese were reluctant to talk, much less agree upon, the lessening of their import-export controls.[35] At the same time, the U.S. Congress continued to debate its own trade policy in the face of Nixon's open-door trade approach. Although the protectionist cause in Congress continued to be compromised by the anti-communist appeal of free trade, it was not destroyed. The strict control of Japanese soybeans entering the U.S. market, for instance, symbolized an early 1970s success story for farm-state lobbying and congressional foreign policy. This angered Tanaka, who urged the Americans to establish some coherence in their trade policy. The battle between Congress and the White House over the meaning of Vietnam and the corruption of Watergate implied to the Japanese that U.S. trade policy was also a political football between the legislative and executive branches. Because of this situation and the soybean embargo, the White House worried if the Japanese would retaliate, in some way, relevant to Pacific security and defense matters.[36]

In the summer of 1973, Tanaka would visit Nixon once again. Coinciding with the televised hearings of the Senate Watergate Investigative Committee, the Nixon-Tanaka meeting was largely designed to demonstrate the president's strength as a foreign-policy maker. Since Nixon's early 1972 visit to Mao's China, the electorate gave their president high marks for his diplomacy. He needed higher marks now. With that goal in mind, Nixon arranged a frenetic schedule of White House meetings with international leaders throughout the hot summer of 1973.[37] But, with Nixon's popular support slipping to less than 30 percent in the opinion polls, a summer visit from the Japanese prime minister would have little impact on the president's Watergate troubles.

This Nixon-Tanaka meeting covered a wide range of topics, but the Nixon accent remained on educating the Japanese about executive versus legislative branch politics in the United States. Nixon predicted victory over the "protectionist" Democratic Congress, and Tanaka, at least, welcomed his civics lesson on the U.S. government: "I have been blessed with the opportunities of broadening and deepening the dialogue not only with you personally but also with a wide spectrum of your Congressional, mass media, business, civic and other leaders. . . . You gave me a clearer picture of the vast strength and resilience of your country and of the enormous possibilities open for our cooperative endeavors."[38]

But could the early 1970s U.S.-Japan relationship be labeled a "cooperative endeavor?" The Nixon White House was divided on this assessment. Nixon claimed that the lowering of the U.S. flag over Okinawa, for example, symbolized a new era of friendship between the United States and "Pacific peoples." It was exactly the type of "mending fences" message that Kissinger expected from Nixon. But both Alexander Haig and Pat Buchanan worried that Japanese public opinion was swinging away from American friendship and not toward it. They wanted the president to "get tough, even ruthless" with the Japanese; the political benefit at home would be worth it. Predicting a worst-case scenario of anti-American rioting near U.S. military bases, accompanied by a game of "economic hardball" on the part of Japanese business and government interests throughout the world economy, Haig warned the president of bad times ahead. Having commissioned a special USIA survey of Japanese opinion, Haig suggested that he had the data to back his warning.[39]

According to this survey, very few university-educated Japanese "trusted" or "respected" Americans. One-half of all those questioned believed that the United States had "reached its peak" as a nation before Lyndon Johnson and the Vietnam War. Another half said the Soviet Union was the only superpower left on the planet, and one-third doubted America's military competence to defend Japan against a Soviet attack. In general terms, two-thirds of those surveyed said they "did not have considerable confidence" in the United States to maintain either its economic or security commitments following Vietnam. The United States, they concluded, was in decline, "lacking those qualities that make a country outstanding."[40]

Adding fuel to these negative assessments was the rumor that Kadena Air Base on Okinawa stockpiled nuclear weapons in violation of the reversion agreement. If true, this matter would also be a violation of the "cooperative spirit" that the reversion decision was supposed to represent. Indeed, Nixon might have provided a clever interpretation of the reversion accord, claiming that the "necessary defense" of the region required nukes. But few would have accepted the claim.

Although the Nixon administration had no comment on rumors, the press did. Former ambassadors Johnson and Reischauer even told the Japanese media that they distrusted Nixon on the nuclear issue. Meanwhile, at the Kadena Air Base hospital on Okinawa, ailing U.S. Air Force personnel were routinely asked if they had been "working with nuclear materials." The U.S. Air Force claimed that the question was simply a procedural one, equal to that of asking for one's name and address. Most Japanese doubted it.

America's cryptic responses and Japan's doubt would become something of a tradition in U.S.-Japan nuclear relations for the remaining years of the Cold War. From the beginning, the Japanese government did not want to press the U.S. government too hard on the matter, for fear of losing the White House's favorable position on imports. Nixon and Kissinger had hoped the issue would just go away, while the United States shored-up its post-Vietnam Pacific defenses. Tanaka obliged, to a degree, but the Japanese press kept the nuclear matter alive and well. Although Washington and Tokyo never admitted it, America's continuing interest in proper anti-communist defense versus Japan's economic-policy priorities played well together at times. The potentially damaging nuclear issue, for instance, was never permitted to become too harmful to the Tokyo-Washington detente.[41]

But did the Nixon administration accept the fact that economic diplomacy could now play a priority role in any democratic foreign policy? The withdrawal of U.S. forces from Vietnam did not alter the Nixon administration's vigilant anti-communism, and Kissinger still saw America's triumph in the Cold War as as important as ever. Nevertheless, to State Department advisers on Japan R. C. Brewster, Winthrop G. Brown, and others, American foreign policy needed a quick post-Vietnam adjustment. Sponsoring a secret colloquium on U.S.-Japan relations, the State Department's Far East specialists vented their anger at status quo diplomacy. The United States, they said, was unprepared for Japanese "economic offensives" or "predatory capitalism." It was not too late to embrace "some dollar diplomacy of our own."

> America is seized with a good deal of self-doubt, a kind of weariness and querulousness, with a certain withdrawal; whereas Japan is more self-confident, more assertive, more determined to find a broader role. And a younger generation of Japanese does not mind comparison with the advanced West or with others. But there is going to be a new questioning of American will and credibility, and this is going to take place in the context of a Japan that either seeks superior relationships with many of the states around it, or at least some new relationship.[42]

Kissinger was impressed with "the depth and balance of thought as well as the measure of agreement that emerged from the meeting." But he still preferred "focus," and that meant continuing to pursue

Truman Doctrine objectives. A renaissance in economic diplomacy was not necessary, and more rather than less commitment to free-trade principles was within the best traditions of post–World War II American capitalism.[43]

To Richard Nixon, academic-style debates over the place of economics within U.S. foreign policy were a luxury. Fighting for his political life as the Watergate scandal unraveled around him, Nixon spent much of his working day in 1974 trying to stay above the fray. That also meant *looking* like one was above the fray, and Japan relations had a role to play in the effort. For instance, Ron Ziegler announced that the president had been the motivating factor in the Japanese decision to eliminate the Buy Japan decree. Dating back to September 1963, the Diet's Buy Japan legislation "encouraged the use of domestic products in order to utilize foreign currencies efficiently." Although Nixon doubted the truth of the administration's spin on the announcement, Ziegler was instructed to tell the press that the way was now open for U.S. products to compete in Japan. The necessity of Nixon's leadership was demonstrated once again, Ziegler implied.

In reality, the Buy Japan decree might have gone by the wayside, but computers and most U.S. export goods were not affected by its demise. The Ziegler announcement was designed to influence American public opinion concerned about a flagging, "Watergated" economy. It did little good.[44]

Without question, the Watergate scandal kept the U.S.-Japan relationship on edge. Concerned about the American president's political troubles, the Japanese government especially noted its worries in the executive meetings of the Japan-U.S. Economic Council and the Advisory Council on Japan–U.S. Economic Relations. As the U.S. Congress moved toward the impeachment of the president, the Japanese delegation to the joint economic council wondered, as did many Americans, if U.S. government policymaking still existed. After years of debate between the Congress and the White House, U.S. trade policy still remained difficult to define. To the Japanese, the only concrete example of fast-moving U.S. action on economic matters was not dollar devaluation but the soybean embargo. The U.S. delegation to the joint economic council disagreed, suggesting that the Japanese planned to flood the U.S. market, make an unholy profit, and then use it to buy oil from the same Middle East oil producers who were hold-ing much of the non-communist world to "economic ransom." The Americans were implying grossly unethical, if not politically criminal, behavior on the part of the Japanese government. The latter flatly de-nied the charge.[45]

Nixon's August 1974 resignation offered the hope that reason and policymaking might better typify the mid-1970s Tokyo-Washington dialogue. Yet this besieged president left a record of accomplishment. Challenged by continuing Cold War concerns as well as Watergate, Nixon's Japan policy had, in the atmosphere of detente and "fence mending," welcomed Japan's "miracle economy" into the U.S. domes-tic agenda. At the same time, it ended the years-long argument over Ryukyus reversion. These were no small feats. But Nixon owed much to the groundwork laid by Presidents Kennedy and Johnson.

Guided by what some have called "the Watergate malaise," Nixon seemed more interested in the use or misuse of "executive privilege" than the policy-making mechanics of U.S.-Japan policy. From the carefully planned "golf-ball" diplomacy to "deep-sixing" Wilbur Mills and to playing hardball politics with U.S.-Japan relations, the Nixon White House elevated scams, schemes, and belligerent press releases to a fine art. Indeed, Nixon never divorced himself from controversy. Then in August 1974 it became President Gerald Ford's turn to move the Washington-Tokyo relationship forward. The new president prom-ised quiet diplomacy, not controversy. The new occupant of the Oval Office said he was "a Ford and not a Lincoln." Most Americans liked the cute analogy. Exhausted by Watergate, they wanted old problems resolved and new issues addressed.[46] Ford would have little time to do it.

As the longtime Republican minority leader in the House of Rep-resentatives, Ford had maintained a quiet presence on Capitol Hill. Although sharing most of Nixon's political views, including the at-tachment to "executive privilege," Ford, a Michigan native, also cham-pioned "honest Midwest values." The latter offered great hope to the Watergate-wracked Republican Party. Nixon's landslide 1972 victory over liberal Senator George McGovern had suggested, to some, that the Republican Party was about to become the nation's dominant po-litical party. Could Ford resume this march to dominance?

At best, the Ford administration assumed the role of crisis manager. Beyond the trying task of restoring public confidence in government, the Ford team had to cope with runaway inflation and unemployment, growing tension in the Middle East, dwindling energy supplies, and a Vietnam-centered economy and political reality that had lost its center. As in the case of Japan's Sato-Tanaka transition, following the Nixon resignation the pitcher changed but much of the team stayed the same. In foreign policy, this meant Kissinger's continuing leadership. In U.S.-Japan relations, this meant an effort to resume Tokyo-Washington detente.

Nearly a year before the end of his presidency, Nixon had promised to meet with Tanaka in Japan. Watergate canceled this plan. Ford resurrected it, noting that the trip was "long overdue" and that U.S.-Japan relations needed to be "saved." Symbolically, this trip had great significance for the Japanese. Ford would be the first U.S. president to visit Japan, and that fact was not lost on the Japanese people. In the United States, it was a different matter. Urging Ford to take care of America's pressing domestic problems, most newspapers said he had no business flying off to Japan. Ford disagreed, explaining that healthy U.S.-Japan economic relations would only benefit the American consumer.[47]

In Japan, Ford had no intention of apologizing for Nixon policies, but he did want to establish a much more cooperative relationship. Like the Japanese, Ford believed that Nixon had not been open and informative about all issues relevant to U.S.-Japan relations.[48] He even stressed that point in a brief meeting with Emperor Hirohito, but it meant little to Tanaka. Whereas Nixon saw so much of himself in the abrasive Tanaka, Ford saw nothing but trouble ahead:

A burly, aggressive man whose nickname was Tiger, Tanaka never let diplomatic niceties stand in the way of blunt speech. Although our relations were formal and correct, he was not the kind of man to whom I could warm up easily. Even before our arrival, Japanese newspapers had carried reports that he was involved in questionable financial activities. Kissinger and I concluded that Tanaka probably would have to resign soon, but in our discussions with him the matter never came up.[49]

Ford's reference to "Japanese newspapers" was, in reality, a reference to *Bungei Shunju*, Tokyo's most prestigious monthly magazine. With its reporters proudly employing Watergate-influenced investigative techniques, *Bungei Shunju* had uncovered Tanaka's career-long history of corruption. Indeed, the magazine demonstrated (assigning more than twenty reporters in a months-long investigation) that Tanaka (who often boasted of his modest means) hid his true wealth in a web of phony "ghost corporations" designed to evade Japanese income-tax laws. The investigation was prompted by Tanaka's strange and angry denunciation of Dr. Jerome Cohen, a Harvard professor, who accused the prime minister of taking bribes from the South Korean government. But Tanaka did take bribes, *Bungei Shunju* concluded, from dozens of sources, concealing his wealth in six different chemical and transportation companies, $8 million in Tokyo real estate, and three summer villas.[50]

There had never been a tradition of hard-hitting, investigative reporting in the history of the Japanese press; consequently, *Bungei Shunju's* work had a profound impact on Japanese opinion.[51] But what did it mean for the U.S.-Japan relationship?

Before leaving to meet with Tanaka, Ford worried that, somehow, his former colleagues in Congress, and U.S. public opinion, might conclude that his interests in a corrupt foreign leader were stronger than his interests in ethical domestic policy.[52] The Congress had already delayed its hearings for his choice as vice president, Nelson Rockefeller, and he was also concerned about the fate of the U.S.-Japan Cultural Aid Bill. If defeated or compromised to death, it would have a most unfortunate effect on the latest "fence mending" effort with Tokyo.

The U.S.-Japan Cultural Aid Bill dated back to a 1962 commitment of the Kennedy administration. Reaffirmed by Nixon in 1973, this commitment involved the use of Japanese postwar Occupation payments for U.S.-Japanese cultural-exchange programs. Kissinger believed that the announcement would be enthusiastically received in Japan, reciprocating early 1970s Japanese grants to American universities. The NSC, on the other hand, opposed the legislation, insisting that the postwar payments were defense-related and, therefore, should be used for defense-related matters. Ford's domestic policy advisers also opposed the effort, noting that cultural arrangements were a luxury during bad economic times. The United States could still use the money as it desired. Spending it on domestic economic-recovery projects would warm the Ford administration to concerned American workers. Even if passed, Ford's staffers warned, the new U.S.-Japan Cultural Bill would take a new bureaucracy to administer it. They reminded the president that he was supposed to be opposed to "creeping bureaucracy." The Watergate-era voter was not interested in more faceless, mysterious civil servants, they concluded. And would this new bureaucracy be working on behalf of America's Japanese competition?[53]

Ford thanked his advisers for their candor, but agreed to disagree with them. Meanwhile, these in-house arguments foreshadowed a larger debate with Congress. Jacob Javits, New York's renowned liberal-Republican senator, said he had the answer to Ford's problems, but it was not the answer the president wanted to hear. Like so many of his Senate colleagues, Javits opposed "the cult of executive privilege." Congress, he said, needed a role in the Cultural Aid legislation. Hence, he proposed a much larger program. In addition to congressional leadership in administering the funds of the president's original bill, a new U.S.-Japan cultural commission, run by congressional staff, along with a sprinkling of White House aides and private-sector academics, would be established to further educational/cultural ties. Meanwhile, the U.S. Congress would authorize the funding of programs in Japanese studies in U.S. universities. This, Javits said, "would make a difference" in the U.S.-Japan relationship, as well as excite pro-American sentiment throughout Japan. Especially attracted to the congressional versus executive branch construction of the Javits initiative, dozens of House members joined Javits, voicing their support for it.

With Kissinger's close consultation, Ford denounced the congressional effort as too expensive. He also explained that congressional interference in this aging foreign-policy issue raised serious constitutional problems. "No one," he believed, wanted an executive versus legislative showdown over cultural legislation. At stake was the original $15 million involved, and that was all, Ford said. It was his final word, although it made him look, particularly in Japan, opposed to improvements in cultural ties. To Ford, the bottom line of this argument involved the White House's right to define aspects of its foreign policy as it saw fit.[54] This time, the executive branch won. Ford beat back the Congress here, following through with the 1962 commitment, the 1973 reaffirmation, and the $15 million bill. Sadly, the goodwill of the original initiative was lost in the process.

In a different time, and given the Japanese fascination with cultural issues, the American debate over U.S.-Japan cultural ties would have added serious strains to the Tokyo-Washington relationship. Instead, it remained a minor issue in the face of the many corruption charges against Prime Minister Tanaka. Only one charge interested the U.S. president, and it involved the Lockheed Aircraft Corporation's $2 million "gift to promote its sale of airplanes."[55] The dimension of the problem went beyond a "gift" (Lockheed's terminology). It became Edward Schmults's job to find out what those dimensions were, and how the "Lockheed Scandal" might impact the Ford administration's Japan policy. As Ford's deputy counsel, Schmults was ordered "to investigate, control, or otherwise halt questionable corporate payments abroad."[56] It soon became an unyielding assignment, always underlying the U.S.-Japan relationship throughout the Ford presidency.

The last thing Ford wanted was a foreign policy linked to Watergate-like problems. Ford had intended to relegate the Watergate era to history. But his 1974 pardon of Richard Nixon raised questions, among some voters, of yet another corrupt deal. The Lockheed investigation also raised Watergate-like issues of corruption and unethical behavior, but it gave Ford the opportunity to denounce that behavior, show his best ethical side, and move the U.S.-Japan relationship forward at the same time. Or so he hoped.[57] To the Ford team, the important thing was not what happened in the Lockheed-Japanese government affair (for they were never sure), but that corrupt deals beneath the noses of the American government never happen again.

As late as spring 1976 and the approaching Democratic Party nomination of Jimmy Carter for president, the Ford administration admitted "having difficulty in deciding how to handle concerns raised by the practice of certain U.S. corporations in Japan." Privately, Schmults, now heading a special Oval Office-commissioned task force looking into the problem, came up with several recommendations to overhaul U.S.-Japan business relations, end the bribes, and restore ethical conduct. With the U.S. Congress, the Organization for Economic Co-operation and Development (OECD), and even the United Nations also interested in this issue, Schmults was not alone. Especially by mid-1976, his mission became more and more involved in the effort to make President Ford "look presidential" in the Lockheed investigative mania. He met limited success.

On November 12, 1975, Senate Resolution 265 had already committed the U.S. government (and especially U.S. defense-contracted industries doing business abroad) to a new code of conduct covering international bribery, indirect payments, kickbacks, unethical political contributions, and "other disreputable activities." The resolution became part of the ongoing GATT multilateral trade negotiations and was tacked on to the Trade Act of 1974. In October 1975, the OECD adopted a resolution demanding that its members "observe the highest standards of behavior," while a UN resolution of December 15, 1975 condemned "corrupt corporate practices."

Although these initiatives received decent press attention, the up-staged Ford administration pointed out that resolutions carried little significance beyond the force of opinion. Ford said he was more interested in "enforcement" than opinion; hence, the onus to do something as the general election neared. Ford and Schmults favored a "three point plan." First of all, the Departments of State, Defense, and Commerce, along with the Federal Trade Commission (FTC), the Emergency Loan Guarantee Board, the Justice Department's antitrust division, the Securities and Exchange Commission (SEC), and the IRS were ordered to conduct investigations and halt all illegal payments by U.S. companies to Japanese and other foreign officials. Second, Schmults estimated that fifty major U.S. corporations maintained international bribery funds as a matter of course. He promised to become more specific, naming names publicly with follow-up IRS and SEC investigations and court action. Finally, Ford called for acts of Congress, not anti–"executive privilege" influenced or election-influenced resolutions, requiring public disclosure of fees paid to agents or officials abroad over the years, official apologies, and corporate reform.[58]

There were problems with all three of Ford's initiatives. Did the Justice Department want to handle what might become an endless number of antitrust cases? Would the Japanese and other foreign governments use America's new disclosures and business ethics legislation to retaliate, in some way, against U.S. policy? Would the Japanese regard America's "coming clean" as a threat to the very secret world of MITI specifically, and to Japanese business life in general? Did U.S. legislation mean to force the Japanese into identical legislative efforts, and could America's "coming clean" work without true international reciprocity? What would the precise impact be on U.S.-Japan trade, and which "side" would be the most hurt by it?

There were no easy answers to these Lockheed-stimulated matters. Because of that fact, Ford gave Schmults a bigger budget and more cabinet-level support and personnel (Commerce and Treasury Departments) to find those answers. This offered the issue even more media visibility, but few in the press were fascinated by this long-drawn-out affair. The public had been "Watergated" enough, and, sadly for President Ford, the media appeared more enthralled with Jimmy Carter's smile than the mechanics of post-Lockheed reform.

The Japanese government and people went through their own period of soul-searching over the "ethics issue." As deep-rooted a discussion as America's Watergate debate, the Lockheed scandal also placed Washington-Tokyo relations in a period of flux. Although few on either side of the Pacific believed that the soul-searching would lead to Western-styled reform of Japanese government and business practice, the Ford administration did believe that Japanese politics had become more predictable than at any time in recent memory. Kissinger called it an "interlude," but an "interlude" to what also remained unclear.[59]

In February 1976, for example, the Diet passed a resolution urging domestic "political trust" and "ethical business practice," but, at the same time, they condemned the Lockheed corporation. Urging the Ford administration to volunteer the names of corrupt officials, the Diet claimed that "the true friendship between Japan and the United States" could not be continued until America ended its unsavory intervention in Japanese corporate and political life.[60]

Three-quarters of the Diet resolution was dedicated to attacking U.S. institutions versus addressing the primary issues of "political trust" and "ethical business practice." This type of politics took the

Ford administration by surprise. Whereas Okinawan reversion had offered a certain focus and direction to anti-Americanism, the Lockheed-generated anger seemed to have no obvious goal. The "Kissinger flap" was a case in point.

A favorite topic of the Japanese press became Henry Kissinger's alleged anti-Japanese racism. According to these reports (the so-called "Kissinger flap"), Kissinger, now the U.S. secretary of state, always referred to Japanese government officials as "Japs." Japan, he supposedly said, could be relied upon as "America's keystone in the Far East" because Tokyo would always bend under U.S. pressure. Consequently, the Japanese people, like so many sheep, would forever follow Washington's lead in the Pacific.[61]

The anti-Kissinger press reports were accompanied by further attacks on U.S. nuclear policy, whereby large public demonstrations met the USS *Midway,* an aircraft carrier home-ported at the U.S. Navy base in Yokosuka, to protest its alleged "huge stockpile of nuclear weapons on board."[62] From trade policy to energy policy, Japan accused the United States of fostering "ill will," although, again, the precise charge remained difficult for the Ford administration to define.

From allegations of Kissinger racism to those of huge stockpiles of nukes, there was little evidence to support many of the mid-1970s Japanese claims. As disturbed by these developments as was the White House, the Senate majority leader, Mike Mansfield, went to Japan to find out for himself, and the U.S. government, what truly was happening in the stalled U.S.-Japan relationship. This future U.S. ambassador to Japan for Presidents Carter and Reagan enjoyed an elder-statesman role that the Japanese respected. His mission to Tokyo was well-timed. A longtime proponent of U.S.-Japan cooperation, Mansfield, Montana's senior senator, had encouraged the Mitsui Mining Corporation to purchase coal from Montana strip mines for Japanese domestic use. Local environmentalists and ranchers had opposed this Japanese "invasion" on a variety of grounds and won their case. Mansfield had represented a certain voice of reason during the Montana debate, winning, amazingly, the respect of both the Japanese and the anti-Mitsui activists.

Once in Japan, Mansfield discovered a government in turmoil. Political polarization seemed to be at the heart of the new Japanese anti-

Americanism, and Mansfield found no easy way to ease the tension. Although the future ambassador brought home nothing new for the Ford team to consider, he did believe that, like the United States during Watergate, Japan was "soon destined to move out of its Lockheed doldrums."[63]

The first victim of those "doldrums" had been Tanaka himself. Forced to resign in December 1974, the Tiger was replaced by veteran LDP politician Takeo Miki. For twenty-five years, Miki had advocated a stronger degree of ethics in Japanese politics and business. Few listened, and his struggling power-base symbolized that fact. He formed the weakest government the LDP had ever seen, the LDP leadership saw him as their "sole remaining trump card." The alternative was to see their once unassailable political party collapse under the weight of scandal and even unforeseen economic troubles.

Miki's weak position was made even weaker by his own political contradictions. Although the champion of ethical reform, he also engaged in the age-old Japanese political tradition of collecting and dispensing large sums of money. Shortly after Miki came to power, the Japanese Communist Party formed six investigative committees to find out where the prime minister's money came from and how much of it did he keep for his own pleasure.

In the midst of this particular problem, Yasuhiro Nakasone, a future prime minister himself, became the secretary-general of the LDP. Largely in charge of shoring up Miki's tottering government, Nakasone was, in fact, a rival of Miki's, and the press quickly predicted that Miki's future was a limited one. But, the sixty-seven-year-old Miki proved to be more resilient than expected. His grandfatherly manner, his sometimes passionate rhetoric in favor of reform, and the blatantly anti-Miki activities of some of his own LDP colleagues won the prime minister early approval from Japanese public opinion.[64] But a further test of his leadership would come in reference to economic policy, and this presented as much of a challenge as political reform.

Like the United States, Japan suffered from a rising inflation rate in the mid-1970s; however, Japan had the rare distinction of enjoying the worst inflationary spiral among "advanced countries." Japan's 25.8 percent consumer price rise was more than twice the U.S. figure of 12.2

percent in 1974. Unemployment hovered at 2 percent. To the Americans, 2 percent was next to nothing. But for the Japanese "miracle economy," the figure was an intolerable one. That ugly figure combined with Tanaka's brief and failed effort to move Japan away from its export economy and balance it with better domestic, consumer-friendly policies. Miki had to deal with the fallout from Tanaka's short-lived "personal economy." This confusion of economic purpose, met by oil prices that cost the consumer four times more than a few years earlier, also helped explain the anger in the Japanese ranks when the Ford administration accused Miki of unfair trading practice in items ranging from steel to color TVs.[65]

Despite Japanese charges to the contrary, Ford was far from protectionist. A number of troubled American industries asked for immediate presidential action to protect them from "Japanese attack." Effectively demonstrating his free-trader view, Ford denounced, for instance, Chicago's Zenith Corporation and its demand for White House protection against Japanese electronics goods. He hoped Japan would receive the proper free-trade message because of it.[66] But, in the era of post–Watergate/Lockheed soul-searching, the usual gentlemanly decorum that characterizes most diplomatic encounters was difficult to find in Tokyo or Washington. Henry Kissinger even addressed that problem in an out-of-character, rambling speech to the Japan Society in New York.

Insisting that it was "time to be frank," Kissinger used a Japan Society annual conference as the forum for a "call to reason" in U.S.-Japan relations. Kissinger admitted that cultural misunderstanding played a new, bitter role in the post-Watergate, post-Lockheed detente, but he also predicted a warmer relationship in the near future. The key to that new era, he said, might be the upcoming, long-planned, and unprecedented visit to America by Emperor Hirohito, combined with a pledge by both Ford and Miki to discuss differences more often.

Japan's evolution over the last thirty years into a major factor on the world scene inevitably has brought changes in the style of our relations even as the community of our mutual interests has grown. Adjustments in United States economic policies and a new policy toward China in 1971 led to painful but transitory misunderstandings to which—let us be frank—our own tactics contributed. We have learned from experience; these strains are behind us; our policies are moving in harmony in these areas; our consultations on all major issues are now close, frequent and frank.[67]

Kissinger would be proven correct. The shouting match did, indeed, die down. Emperor Hirohito visited twenty-one locations in the United States during his whirlwind tour. His goodwill message was pleasing to many Americans, although, to some diehard protectionists, his visit symbolized the arrival of the Japanese economy in the United States.[68] Meanwhile, Ford's presiding over Japanese-attended American Bicentennial celebrations, and the warm cooperation between the U.S. and Japanese teams at the summer Olympic Games in Montreal, also helped tone down the belligerent rhetoric. The U.S. ambassador to Japan, Robert Ingersol, had especially favored the new era of calm, cooperative dialogue. His low-key approach and gracious rhetoric added to the rapprochement.

As the Ford administration plunged headlong into the 1976 election, many voters desired a peaceful, quiet campaign season. Just four years before, the United States was still divided over the Vietnam War, Watergate already loomed on the horizon, and economic change raised more questions than answers. Certainly, this time, the political community could provide a less divisive campaign and a hefty dose of optimism. Discussing the differences in U.S.-Japan relations became too reminiscent of the ugly, Vietnam-related politics of the late 1960s and early 1970s. In the quiet reflection of America's Bicentennial celebration, political discord was never welcomed.

Jimmy Carter understood this desire for political peace better than Gerald Ford, and the latter would pay the price. At best, Ford represented a footnote to the Nixon era in a variety of policy-making areas. In U.S.-Japan relations, he kept the Washington-Tokyo dialogue alive during a resurgence of anti-Americanism in Japan, and alongside the growing distrust of American public opinion for Japan's success in the U.S. market. Both governments faced political fallout from scandals that shook public confidence. Cynicism and emotional charges and countercharges often overtook reason and analytical policymaking.

Nixon and Tanaka had much to do with this development, but their successors remained hard-pressed to move beyond the accomplishments of the early 1970s.

The time was right for a new look at the U.S.-Japan relationship. Miki's short flirtation with reform ended on Christmas Eve 1976. A new government, led by Takeo Fukuda, promised less soul-searching and more "traditional," conservative policymaking. At the same time, and with remarkable candor, America's Jimmy Carter implied that the warm Tokyo-Washington relationship predicted by Kissinger might not be possible because Kissinger himself was an obstruction to it.[69]

If Nixon never had been "the One" to lead the U.S.-Japan relationship, and Ford remained too caught-up in Watergate/Lockheed events to make a difference, then what was next? The answer, a majority of the American electorate agreed, might be found in Carter's promises of open government, honesty, realistic policy goals, compassion, and less cold warriorism. The postdetente era in U.S.-Japan relations was about to begin.

4

What to Do?

Jimmy Carter and Post-Vietnam
Japan Policy, 1977–1981

*Being point-man for U.S.-Japan policy is a responsible position. It
also beats retirement.* [1]

APPOINTED AMBASSADOR to Japan shortly after the inaugural of
Jimmy Carter, Senate Majority Leader Mike Mansfield answered the
call with characteristic good humor. Having already served his country for a half century, either in the armed forces or in the U.S. Congress, Mansfield might have preferred a posting to the prestigious
Court of St. James in London over Tokyo. As Mansfield's above comment suggested to all concerned, Japanese policy had never been his
forte in public life. Like many Americans, he would learn that ignor-
ing Japan's rise to power posed many problems. The United States
needed a working and healthy relationship with this new symbol of
world economic clout, and Mansfield soon proved more than up to
the task. His boss, President Carter, was another matter, for America's
first post-Vietnam leader represented all the hope and confusion of a
nation haunted by a long, disastrous war.

To Jimmy Carter, Japan was, as Hollywood long depicted it, "the
mysterious East." In this regard, he had much in common with most
Americans. On the other hand, he was the president, and the mystified

electorate expected him to figure out this enigma and move forward in the name of American national self-interest. It would always be easier said than done.

When the Carter team took control of the White House in 1977, Secretary of State Cyrus Vance viewed Japan, like so many of his predecessors, as a "stationary aircraft carrier." It remained a bastion of U.S. military basing privileges in the Far East. Beyond that, Vance believed that U.S. foreign policy had become too Eurocentered, Vietnam or no Vietnam, after World War II. Japan was now a significant economic power. The United States should recognize that reality and encourage greater Japanese participation in the world community. Such participation might even involve United Nations peacekeeping operations, if the Japanese saw fit to amend their pacifist constitution. These were all negotiable technicalities to Vance, and his ideas on a more militant constitution for Japan were a decade ahead of their time. He seemed quite pleased with his observations. He even reiterated the point in his 1983-published memoirs that he had the "vision" to predict Japan's new value to the international community.[2] In the meantime, the world remained a bipolar one, and America soldiered on, as Vance saw it, with its role as the unassailable superpower.

At the least, Vance's outlook underestimated the significance of Japanese economic power and overestimated the continuation of a global balance of power defined by Americans and Soviets alone. Japan continued to be seen as an important supporter of U.S. security interests in the Asian/Pacific region, whose peaceful outlook on international affairs would prompt an enthusiastic endorsement for the "human rights" cause.[3] The latter represented the thrust of Carter diplomacy; that is, that the U.S. had unduly stressed anti-communist commitments over moral ones. America, Carter often said, was a "good" country rather than a "great" one. After Vietnam, Carter's lack of arrogance and belligerency when discussing the United States' role in the world brought war-weary Americans to their feet. He promised them a foreign policy "as good as the people."[4] But what did that mean?

As the Carter White House soon discovered, the U.S.-Japan relationship was much more complex than a campaign speech. The Tokyo-Washington arguments over security, trade, and American-led causes, humane or not, would reach a fever pitch in the late 1970s. Always using the Kennedy administration as a mythical model for a caring yet efficient government, Carter hoped that an innovative, sweeping (i.e., Kennedyesque) economic foreign policy might replace America's Cold War sword rattling of the past. That meant a warmer relationship with "Japan, Inc.," and Carter believed his denunciations of global "human rights" violations, international racism, and nuclear war might appeal to Japan's pacifist, moral side.[5]

Coinciding with the Carter inaugural, the United Nations issued a report on international relations that reflected the Carter point of view. Urging that the advanced industrial states concentrate on improving their relations, the report specifically mentioned the Tokyo-Washington dialogue. The international community, the United Nations implied, could not afford any further squabbling. Economic cooperation was the key. Carter agreed, but he also saw America leading its trading partners into a new era of economic cooperation based, of course, on U.S. economic self-interest. With militarism rejected by post-Vietnam U.S. voters, Carter saw economics in a new light. "Dollar diplomacy" could help reestablish a sense of purpose in U.S. foreign policy. To many, American foreign policy, divorced from its longtime commitment to military victory in Southeast Asia, had no direction. Beyond complaints over "human rights" violations in a variety of countries, Carter promised a certain renaissance in the field of economic foreign policy:

> It is important that strong countries, the United States and Japan, work together to expand as rapidly as is consistent with sustained growth and the control of inflation. By adopting this stimulus program, the United States will be asserting leadership and providing a better international economic climate. We will then ask Japan to follow suit. This program itself implicitly calls on them to undertake stimulus efforts of proportionately similar amounts to ours.[6]

The Japanese government's answer to Carter was less than enthusiastic. Reminding the U.S. president that imperialism comes in many forms, the Diet suggested that the Carter administration was calling for an American right of intervention in Japanese business policy and practice. This was unfortunate, they said, also noting that the United

Nations' report was overly alarmist and that few Japanese or any nationality sought an American czar of the global economy. The devaluation of the U.S. dollar, the rise of the Third World, the success of export economies like Japan's, and the failure of America's anti-communist stress in Southeast Asia and elsewhere all pointed to dramatic change. That change, the Japanese believed, might not be as fast-moving as a military offensive, but the world economy would soon adjust accordingly.[7] American leadership was not requested or required.

Naturally, the Japanese government's primary concern was its own economic self-interest. But, they also enjoyed the indirect support of much of the U.S. political establishment. A wide-sweeping, international economic policy shepherded by a just-inaugurated president smacked, once again, of Kennedy's defunct New Pacific Community organization plan. Arthur Burns, the chairman of the Board of Governors of the Federal Reserve System, most of his colleagues on the board, a majority of U.S. senators and representatives, and members of the press complained that the United States did not need a government-led international economic-stimulus program. The world economy, Burns once explained, was improving, and it would be a bad precedent for the free flow of capitalism if the American president ended up spearheading U.S. business interests abroad.[8]

Whereas Americans interpreted Carter's interest in "dollar diplomacy" to mean a coming marriage of government and business adventures overseas for the benefit of post-Vietnam economic recovery, the Japanese saw an American plot to coordinate the world economy and destroy hard-fought-for Japanese gains within it.[9] Both complaints were severe enough to force Carter to retract his statements on economics before they developed into a policy. By April 1977, after serving fewer than a hundred days as president, Carter abandoned what he labeled "the American stimulus program." The Japanese government hailed the decision as a victory for "free trade" (i.e., the status quo of growing Japanese influence in the American economy and elsewhere). The U.S. political and business community hailed it as a victory for the "traditions of American capitalism" (i.e., the long-standing separation of business and government policies). Both these sources of complaint had exaggerated Carter's comments, for the president had been nowhere near enacting a new global economic policy.

Nevertheless, Carter insisted that the United States and Japan, which together represented the thrust of global economic power, had "a special responsibility" to accelerate the growth of their economies even faster. The world economy still suffered from a recession, and the Third World still demanded greater assistance from major economic powers. In short, the United States and Japan had a "moral" obligation to align their economic interests for the benefit of their own citizens and any nation who embraced the capitalist system.[10]

Carter's commitment to moral policy, or his own interpretation of doing the right thing, was sincere. It also helped explain his rise to power. Echoing John Kennedy in 1961, Carter, sixteen years later, saw his administration as a "first step" to a new era of political excitement. Although he often yearned for the "innocence" of his multimillion-dollar peanut farming business or for the lackluster years of his governorship in Georgia, Carter also believed it was time for the New South—the Southern U.S. states—to rescue a struggling nation.[11] He enjoyed the irony of his once-laughed-at region of the country now representing economic growth and success. In 1978, he would tell the Japanese prime minister, Masayoshi Ohria, that Georgia and Japan had much in common. Both were once declared "dead and gone" by economic experts and political analysts. Both now represented amazing success in the face of adversity. Both should reflect on that success and work together.[12]

Reflective by nature, Carter had been especially moved by the civil-rights movement of his home state during the 1950s and 1960s. Jousting against nearly a century of state law that enshrined legal discrimination, young black Georgians helped overturn a sad era of misery. Pursuing his own education and business interests during the height of this civil-rights activity, Carter nevertheless made it clear that he favored the new Georgia over the old. Although he also admired President Johnson's assistance to the civil-rights struggle, Carter, as a businessman with an interest in state government, viewed federal government influence over state and regional matters as too intrusive. Unlike Johnson, Carter never viewed the New Deal as America's greatest moment. It was "right," he believed, for the federal government to guarantee civil rights/civil liberties and rescue the downtrodden at home or abroad when no one else could. Otherwise, he had little use for the power and influence of Washington, D.C. and the legacy of interventionism represented by Roosevelt's New Deal or Johnson's Great Society.[13]

Given these views, the *Atlanta Constitution* coined the term *New Democrat* to describe the Carter outlook. Others, of course, interpreted New Democrat to mean "old conservative." But this dismissed Carter's complexity much too quickly. Proud of his academic expertise in both economics and engineering, Carter was quick to compare his intellectual prowess to the analytical mind of John Kennedy. Proud of his commitment to the "best aspects of the Democratic Party" (i.e., the Democrats' view on the moral responsibility of government), Carter explained that rejecting federal government interventionism in the domestic economy and rejecting U.S. military interventionism abroad equaled the recognition of Washington's "limited powers."

In its day, Carter's assault on the unlimited power of the federal government, and even the Democratic Party that largely administered it, was daring and controversial. For decades, the U.S. electorate had grown used to its public officials touting the glories of interventionism. Wrapped, as it invariably was, in a tight, patriotic package, the power and privilege of Washington, D.C. was always associated with the proper approach to winning the Cold War and running a domestic economy.

Given the American disgust over both Watergate and Vietnam, Carter's presidential campaign announcement that the only time he had visited Washington had been "as a tourist" resulted in cheers rather than jeers. Times had changed, but Carter's transition from the anti-Establishment candidate to Establishment itself would not be easy.

One of the most important components within this transition, he proclaimed in his inaugural address, was the creation of a post-Vietnam foreign policy. Gesturing toward the commonly held Japanese belief that the Vietnam War had been a racist, anti-Asian one, Carter noted that his old, unswerving commitment to civil-rights reform in the U.S. South applied to his special interest in similar reforms around the world. Promising an "open government," whereby Watergate-styled crises remained unlikely, Carter also promised that his relationship with Japan would remain very much in the public arena as well.[14]

"Our people are troubled, confused and sometimes angry" over the direction of American foreign policy, Carter told the Foreign Policy Association during the 1976 campaign. There had been "too much interest in transient spectaculars and too little on substance," he noted. Vietnam had eroded "the focus and morality of our foreign policy." He promised to change that focus, and, in a 1970s version of JFK, "get America moving again."[15] But, it would be "moving" away from "massive retaliation" and Cold War sword rattling. It would be a gentler America than JFK would have remembered; however, like many Democrats who redefined Kennedy's New Frontier as time went by, Carter believed that the peaceful world Kennedy dreamed about after the Cuban missile crisis had been simply sidetracked and delayed by the misguided adventure in Vietnam. Carter planned to continue the task of realigning U.S. foreign policy with the forces of morality, human rights, and democratic harmony. The days of "playing Lone Ranger" in the world, he promised, were over.[16] "We simply must have an international policy of democratic leadership, and we must stop trying to play a lonely game of power politics. We must evolve and consummate our foreign policy openly and frankly. There must be bipartisan harmony and collaboration between the President and the Congress, and we must reestablish a spirit of common purpose among democratic nations."[17]

Following the early collapse of his vaguely described global economic leadership initiative—the "stimulus"—Carter still worked hard to find that "common purpose among democratic nations." Proclaiming the U.S.-Japan economic relationship "the world's most important" one, Carter continued to urge the Japanese government to pursue economic growth programs and welcome American-like definitions of fair play within its trade policy.[18]

In May 1977, Carter met, for the first time, with the political leaders of the world's major capitalist powers. At the gathering—dubbed the London Economic Summit Conference—one prime minister or chancellor or president after another swore their allegiance to economic growth and "ethical" free-trade practices. The Japanese government even "promised" to improve its rate of economic growth by 6.7 percent, "consider" investing its economic surplus in struggling Third World countries (and under U.S. guidance), as well as "consider" opening its own market to U.S. products. Carter hailed these Japanese pronouncements as the most significant development of the conference. He also waxed poetic on the significance of "dollar diplomacy," the warm relations between capitalist democracies, and the "beauty" of American-Japanese friendship.[19] Within a year, Japan reported only a 5 percent growth of its economy. There were no plans to embark on a Third World infrastructure assistance program, and opening the domestic market to benefit U.S. competitive industries was never "considered." Meanwhile, the United States reported a $20 billion deficit and Japan proudly proclaimed a $10 billion surplus. Carter's leadership in this area had proven most ineffective, and the failure was especially glaring in light of his glowing comments in London.

Labeling the matter a temporary setback, Carter announced in February 1978 that his administration's stress of "dollars over bombs" would continue; but different tactics were required. In the effort to end a worldwide recession, stimulate Third World investment, and establish true, working commitments to free trade, the "locomotive tactic," as Carter called it, was no longer the proper approach.

In fact, Carter had offered the press an economic "locomotive" analogy early in his presidency. By quickly coordinating the economic policies of the major capitalist powers, the president had stressed, the United States would also lead the world out of recession, toward Third World pump priming, as well as open the Japanese market at the same time. Like a "speeding locomotive" the United States would establish a new world economy and its new post-Vietnam leadership.[20]

Perhaps too conditioned by angry, Cold War rhetoric and the political/military priorities of anti-communism, few Americans noticed Carter's "dollar diplomacy." On the other hand, the president's promise to be "open" with the American people forced him to admit his failure on the "locomotive" policy. His commitment to candor played well as Candidate Carter, but President Carter now endured lower support in the public opinion polls because of it. He promised to make up for his "mistakes." "Dollar diplomacy" would work, he said, asking for the "trust" of the American people.[21]

Carter now spoke of a "convoy" approach to American leadership in the world economy. "Locomotives" were out. According to the new policy, "convalescent" economies—namely, Italy, Britain, and France—would be asked to expand their economies in a rapid fashion and in coordination with Japan and the United States. A variety of happy results was predicted by the White House, ranging from the death of recession to specific infrastructure assistance programs across Latin America, Asia, and Africa. "Expansion and coordination" was the key to success, Carter explained, and the United States would always be there for the proper guidance. Formally, the new initiative was called the Coordination Reflation Action Program. The Japanese government simply refused any role in it. Without a coordination partner, the Carter administration was humbled into announcing another foreign-policy failure. This was second time around, and the world press found great significance in the struggles of the U.S. president. They also found humor in the acronym of his failed program: CRAP.[22]

Carter's failures meant the United States had no working economic foreign policy beyond a rising deficit. Since he had placed great confidence in lessening U.S.-Japan tensions by offering the Japanese a leadership role side by side with the United States in his economic plans, Carter found Tokyo's position especially frustrating. In answer to the Carter administration's concerns, the Japanese government announced that it had similar interests in ending recession and seeing a happier Third World. It did not like the "interference" of the Carter administration in Japanese domestic policy and, therefore, could never adhere to the larger American-instigated policy.

Carter's answer to Japan was a very public campaign opposed to Japanese "selfishness," urging the reduction of their market surplus. He also permitted the dollar to fluctuate in the world financial market. Concerned that U.S.-Japan relations had reached a new low, the administration reshuffled a number of cabinet portfolios and offered an apology to Washington for any ill will that might have been caused over the past year. It was now left to Carter to accept the apology or keep pressing for a Japanese surplus reduction and open market. He opted for more pressure tactics, but took his time in deciding what those tactics might entail.[23] In the meantime, criticism of his "dollar diplomacy" mounted; and, to his surprise, his leading critic came from Europe, not the Pacific.

West Germany's chancellor, Helmut Schmidt, found the American-Japanese squabble especially annoying and bizarre. Carter, he observed, had created this awkward situation. The world economy hung in the balance, he noted with disgust, while the Americans debated their next move. For many, West Germany's rise to economic power had always been as dramatic as Japan's. Throughout Carter's first year in office, Schmidt suggested, and often in public, that the Washington-Tokyo dialogue was too narrow and unfortunate. Instead, he called for an active alliance between Tokyo, Washington, and Bonn on economic issues. Carter's fear of appearing too Eurocentric, Schmidt noted, had driven the White House away from West Germany and toward Japan alone. The West Germany–United States dialogue had always been a happier, more cooperative one than the Washington-Tokyo relationship; but it should never, the West German chancellor insisted, be taken for granted.[24]

Schmidt did not define the mechanics of this proposed new triumvirate of economic-superpower relations, but he was quick to denounce Carter's "locomotive" and "convoy" ideas as foolish and naive. Suggesting that Carter simply hoped to replace recession with wild inflation, Schmidt announced that America was too much of the "amateur" in world economic policy to be trusted. Proudly, the West German chancellor explained that his country earned the right to be declared the world's leading economic power. While America was focused on Vietnam, he said, West Germany had stressed international economic relationships, and without the prejudices, market peculiarities, and legal limitations of the New Japan. Given Carter's stumbling and bumbling, Schmidt announced that international financiers, bankers, and economic planners around the world should turn to West Germany for guidance. The Americans, he noted, needed more time to recover from their Vietnam nightmare. Sadly, he predicted, that recovery might remain elusive.[25]

Schmidt's conclusions shocked the world. No significant Free World leader, and certainly not a German one, had ever suggested that the

"American Century" was over. Soon to be further enhanced by the Carter administration's troubles during the Iranian hostage crisis and the Soviet invasion of Afghanistan, Schmidt's conclusions set off a series of international discussions about the competence of the Carter administration. They also stimulated a considerable amount of soul-searching in the Carter White House itself.

Both Vance and Carter agreed that the best response to Schmidt would be to ignore his charges. This might offer the image to the world that the United States still regarded the opinion of nations such as West Germany less than significant to world economic planning—with the consequent suggestion of the image of a still-all-powerful America. If wedded to a "get-tough" policy on Japan, the Carter team could effectively isolate America's uppity, old World War II foes, flaunt Washington's power, and continue to pursue their "dollar diplomacy" interests. With this in mind, Carter demanded that Tokyo, and in only three weeks time, detail how it planned to reduce its surplus and open its market to U.S. competition.[26]

The Japanese Diet's reaction to the Carter demand remained unsurprising to veteran Japan watchers. Their official response stressed the point that Japan was still a "vulnerable" nation, quickly moving from "developing" to "superpower" status. For a longtime superpower, such as the United States, to "bully" Japan after supposedly learning the "hard lessons of defeated arrogance" in Vietnam, was difficult to accept, the Diet pointed out. Meanwhile, "structural difficulties," they concluded, made it impossible for the Japanese government to adhere to American demands in the first place. In the second place, the United States was still refusing to understand Japan's interest in protecting its market from foreign competition.[27]

With American-Japanese relations reduced, yet another time, to mudslinging, and no economic dialogue in sight, the U.S. dollar plunged in direct proportion to the rise of the Japanese yen. This latest embarrassment, Carter reasoned, might be good for the American economy in the long run. "Benign neglect" became the Carter team's official economic foreign policy. The continuing slide of the U.S. dollar against the yen and other currencies, the American president predicted, would make "their" products more expensive in the U.S. market and "our" imports more tempting to overseas consumers.

Such a policy would lower the deficit and stimulate international interest in American goods. Hence, as Vance put it, the twisted political joke, usually leveled by activist, liberal Democrats against steadfast, conservative Republicans, held new significance: "Don't just stand there, do nothing."[28]

Although a similar policy would be adopted by the Clinton administration nearly twenty years later and barely cause a ripple in political opinion, the American public reaction to "benign neglect" was damning in 1978. Much of the U.S. press, and an eager Republican opposition, accused Carter of "taking the American dollar down" in a fit of administrative incompetence. Later admitting that he never anticipated an angry public reaction, Carter mused that that reaction was due to a confused America.[29] On the one hand, the American electorate desired a quieter, gentler foreign policy after the misery of Vietnam. On the other hand, they were nostalgic for the days of the all-powerful U.S. military and "sound as a dollar" currency. A foreign policy that combined aspects of both sentiments required a miracle, Carter believed, and, as the search for a workable policy continued, his administration remained trapped in a cross fire of domestic criticism and international complaint.

In Japan, public opinion grew deeply concerned about the growing Tokyo-Washington tension. By 1978, most opinion polls blamed Carter for the problem, but the country was far from united on the best policy to follow in relations with the United States. Billed as the most important public opinion survey in the postwar era, Tokyo's well-read and prestigious *Asahi Shimbun* newspaper reported that 37 percent of their countrymen regarded a friendly U.S.-Japan dialogue as the most important issue facing the nation. Yet an unprecedented number (20 percent) believed that the Carter administration was incompetent, and that their government should concentrate its trade policies on China. America was not worth the trouble. This type of sentiment was easily translated into defense-related issues, and the *Asahi Shimbun* noted that more than 37 percent of Japan's population found the U.S. military bases in their country "a serious threat to peace." Nearly 52 percent saw America's continuing Cold War position around the world as an invitation to World War III.[30]

Among America's anti-communist allies, the Japanese shared the highest level of doubt over Washington's Cold War leadership and political/economic competence. Helmut Schmidt might have accented issues of doubt and competence in his various public utterances, but only 13 percent of his countrymen shared his concerns. To the Japanese, the United States had become a bumbling ex-superpower, even though Tokyo's "miracle export economy" still required the buying power of the American consumer to continue the "boom years." This love-hate relationship posed certain dilemmas to Japanese policymakers, for a truly significant anti-Japanese backlash in U.S. public opinion would mean the dreaded return of American protectionism.

As an on-call adviser to the Carter White House, former CIA director William Colby explained to the president that it certainly would take only a short period of time for a diplomatic love-hate relationship to develop into a serious security crisis for the United States. Predicting that Japan had the potential to kill the significance of the U.S. dollar in the world market, Colby suggested that Japan sought "dominance" in world economic matters and not "market share." The ultimate casualty in this power play would be U.S. power itself. America was on the threshold, he concluded, of either continuing its superpower status or following the British and the French as yesterday's world powers. U.S. survival in the new post-Vietnam era— the era of a withering Cold War—required the intimate tying together of the Japanese and American economies. "As long as two separate political frameworks exist," Colby warned Carter, "competition in the economic field will be reflected in the political field, and the temptation will arise to use political tools to suppress economic competition."[31] Unless Carter considered offering recognition to Japan as the soon-to-be unassailable superpower of the 1980s and 1990s, Colby said there was no real alternative to his political/economic integration suggestion.

To Carter, Colby's conclusions about impending doom on the one hand reflected the disgust, shared by many aging cold warriors, over the Vietnam defeat and the lack of interest among America's youth for anti-communist crusading. On the other hand, Colby's integration ideas interested the president, reflecting his own belief that the coming new global economy required less commitment to nationalist politics and more gestures toward internationalism.[32] Despite this attraction to at least part of the former CIA director's thesis, legendary Cold War veterans like Colby were not the president's cup of tea.

Although, unlike John Kennedy with Arthur Schlesinger, Carter had no in-house intellectual advisers, he admired Kennedy for having "the brightest and best" in academe close at hand. Like Kennedy, Carter enjoyed a fine intellectual argument. Few observers of the Carter administration, at the time, were willing to credit the president for his intellectual prowess. The press remained fascinated by Carter's blue-collar brother Billy, who forever lent a country-bumpkin image to the White House. They also complained about the "Georgia Mafia," a reference to Carter's inner circle of Atlanta area born-and-bred advisers. Consequently, the Carter White House was accused of maintaining a weak foundation to study and conclude policy on the complexities of U.S.-Japan relations.[33]

To a large degree, the public complaints of Carter's struggles in U.S.-Japan policymaking, and other fields of endeavor, constituted the infamous "low blow." From Ambassador Mike Mansfield to Edmund Muskie on the Senate Foreign Relations Committee, or Warren Christopher at the Middle East desk in the State Department, Carter welcomed the competent advice of experienced policymakers. More than anyone, Carter understood his own liabilities as a former official at state government level now in a world leadership role.[34] In any event, he was not required to enjoy the company of D.C.'s power elite. He was most comfortable with his New South staff and early campaign supporters in academe. The latter also had something to offer his Japan policy.

The person in the Carter administration closest to being "expert" on things Japanese, and who also had the academic pedigree to suggest such credentials, was the director of the State Department's policy-planning staff, Professor Anthony Lake, from Holy Cross College in Massachusetts. Lake's 1976 work *The Vietnam Legacy* had a profound influence on candidate Carter. Its thesis stressed the new limitations on American power in the Pacific, urging a shoring-up of defense relationships in the region. It predicted, like many who supported Henry Kissinger's identical concerns, a renewed communist challenge in the Third World due to America's Vietnam defeat. On the other hand, it also recommended a Pacific policy that stressed the uplifting of human rights. Lake noted vaguely that "our allies" must now play a role in this great endeavor, implying a new role for rising Japan.[35]

Carter was attracted to the Lake thesis, but not because of its vague suggestions of a new role for Japan. The attraction for Carter was based on the legacy of JFK's success in using innovative foreign-policy slogans in the 1960 presidential campaign to gain a media-spotlight advantage over his traditional cold-warrior opponent Richard Nixon. To Kennedy, the catchall slogans ranged from "missile gap" complaints to attacking America's "Ugly American" image in the Third World. To Carter, the catchall slogan stressed humane government at home and human rights abroad. In contrast to 1960, Carter's foreign-affairs comments remained limited. The electorate in 1976 seemed not to prefer a specific stand from its Democratic Party candidate on issues such as Japan.[36] The mechanics of championing human rights in the Asian/Pacific region, and a role Japan might play within it, was not a matter of concern to voters. Consequently, Lake's influence and the influence of academic Japan watchers such as Charles E. Neu, author of the probing 1975 work *The Troubled Encounter,* were ignored. Neu's book predicted the growing tensions between the United States and Japan in the 1980s and made recommendations to head off these "troubles" by reinventing a serious economic foreign policy for the United States. Neu, like many Democratic Party–leaning academics in 1976 who were smitten with Potomac Fever for the first time in nearly a decade, applied for a policy-making job with President-elect Carter. The application was rejected.[37]

Forever candid, Carter suggested that his staff was a mixture of "good ol' boy" loyalists and brilliant, no-nonsense advisers.[38] After the revelations of White House staff criminality during Watergate, the electorate remained attentive to the issue of competent, ethical bureaucracy. Carter promised to "do better," and appointment of Mansfield as ambassador to Japan symbolized that commitment.

Well beyond mandatory retirement age, Mansfield had served as majority leader since LBJ joined the John Kennedy ticket in 1960. More than seventy years old and looking every year of it, Mansfield responded to his nomination as ambassador with characteristic deadpan style. Insisting that the ambassadorial corps had long been "an old folks home" anyway, he promised "to stay awake" as Japan and America "constructed a new relationship."[39] It was one of the greatest political understatements of the 1970s.

To many Americans, Mansfield was a Democratic Party warhorse heading overseas. To the Japanese, he represented a keen analytical mind and a forceful personality worthy of respect and careful watching.[40] Along with his closest Senate colleague, Edmund Muskie, Mansfield had made a series of speeches in 1972 warning the country about the economic prowess of Japan and what it might mean for America and the world. Mansfield, addressing the Defense Appropriations Subcommittee, following the reversion of sovereignty to Japan of the Ryukyu Islands in January 1972, complained that the United States had been too willing to ignore the interest of the locals, especially on Okinawa, during the reversion process.[41]

"Doing the right thing" had been an important political issue for Mansfield long before the Carter career. The new president admired Mansfield's dedication and welcomed his advice. Japan policy, Mansfield warned Carter, would not be easy; it required greater presidential attention than ever before. The Ryukyus issue, he predicted, was not over. An ugly state of mind remained, and it threatened most aspects of the U.S.-Japan relationship. Mansfield had visited the Ryukyus in 1972, and he found a distinct Ryukyuan identity. It was an identity partially molded through U.S. postwar commitments to civil rights and civil liberties there. The more the United States recognized the Ryukyus' democratic growth, the more Japan would complain of U.S. colonialism in the Pacific. The latter, Mansfield suggested, might even lead to the complete breakdown of the Tokyo-Washington detente. But could the United States ignore the Ryukyus' lingering desire for full civil-rights benefits in favor of Tokyo's lack of concern and economic-based agenda? U.S.-Japan relations, Mansfield implied, should be more than squabbles over imported goods from Japan and U.S. military bases in Japan.[42] Carter's "human rights" commitment should be applied to Japan as well.

Mansfield, a clever and cautious politician, was not advocating a Washington war of words leveled against Tokyo's Ryukyus policy. But he did suggest that the U.S. commitment to "human rights," even if it meant the insistence on Japanese equal treatment of Ryukyus residents, might even be respected in Japan as an American postcolonial statement. Japanese politics, like the post-Vietnam era itself, Mansfield noted, were complicated and involved. Washington had more to gain from dissecting the intricacies of Japanese politics than insisting upon Japanese loyalty to U.S.-set goals in Pacific policy. The Ryukyus issue, he said, had become a symbol of cross-cultural misunderstanding. There would be many more such symbols if America did not study and anticipate the goals of Japanese government and business.[43]

Mansfield's recognition of the cultural-misunderstanding issue won him instant respect in Japan, and his concern for "human rights" everywhere, including the Ryukyus, won him special praise from Japanese liberals and pacifists. For the first time since the early Reischauer era, an American ambassador was a hit in Tokyo. The fact that his policy position was also Washington's policy position mattered little in the Japanese press's fascination with Mansfield's every move. Ironically, Carter did not enjoy the same praise in the Japanese press. For both Mansfield and Carter, being candid often worked, but, in contrast to Mansfield, Carter also admitted ignorance of recent Japanese politics, life, and culture. These latter admissions won him few admirers in Japanese public opinion. For example, he once admitted in an interview with *Asahi Shimbun* that he had no idea Tachikawa Air Base west of Tokyo had been closed shortly before he took office. Given its significance to the U.S. air war over North Vietnam, Tachikawa still symbolized American anti-Asian racism to many Japanese. This "issue," along with Carter's odd comments about the "liberalism" of the always conservative LDP, led *Asahi Shimbun* to editorialize on "the ignorance factor" in the new Carter White House.[44]

Throughout 1977, Mansfield still supported the idea of uplifting civil rights/civil liberties for "all" Japanese citizens, and made that very clear to his host government. He insisted that the United States was not retreating from the Pacific and urged the Japanese Diet to work with the Carter White House in building a new post-Vietnam relationship. Unfortunately, the Japanese press and much of the Diet sometimes concluded that Mansfield rather than Carter represented the real policy-making power of the U.S. government.[45]

In his own folksy, yet gentlemanly style, Mansfield also told the Japanese government to beware of those who interpret America's position in the world as faltering, either militarily or economically. He reminded the Japanese that America, too, had its eager "extremists," ready to take advantage of the divisions caused by Vietnam and Watergate, and advance their own careers. He warned the Diet to reject the political Right that called for the end of the "incompetent, defeated" U.S. military presence in Japan and its replacement with the resurrection of a Bushido (warrior's code of honor), and, recalling the terminology of the 1930s, a new "coprosperity sphere." Mansfield warned them of the youthful political Left, eager to destroy the excesses of the Japan Inc. lifestyle, but without a better replacement for it than Soviet communism.[46]

As always, Mansfield claimed he was never an expert on Japan, but his warnings to the Diet and follow-up recommendations to Carter suggested, at the least, that he was a remarkably fast learner. A different personality, younger, less gruff, less experienced, would have been accused of shameless paternalism in his treatment of the Japanese Diet. But Mansfield's comments continued to command grand attention in Japanese politics, the media, and academe. Lacking the elitist polish and language skills of a Reischauer, preferring Sapporo beer to Dom Perignon, Mansfield, nevertheless, reminded some veteran politicos in the Diet of Douglas MacArthur. Paternalism was a plus in this case, and the Japanese government took Mansfield's invitation to work with the new post-Vietnam America most seriously.

"I expect you to report with directness and candor," Carter had told Mansfield before he left for Japan. This did not mean that the former Senate majority leader had a green light to move forward with his own policy-making agenda. Zbigniew Brzezinski, Carter's NSC chief, worried that Secretary Vance may offer certain ambassadors— namely, Mansfield—an overly long leash. In Carter's foreign policy-making team, Brzezinski remained the most-concerned about the diminishing of U.S. power and allied reaction to it. He urged Carter to remain a vigilant cold warrior, and that meant a coherent, efficient foreign policy. Suspicious that the State Department did not have a strong commitment to continuing the anti-communism cause, Brzezinski saw his NSC more essential to foreign-policy making than anyone in the Vance-led bureaucracy. This attitude was nothing new at the NSC; however, Brzezinski linked his own ambition to the NSC's fortunes. Carter admired his hard-nosed realism and fine intellectual credentials. Yet he never saw him as a dominant member of his foreign-policy-making staff.[47]

According to Brzezinski, Mansfield was preparing to lead America's Japan policy. Carter was expected to follow along, and, sooner rather than later, the allies would be denouncing the utter collapse of presidential power. Brzezinski based his predictions on the Grew-Roosevelt relationship of the 1930s. But Mansfield was not a Joseph Grew and Carter was not a Franklin Roosevelt. Brzezinski also exaggerated his case. Grew had been FDR's ambassador to Japan in the dark days before World War II. Forever playing golf with the leadership of the Japanese government, Grew was on a first-name basis with the architects of the Pearl Harbor attack plan. The friendly and candid conversations that resulted from these warm relationships were dutifully reported back to FDR, and policy decisions were made accordingly. FDR preferred his ambassadors to be, to a degree, independent-minded and offer him the best alternatives in policy. FDR's successor, Harry Truman, preferred coordinated efficiency to independence and conflicting ideas in the ambassadorial corps. Carter had often said in the 1976 campaign that his favorite modern president had been Harry Truman, and Brzezinski reminded him of that point in direct reference to the ambassadorial corps. Japanese-American relations were delicate, and Mansfield's approach and policy recommendations bordered on the extreme, the NSC warned Carter.[48]

Mansfield's real test of fire came in late 1977 and early 1978. Although it received little press in America, and was rated well beneath the military basing/economic policy priorities of the Carter administration, the issue of nuclear disarmament was still an important one to the Japanese political community. In February 1978, after nearly a year of lobbying, petition gathering, and news spotlights, the Japanese antinuclear movement offered a petition, signed by a majority of the Japanese population, that called for a nuclear free Pacific and the exit of U.S. nuclear vessels from the vicinity of Japan. The big U.S. navy bases, particularly the submarine pens at Sasebo, near Nagasaki, and the WESTPAC headquarters at Yokosuka, near Yokohama, were targets of large demonstrations during the first Carter year in office.

The navy always denied that nuclear weapons were present on these bases. Nuclear-powered vessels never posed threats to Japan, they said. But the growing antinuclear movement remained skeptical. While in Congress, Mansfield had denounced the nuclear arms race, and Japanese antinuclear activists hoped they had a friend in Mansfield.[49]

Brzezinski worried that, sooner or later, Mansfield would embarrass America's already weak national security position in the Far East by supporting the antinuclear movement. Opposing nukes could be considered within a "human rights" agenda, and to Brzezinski that agenda was more trouble than it was worth. But Brzezinski was wrong. Although he decried nuclear solutions, Mansfield backed-up the claims of the navy, called for calm and a working dialogue between the U.S. government and the Japanese antinuclear movement, and emerged as a statesman on the issue. Noting that the antinuclear movement was not going to disappear, he urged Carter to "do something" that might please "this next generation of Japanese leadership."[50]

Becoming more and more responsive to the antinuclear movement, the ruling Liberal Democratic Party appeared on the verge of wedding its fortunes to the movement's popularity. By late 1978, the Diet insisted that spent fuel stockpiled in Japan from U.S. nuclear powered vessels be immediately removed from the country. This insistence was greeted with enthusiasm across Japan, and Carter, to the surprise of the antinuclear movement, agreed to the transfer. Perhaps as a gesture to America's national self-interest concerns, Carter said he reserved the right to be "flexible" in future decisions of nuclear-fuel transfers, and that comment was poorly received in Japan. But Carter's general comments in favor of the transfer stressed the "basic human right to safety," and this won him considerable respect from a nation used to expressions of American power and not "safety."

This type of expression suggested to Japan's Carter watchers that U.S. policy was truly in transition.[51] They awaited more substance to that transition. Without question, the Carter team did nothing to suggest otherwise. A new era of U.S.-Japan relations was about to begin, they implied. In reference to the growing number of anti-Japanese auto and electronics industry protectionist measures being proposed in Congress, Secretary Vance made it quite clear that he would be "undertaking a cooperative effort with Congress to make a comprehensive revision of those laws during the next session" (1978). He would be engaging in this effort "personally," he told the press, describing this State Department–Congress effort as "unprecedented."[52] In terms of multilateral trade negotiations, Vance admitted that disagreements over trade would probably remain disagreements for the time being, but he refused to point fingers at Japan or any other nation as being more responsible for America's weakening trade position. "Our trade deficit," he noted in August 1978, "results from continuing high demand for oil imports and the faster pace of economic recovery in the U.S. than in the rest of the world." He did admit, on the other hand, that a "reduction in trade barriers and increased opportunities for U.S. firms to compete" in the Japanese market would make sense.[53]

Vance's approach made it very clear to Japan that the Carter administration had no opposition to free trade, that the Democratic-controlled Congress could be leashed by dedicated antiprotectionist Carter White House forces, and that a decent Japanese gesture toward America's interest in penetrating their domestic market would be welcome. Unfortunately, Vance's matter-of-fact comments were taken quite literally by the Japanese government. By 1980, when nothing in the Tokyo-Washington relationship had advanced beyond American complaints against the closed Japanese market, the competence of the Carter administration would in itself be an issue.

Ironically, the possibility of U.S.-Japan relations reaching an all-time high point of cordiality had always existed in the late 1970s. Prime Minister Masayoshi Ohira had first met Carter during an international energy conference in 1975. Given the fact that both men championed new energy policies in their respective countries, and given the fact that both had been derided by their respective political parties for these "pet projects," Carter and Ohira became friends. So did their families. Carter's young daughter, Amy, became especially close to the Ohiras. In 1979, when Amy was overheard by the Japanese press denouncing the Tokyo area's horrible pollution, Prime Minister Ohira rushed to her protection after the press began a countertirade against polluted American cities. Explaining that Amy was right on the mark, and that no honorable, ethical person would ever attack the daughter of his friend the U.S. president, Ohira became especially endeared to the Carters.[54]

The friendly Carter-Ohira dialogue was unique in twentieth-century diplomacy, and Carter likened it to the famous friendship of Franklin Roosevelt and Winston Churchill. Great developments in the history of democracy stemmed from that relationship, the president once noted, and much could develop from the Ohira-Carter relationship as well.

Carter exaggerated the Roosevelt-Churchill parallel.[55] Carter and Ohira never even agreed on the priority issues facing U.S.-Japan relations; nor did they view those issues in the same light. For Japan, the post-Vietnam U.S. "retreat" from Asian/Pacific defense was real, and America's growing reliance on nuclear defense capability over conventional forces in the Asian/Pacific region was symbolic of that "retreat."

In economic matters, Ohira's Liberal Democratic Party viewed Carter's Democratic Party as the party of protectionism. The U.S. Congress, smarting from a continuing energy crisis as well as from the continued failures of a domestic automobile and electronics industry that could not withstand the onslaught of Japanese competition, blamed Japan for its troubles. The 1980s promised a rocky Tokyo-Washington relationship because of this Congress, and because Carter's party was in charge of it. Meanwhile, Carter's insistence on "human rights" commitments from old allies, like Japan, implied to the Japanese Diet that the Americans would soon be pressuring them to accept a large influx of Cambodian and other Southeast Asian refugees, as well as joining in American-defined "peacekeeping" missions in the near future.[56]

The Diet's concerns and fears suggested that there was no reason why a warm U.S.-Japan dialogue should exist. To compound matters further, Carter announced in the summer of 1979 that the American bases on Okinawa would now be hiring Ryukyu islanders who had been denied jobs on the Japanese mainland because of Japanese "racism."[57] The Diet saw this as undue U.S. influence in domestic Japanese affairs, and it kept the old catchall Ryukyus issue alive—an issue the Carter administration never fully understood.

Carter saw himself as a diehard free trader, acting in the tradition of Franklin Roosevelt's assault on "Republican Protectionism" a generation earlier. Moreover, he saw the Congress as a growing obstruction to friendly Japanese relations, and he saw himself in a

Wilsonian-styled role. Whereas Wilson, a former professor, took it upon himself to "educate" Americans into accepting the concept of world responsibility during the era of World War I, Carter hoped to "educate" the American people into accepting the "limits of American power" at home and abroad. No more Vietnams, he promised; and America's energy supply was not unlimited, he stressed as well. It was the lack of an energy policy that had harmed the 1970s economy, Carter believed, not the trade imbalance with Japan. The United States could rebound in the effort to take on Japan product for product, but it could not rebound from an exhausted energy supply.[58]

When asked by the press when the United States would indeed bounce back from an economy "flooded" with Japanese cars and electronic goods, Carter avoided glib comments about slackened American quality and the need to change that situation. Instead, his stock answer was always in the format of his forever-languishing energy bill. Calling for strict control of existing domestic energy supplies, federal government incentives for domestic energy exploration, and inventive conservation methods, Carter called upon every citizen to participate in this endeavor with Kennedyesque Peace Corps–styled volunteerism. Nevertheless, the energy bill was viewed by many congressmen as too demanding, too expensive, and too bizarre. Undaunted by the critics, the president insisted that the Japanese trade imbalance would be addressed on the day after the Congress passed his energy bill. "Our huge appetite for foreign oil," he told a news conference in August 1978, "is the major cause of our trade deficit. There are other factors, but if we can get a handle on this we will be in good shape."[59]

America's worries over Japanese market power were unnecessary, Carter suggested. Meeting with a variety of world leaders in Bonn during 1978, Carter had explained that increased economic growth in Japan, West Germany, and elsewhere would soon stimulate greater demand for U.S. exports. A successful conclusion to a serious round of trade negotiations with the Japanese, which he envisioned taking place in 1979 and 1980, would bring about a reduction in trade barriers and give American firms increased opportunities to compete in the Japanese market itself.[60] The president's 1978 comments implied the upcoming negotiations would be more time-consuming than difficult, and that a happy conclusion for both American industries and consumers was inevitable.

Some of Carter's optimism over trade negotiations and the basic issue of U.S.-Japan trade negotiations was attributable to Vance. The secretary of state's major concern was America's military posturing in Japan, not economic sparring with the Japanese. The military matter was a dilemma to him; the latter was easy. Put in the framework of a continuing Cold War with the Soviets, U.S.-Japan disagreements over economic matters was a forgettable, although occasionally frustrating, concern to Vance. Holding the line against the growing power of the anti-American, anti-U.S. bases, antinuclear movements in Japan remained a Vance priority. Dispersing the U.S. military presence in Japan, rather than withdrawing it, was Vance's answer. The U.S. bases, with more than forty thousand active-duty military personnel associated with them, were "too visible." Hence, the number of patrols made by nuclear submarines that made port in Sasebo was reduced, and the secret naval intelligence operations of the fleet headquarters at Yokosuka were transferred to the isolated and sleepy navy base at Kamiseya. Meanwhile, the jet fighter wings attached to Yokota Air Base outside Tokyo were transferred to Kadena Air Base on Okinawa, leaving Yokota under the administration of Military Airlift Command (MAC), which was occupied with routine transportation/re-supply duties.[61]

Vance's "out of sight, out of mind" approach to the post-Vietnam presence in Japan was supposed to suggest a calm, peacetime U.S. presence to the Japanese citizenry, and, perhaps, take the wind out of the sails of antinuclear protests; in short, why protest a boring U.S. air base like Yokota? To Zbigniew Brzezinski and the NSC, attempting to hide forty thousand troops and disregarding Japan's growing power in the world economy was a ridiculous maneuver. Brzezinski argued that Japan would soon constitute something of the Fifth Column in the United States. Always the passionate cold warrior, Brzezinski believed that as the Soviet Union continued to turn toward old Stalinist solutions to problems in both domestic and foreign affairs, the U.S.-USSR relationship was destined to sour even further. If America was forced to return to a 1950s-style confrontational foreign policy because of Soviet developments, it would be a return with a big difference. In the 1950s, the U.S. economy was unassailable, producing balanced budgets in 1957 and 1960. In 1980, Japan would control a significant share of a flagging economy now gearing up for yet another decade of Soviet confrontation.

Brzezinski wanted the protection of key defense-related technologies in key U.S. industries. He wanted anything associated with the manufacturing of American defense capability declared off-limits to Japanese economic penetration. How far had the Japanese penetrated that industry already?[62] Brzezinski was not sure of the answer, but he recommended that a special, top-secret task force be established to find it and then safeguard the rest of the defense industry. In short, Brzezinski distrusted MITI. Given the growth of anti-Americanism in even conservative Japanese business circles, Brzezinski was taken aback by some of the wording of MITI policies; for example, "frontal attacks on General Motors"; "total envelopment technologies" to surround and "interlock" the American consumer with Japanese-only electronic products and Japanese-only replacement parts for those products. To Brzezinski, the Japanese were posing a security threat through their very success in America. That success could work against U.S. foreign policy if Japan became cozier with the Soviet Union than would be the White House's preference.

Vance and Carter saw no use for a hush-hush organization that would, for instance, spy on foreign competitors in the U.S. market.[63] It smacked of the type of Watergate-influenced imperial presidency that Carter campaigned against in 1976. Ed Muskie, soon after he replaced Vance as secretary of state, would applaud much of Brzezinski's efforts. Nevertheless, Muskie's interests in keeping close watch on Japanese developments in America were more out of raw concern for his country's economic future than connected to Brzezinski's classic Cold War assessments. Vance, although he resigned over the Carter administration's failed efforts to rescue U.S. hostages in Iran, also expressed a certain disgust for the NSC's Cold War influence on the presidency. But it would be the Reagan administration that implemented the Brzezinski-instigated plan with the code name of Operation SOCRATES. Reagan's secretary of state, George Shultz, would share Brzezinski's concerns.[64]

Meanwhile, Carter's vision of a serious round of trade negotiations with Japan came true in 1979 and 1980. It was a learning experience for the Carter team, and they emerged from these talks in late

1980 as knowledgeable about Japan as they should have been in 1977.

A nation's strength rests heavily on the strength of individual families and individual communities, Carter believed, be it in Japan or America. "That's the reason Japan has made such great progress," the president told a group of Japanese farmers in June 1979. "That's the reason why you are one of the greatest nations on earth, the strong family."[65] With these comments, Carter was alluding to the issue of U.S. agricultural imports to Japan. Those imports had met a hostile reception by the Japanese farming community and by patriotic sympathizers resident in Japan's big cities. As a successful peanut farmer, Carter had been intrigued, early in his administration, by the Japanese interest in U.S. farming products (tangerines and oranges). His data suggested that the Japanese consumer had a lust for these items, and he could not understand why his predecessors had not satisfied the Japanese demand with American products. Hoping to saturate the Japanese market with quality produce, Carter saw this as the opening salvo against the trade imbalance with Japan, as well as a clever answer to Japanese inroads in the U.S. electronics and automobile markets.

By 1979, American citrus products were penetrating the Japanese home market, after a year of wrangling with the Japanese Diet. A frustrated Mansfield, nervous over the possibility of losing entirely to Japanese protectionism, agreed to a scenario whereby U.S. citrus-product sales would never equal more than 2 percent of Japanese domestic production between the late 1970s and 1983. Carter reasoned that, at the least, America would penetrate the Japanese market, wow the Japanese consumer with American quality, and the trade barriers would be lifted after the 1983 2 percent "quarantine" expired.[66] Jimmy Carter would become the president who broke America into the Japanese market, courtesy of his expertise as a wheeler-dealer Georgia farmer, and the American voter would reward the Democratic Party successor to the savvy Carter in 1984. Like so many of the "good intentions" of the Carter presidency, there was no reason for this optimism.

Japan's citrus production—tangerines, grapefruit, oranges, and lemons—totaled nearly four million tons per year, and the Japanese consumer considered this a sad misfortune. The Japanese eat a *lot* of citrus: consumer demand in Japan outnumbered America's domestic citrus sales by a ratio of eleven to one. But the 1978 appearance of American citrus products did not have the impact Carter envisioned. Japanese dock workers, often in solidarity with enraged Japanese citrus farmers, sometimes left American goods to rot. If a neatly wrapped package of tangerines did reach the Japanese supermarket chains, such as Nagasakiya, it was sold separately at the front of the store, the Stars and Stripes tacked onto the displays. If already spoiled, those smelly American products had the opposite effect on the Japanese consumer than the Carter White House desired. If the packages were unspoiled, the sticker-price spoiled the sale. In the Tokyo area, a small package of American tangerines could reach a price as high as—in U.S. dollar equivalent—sixty dollars.[67]

Breaking into the Japanese market was just the beginning, and the Carter administration learned the lesson the hard way. The stress on agricultural products came to be perceived as a "back door" to the Japanese consumer, and it resulted in the growth of Buy Japan patriotic sentiment and a further image of the "unsafe" American product. A better approach would be to break into the same markets that Japan targeted in America, such as high-tech electronics. How? The Carter White House, in its first term, was running out of time in which to encourage such an effort. Too much had been banked on the hope that Japan would open its doors to American products once it bit into a Florida orange. By the summer of 1980, Ohira, Carter's friend, fell to factional infighting within the Liberal Democratic Party, to be was replaced by Zenko Suzuki, a hardliner on the issue of protecting Japan from "cheap American products." Suzuki's popularity soared, making him the second most popular prime minister since World War II. Answering the mounting protests of Japanese farmers and those in solidarity with them, he insisted that a new round of negotiations would have to begin. A friendly trade accord was now impossible.[68] Without question, Carter had hoped that trade problems could be handled via friendly persuasion; after all, these were issues secondary to continuing Cold War concerns. But it was not so to Japan.

Back in the summer of 1979, to usher in the new era of friendly persuasion, the consultative Group on Japan–United States Economic Relations had been formed. Bob Ingersoll, Mansfield's predecessor as ambassador to Japan and CEO of the Chicago-based Borg-Warner

Corporation, was appointed to head the U.S. delegation within the group. Ingersoll's Japanese counterpart was an old chum, Nobuhiko Ushiba. the former ambassador to Washington in the Nixon-Tanaka era. Specializing in trade issues, Ushiba could trace his career back to 1932. Although always in the shadows, this professional bureaucrat helped Ikeda and Miyazawa build the 1960s "miracle economy."

Ingersoll was outmatched in the resulting trade negotiations. The belligerent tone of the U.S. delegation during group meetings soon underlined this fact, as well as drawing attention to the frustration the Americans felt at a growing trade imbalance in the face of a protectionist Japan. Ingersoll had followed Robert Strauss as America's chief negotiator, next to Mansfield, on trade matters. A former chairman of the Democratic Party Executive Committee, Strauss had wanted a role in the development of a post-Vietnam foreign policy. Placing stress on the neglected area of international economic relations had made sense to Strauss; America's new "dollar diplomacy," he said, might also shore up relations with Asian/Pacific countries who had been wounded by America's obsession with Vietnam.

Dealing with the Japanese was not like dealing with the factions of the Democratic Party, although Strauss assumed that would be the case. Strauss had spearheaded the citrus deal, once considering it a grand accomplishment. Mansfield had provided plenty of data during the citrus negotiations to suggest that Japan was more capable of sabotaging the deal than following it through, but Mansfield's "realism" was rejected as not with it. This was an argument reminiscent of the Kennedy cabinet—the rejection of cold, hard facts, such as possible failure at the Bay of Pigs, in favor of macho determination. Getting nowhere with Japan, Strauss switched jobs, preferring the crisis-management work of Palestinian-American-Israeli relations to Japanese trade negotiations. Ingersoll's role, therefore, was expected to be belligerent, and he was expected to demonstrate America's commitment to creating an acceptable, post-Vietnam world economy. But acceptable to whom? Ushiba remained unimpressed. Consequently, the Carter administration would make no inroads in one of the most pressing economic issues facing the world going into the 1980s, the growing collapse of the U.S. industrial economy and the transfer of wealth from the debtor-nation America to the Japanese "miracle."

Carter had hoped for better results on oil, mutual defense, and human rights before his administration became embroiled in the 1980 election. Fate, once again, would not be kind. Meeting in Tokyo in the summer of 1979 with leaders of the seven major industrialized nations, after nearly two years of preparations for the summit, Carter hoped that Ohira would join him in, at the least, a joint U.S.-Japan statement condemning Middle Eastern nations for "terrorist tactics" in holding the industrialized world a virtual hostage to their overflowing oil supply. Carter rarely condemned anyone or any nation, but the Tokyo summit required solidarity before specific arrangements on oil conservation, exploration, and so on could be made. Japan imported every drop of oil it used in feeding its industrial revolution; a statement of cooperation from Ohira would provide the right message. But the days of the United States suggesting policy approaches to Japan, or any nation, had passed, fallen with Saigon. Asked by the press if a joint U.S.-Japan communique was forthcoming, Ohira responded in typically cautious and polite fashion. Noting that friendship is a wonderful thing, Ohira explained that U.S.-Japan friendship would not resolve problems in oil supply; a summit or two could never align the have and have-not nations, but times were certainly changing. Ohria's cryptic comments left the press guessing if Japan still considered itself in the have-not category, and, therefore, would remain extremely cautious in its relationship with Middle Eastern oil suppliers.[69]

If the days of joint U.S.-Japan communiques were over—even before Ohira's fall in 1980—then the days of a guaranteed U.S. defense of Japan might be waning as well. Both Ohira and Suzuki had worried that Japan's 1978 signing of a "Peace and Friendship" treaty with China might be misinterpreted in Washington as an effort to replace U.S. influence in the Asian/Pacific region with a Japanese-Chinese alliance. Although Senator Sam Nunn, of the Armed Services Committee, and others were nervous over Japanese-Chinese connections, Carter was not. According to the president, the friendship treaty was identical in purpose to America's own rapprochement with China early in the 1970s, and that was all. Nunn, on the other hand, supported by a majority of congressmen, saw the treaty as a good reason to keep American troop strength and all Asian/Pacific basing privileges intact. Japan-China connections were not to be trusted, Nunn implied, and America must do everything it could to tell the world that its retreat from Vietnam had not been a rout from world-power status.

Nunn's argument even ran counter to Carter's interest over human rights: it suggested that there must be little difference between U.S. defense policy with Japan and that with Japan's repressive neighbor South Korea. President Park Chung Hee's dictatorship over the Republic of Korea, propped up by more than forty thousand U.S. military personnel, smacked of the type of careless imperialism that led to the Vietnam defeat. Or so Carter concluded. Denouncing Park in his list of world leaders who failed to deserve U.S. support, Carter's comments throughout 1977, 1978, and most of 1979 suggested that a U.S. military withdrawal was pending. Carter denied this suggestion, but the Japanese government worried that a U.S. withdrawal from Korea would be followed by either a withdrawal from Japan or by a heated U.S. argument to increase Japanese defense spending.[70]

The lack of a significant Japanese military structure, combined with the effort to reject the fascist past, had a profound effect on the self-proclaimed New Generation of Japanese young men. More than 80 percent of them claimed in an *Asahi Shimbun* poll that they would not defend their country if attacked. Japan's pacifist agenda lived on. Both Nunn's and the Japanese government's concerns were largely unfounded. The human-rights crusade had its limits, and Carter was not going to destroy America's friendship with Japan over the issue, much less usher in a deadly domestic political battle over the chief executive's alleged defeatist approach to the post-Vietnam Pacific. He announced in 1979 that too much had been made of too little: "Our partnership with Japan has never been more productive. Our security commitment to Korea remains unshakable. We have concluded an agreement with the Philippines, enabling us to maintain stable access to our bases through the next decade. We have increased support for ASEAN. Our Asian policy serves the interests of the United States and its Asian allies well. I have no plan to change it."[71]

The tenor and tone of Carter administration rhetoric vis-à-vis Japan relations would change as the 1980 election loomed, as the hostage crisis in Iran began, and the Soviet invasion of Afghanistan pushed on. Carter had once discussed the issue of higher Japanese expenditures for defense (beyond the all-time high of $10 billion for 1980) with Ohira, as did Mansfield and even Ingersoll, but the usual political/economic objection was given and the Carter White House did not press the issue. A better tactic to win Japan's pledge to a new, post-Vietnam era of American cooperation, Carter concluded, was in the field of Indochinese refugee assistance; that is, the continuing human-rights cause.

Supported by the British colonial government in Hong Kong, which bore the burden of the refugee influx from nearby Vietnam and Cambodia, the Carter administration urged Japan to accept totals ranging from three thousand to fourteen thousand per month. These were conservative figures considering the hundreds of thousands of Indochinese in flight from their homes, but Japan's immigration/refugee laws were the most rigid in the democratic world. More to the point, Japan's "aliens control" laws were designed, at one time, to protect the nation from "race pollution." The scrapping of law was as touchy a subject in Japan as the refusal to accept Hitler's real and imagined enemies had been in the United States during the 1930s. In contrast to Carter's cautious political rhetoric on issues ranging from economics to defense, his position on Japan's role in the human-rights cause was loud and clear: "All countries must play a larger role. The United States is accepting a very large number of refugees, tens of thousands of refugees. Japan has accepted very few. I think when Prime Minister Ohira was over here (1979), the total number of refugees accepted in Japan was three."[72]

Although Ohira had promised, and in public, a more generous Japan in the refugee story, the level of generosity, of course, was left to the Japanese Diet. Echoing his boss, Mansfield's speeches on the need for "moral responsibility" were well received in Japan, reminding some Japanese, more than ever before, of Douglas MacArthur. But, a promise from a Japanese prime minister and a great speech from an American ambassador did not result in the new era of Japanese generosity to Indochinese refugees. Desiring no impediments to its booming economy, and content with its homogeneous society, Japan favored few concessions to America's insistence on "moral responsibility."[73]

As Carter turned to the sad task of responding to a hostage crisis in Iran and the Soviet march through Afghanistan, the topic of human rights for Indochinese refugees took a far-back seat to the priorities at hand. The National Defense Report for fiscal 1981, submitted to Congress in early 1980, painted a picture of an administration that had lost control of its foreign policy years earlier. Still weakened by the Vietnam disaster, America's armed forces, the report claimed, needed allies more than ever if it hoped to "cope" with threats from international terrorists and Soviet communists. "It is difficult for the U.S. alone," this report concluded, "to cope with these threats, due to the decline of its national power. Japan, too, should extend due cooperation, as much as possible."[74]

The National Defense Report envisioned a 1980s America under assault by a variety of once-forgettable powers. The report—as well as the Defense Department and many Americans—assumed that America's Vietnam defeat had triggered this response. Carter's interests in priorities that were not Cold War related, this thesis continued, from human rights to economics and energy, had led to the new challenges, ranging from Islamic fundamentalists to lingering Stalinists in the Kremlin. It was a simple opinion, divorced from the facts that stimulated each individual crisis. But it was the type of opinion that could defeat a presidency. Meanwhile, Carter's new defense policy for the Asian/Pacific region insisted on a shared role by Japan. Called the Swing Strategy, this policy announced in February 1980 called for immediate reinforcements/improvements to the U.S. Seventh Fleet in Japan. All America could hope to do, this Swing Strategy explained, was "cope" with crisis, should it occur, in the Japan defense sector.

Carter had already summarized the Swing Strategy in his 1980 State of the Union address, whereby he vowed to use military power in the Persian Gulf, but then several days later claimed that power could not succeed without the full participation of America's allies. This included Japan. The Japanese Diet responded that it "might" have no objection to "collective defense" should trouble come to Japan, but that expenditures would still remain at a limited level. A national dialogue, they said, would have to be built on the issue; otherwise, there could be no assistance to the Americans.[75]

In the event of a wartime crisis for the United States, the Diet-style debate would be of limited use to Washington's immediate military objectives. Japan's biggest worry, the Diet admitted, was the possibility of a World War centered in the Persian Gulf. The United States might pull out most of its Japan-based troops for the effort, and a resurgent Soviet Union just might take advantage of the situation. The Diet seemed to prefer this worst-case interpretation of events.

To make matters worse, a tired, frustrated Mansfield, envisioning his replacement by a victorious Ronald Reagan after the November 1980 election, broke with his grandfatherly image and assaulted his host government on a number of issues, including its "shameless" position on defense to MITI "plots" against the American economy. Mansfield later dismissed this rhetoric as influenced by trying times, and the Japanese public was in a forgiving mood.[76] Such political Teflon would later be associated with Reagan himself, and the new president would not hesitate in the decision to enlist a fellow "Teflon don" in the Reagan Revolution. Mansfield kept his post.

By 1981, Japan and the United States together produced more than 35 percent of the world's new output and engaged in almost 25 percent of the world's trade. For that reason alone, the two countries' success in maintaining a close, mutually beneficial relationship was not only vital to their own prosperity and security, but critical to the world as a whole. But as the Japan–United States Economic Relations Group admitted in its final 106-page report to Carter during January 1981, the U.S.-Japan relationship was polluted by endless "misunderstandings." Once the two countries understood and accepted each other's cultures, as well as their political and economic ambitions, then the era of cooperation would truly begin.

Jimmy Carter was the first U.S. president to recognize Japan beyond its worth to the Cold War. From Truman through Johnson, the White House saw Japan as Defeated Japan, bastion of U.S. military power in the Far East. During the Nixon and Ford presidencies, Japan was seen as less of the bastion and more of the soon-to-be superpower. What this meant for America's own superpower status was a difficult question to ask for the Nixon-Ford team. Hence, they did their best to avoid asking it. While they connected Cold War priorities to granting the wishes of Japan's export economy, the Nixon and Ford White Houses struggled with the meaning of Vietnam and Watergate.

Carter was free of Vietnam tensions and Watergate scandal. Public opinion now rejected the idea of a "communist monolith" and "massive retaliation" to halt it. Forever paraphrasing John Kennedy after the Cuban missile crisis, most Americans now concluded that one did not win cold wars; one survived them. In this new atmosphere, Washington and Tokyo could discuss their future openly, and this was in keeping with Carter's 1976 promise of "open government." There were priority policies beyond Cold War sparring techniques, and Carter defined them in the Japan relationship. Ranging from raw economic concerns to energy policy and human rights, Carter discussed the new, post-Vietnam agenda with an intrigued Japan.

Without question, the Japanese government was pleased with the lessening of Cold War priorities in U.S. policy, but that did not mean it had to accept America's position on everything from domestic reform to economic competition. In fact, the Diet had little use for Carter's insistence that Japan cooperate the way America saw fit. Like his predecessors, Carter attempted to maneuver Japan away from its nationalist conclusions, but times had changed. The frustrations felt by these failed maneuvers, which would continue on into the Reagan, Bush, and Clinton administrations, made Carter the first president to have dealt with a modern, vibrant, determined Japan that dared to say no to an American president, and more than once.[77]

As the Japan—United States Economic Relations Group implied in the final moments before the Reagan White House began, America needed to renounce its old paternal relationship with the Japanese and recognize the potentially destructive economic power of the New Japan. Japan needed to recognize that diplomacy and cooperation may be essential to its future, rather than staying the course with raw nationalist goals.

Today, as Japan and the United States reach a new century in their relationship, this old Carter message remains barely heard. Power means more than bombs and threats heard around the world, Carter said of the "Good America." The implication here was that a "Great America" must invent a working Japan policy, and that the Cold War–style sword rattling of the past must be relegated to history. Carter's administration gestured toward this procedure, but found that most Americans remained confused by both the Vietnam/Watergate era and the changing world economy. The Japanese, Carter learned too late, shared the same confusion.

Postscript

To some chroniclers of the 1980s, Carter's era of "good intentions" passed to Reagan's era of "anxiety." Reagan's blend of Red Scare nostalgia and post-Vietnam realpolitik provided obvious contradictions to Reagan critics, but not to his many enthusiastic supporters. Yale University's Paul Kennedy, in his highly acclaimed *The Rise and Fall of the Great Powers*, saw Reagan's popularity wrapped in a tale of American confusion that could trace its roots to the 1960s. To Paul Kennedy, America's Japan and other Asian/Pacific connections depended on how well Reagan or the Washington Establishment answered a series of difficult questions, such as "how to 'support the stability and independence of friendly countries' while trying to control the flood of their exports to the American market; how to make the Japanese assume a larger share of the defense of the western Pacific without alarming its various neighbors; how to maintain U.S. bases in, for example, the Philippines without provoking local resentments; how to reduce the American military presence in South Korea without sending the wrong 'signal' to the North."[1] The gap between U.S. capabilities and U.S. interests had become too wide, Kennedy concluded, while critics of Japan's success in the U.S. market and other aspects of U.S. economic policy "failed to note the 'naturalness' of most of these developments."[2]

Indeed, by the 1980s, there were many who believed that there was a certain "natural" order to the troubled U.S.-Japan relationship, and that the important questions raised by that relationship might never be answered. In an effort to put a laissez-faire spin to the growth of Japanese influence in the U.S. economy, Reagan insisted that Japan "simply meant jobs" to a recovering economy. The struggling U.S.-Japan relationship, he implied, was more the product of liberal angst than anything else. But easy labels for the continuing Washington-Tokyo dialogue were hard to find, and blaming Carter and his predecessors for a host of politically incorrect approaches toward Japan did not constitute policy. Reagan would learn this the hard way, and as the U.S.-Japan relationship soldiered on.

During the twenty-year period (1961–1981) that formally marked the reversal of Japan's and America's fortunes, U.S.-Japan relations were defined by a legacy of cultural misunderstanding, concerted and innovative policies on the part of Japan, and a strange game of catchup for American policymakers, who distrusted Japan's intentions as well as disliked distractions from Cold War sparring with the Soviets. No president found the key to calm and collected U.S.-Japan relations behind that front line of the Cold War. No Japanese prime minister could claim full success in the "capturing" of the American market. In reality, few of the leaders, American or Japanese, truly desired to compromise their respective policies. While the Americans worried about their "decline" in the face of a continuing Cold War and a rising Japan, the Japanese fell into the same trap as the United States in the era of the Vietnam War escalation; that is, believing in unlimited influence and power. From the Okinawa issue to free-trade practice, the Japanese governments saw America as both a meddler and a savior at the same time. To Washington, Japan always remained a grand mystery, yet capable of great destructive powers, ranging from Pacific defense to economic coups. And while American and Japanese rhetoric praised the "spirit of harmony" in the Tokyo-Washington relationship, few policymakers viewed that relationship beyond the bounds of mutual necessity.

To John Kennedy and Hayato Ikeda, the World War II past had truly been relegated to history upon their respective rise to national leadership. The future was a bright one, they said, although neither would live to see what that meant to the U.S.-Japan relationship. Not foreseen by either Kennedy or Ikeda, the strains and misery of the Vietnam War took its toll on the Tokyo-Washington dialogue. The resulting debate over proper "fence mending" and detente did little to remedy the tension, and Japan's economic prowess in light of America's struggling post-Vietnam economy added to the confusion. At the least, the United States learned that the world was no longer a bipolar one, while the Japanese learned that power could also be a fragile thing—that balancing their own defense needs with the desire to win big in the American consumer economy required more delicacy than they cared to admit.

Cooperative yet confrontational, the U.S.-Japan relationship of the 1960s and 1970s set precedents in both diplomatic contradiction and determination. Now well into the 1990s, the peace continues, suggesting that today's problems between Tokyo and Washington, without the tensions of the Vietnam era and the growing pains of the New Japan, enjoy a possibility of resolution stronger than ever before. The past, it can always be hoped, points in that positive direction.

Notes

Chapter 1: Partners in Misunderstanding

1. "The United States and Our Future in Asia," excerpts from the remarks of Sen. John F. Kennedy, Senate Files (Hawaii Statehood, 1958), John F. Kennedy Library (hereafter, JFK Library).

2. Memo on "Political Conditions in Japan," Assistant Secretary of State James Thomson to President Kennedy, August 1962, box 18/Far East–Japan, James Thomson Papers, JFK Library.

3. Tsongas public rally, Daniel Webster College, Nashua, New Hampshire, February 1, 1992.

4. Michael Kranish, "Legacy of the Bush years blooming in Clinton era," *Boston Globe*, October 23, 1994, p. 1, 22.

5. "The U.S.-Japan Relationship, January-June 1961," State Department briefing material for the visit of Prime Minister Ikeda, State Department to President Kennedy, June 23, 1961, POF/box 120, JFK Library.

6. Kennedy's can-do rhetoric was carefully rehearsed. See John F. Kennedy, *Public Papers, 1961*, pp. 174–175. It was cabinet meetings on foreign policy, and especially his early ones, that became energetic discussions on how to win the Cold War. A winning strategy, whether favored by the allies or not, was acceptable. This type of approach is skillfully described in Hilsman, *To Move a Nation*, and Parmet, *Jack*, pp. 399–416. See also Kennedy to Secretary of Defense Robert McNamara, January 31 and February 1, 1961, NSF/box 345 and Guam/box 101, JFK Library. Much of this chapter is based on little-known documentation, or documents declassified between 1989 and 1995, at Boston's JFK Library.

7. For a detailed review of how a "proper" foreign policy should be conducted, see the lengthy "Considerations Regarding the Selection of Top Policy-Makers," December 18, 1960, box WH-3a/Chester Bowles, Papers of Arthur M. Schlesinger Jr., special assistant to the president, JFK Library; and Dean

Rusk, "Reflections on Foreign Policy," in Thompson, *The Kennedy Presidency*, pp. 190–201.

8. A major ambition, for instance, remained a quick triumph over all communist challenges in the Far East, and the establishment of an American-run, UN-styled international organization to police the final days of the Cold war there. See my *Kennedy and the New Pacific Community*.

9. Ikeda visit "Briefing Material" (State Department) to Kennedy, June 23, 1961, POF/box 120, JFK Library.

10. "Current or Potential Problems in Asia," (NSC report and review of 1961 events, including Kennedy's cabinet-confidential comments in reference to them), January 11, 1962, NSF/box 283-National Security Council: 1/62, JFK Library.

11. Thomson to Kennedy and reports "Economic Conditions" (Japan), and "The Nature of the Japanese Economy," August 1962, box 18/Far East-Japan, James Thomson Papers, JFK Library.

12. For background on Dulles's view of Japan (which remained unchanged since the early 1950s), see Livingston, Moore, and Oldfather, *Postwar Japan*, pp. 238–241, 245–250. See also the "Dulles Visit" and "Political Conditions" (Japan), Thomson to Kennedy, August 1962, box 18/Far East–Japan, James Thomson Papers, JFK Library.

13. Thomson to Kennedy, August 18, 1962, box 18/Far East–Japan, James Thomson Papers, JFK Library.

14. Roger Hilsman, director, Intelligence and Research, State Department, to Kennedy, October 24, 1963, box 4-6/Far East Trip, Roger Hilsman Papers, JFK Library.

15. "The U.S.-Japan Relationship, January–June 1961," State Department briefing material for the visit of Prime Minister Ikeda, State Department to Kennedy, June 23, 1961, POF/box 120, JFK Library.

16. Edwin O. Reischauer, U.S. ambassador to Japan, to James Thomson, March 1961, box 18/Far East–Japan, James Thomson Papers, JFK Library.

17. Arthur M. Schlesinger, special counsel to the president, to Kennedy, "U.S. Policy Problems Arising from Japanese Trade." This long report was the result of a special investigative trip led by Schlesinger himself, and was offered to JFK, and eventually to the Senate Subcommittee on Foreign Economic Policy, under top-secret classification on November 20, 1961. See also CIA background reports, Kiichi Miyazawa and Hayato Ikeda, box WH-12a/Japan Trip and POF box 120/Japan, JFK Library. See also the opening chapters of Hunsberger, *Japan and the United States*; Allen, *Japan's Economic Recovery*, pp. 97–100; Friedman and LeBard, *The Coming War With Japan*, pp. 136–137. For Brooks Adams's background and relevance to modern foreign-policy making, see Healy, *U.S. Expansionism*, pp. 109, 115–116.

18. "The Nature of the Japanese Economy," special report by James Thom-

son to Kennedy, August 1962, box 18/Far East-Japan, James Thomson Papers, JFK Library.

19. Ibid.

20. "Japan's Economic Relations with the Sino-Soviet Bloc," special report by James Thomson (with comments by Ambassador Reischauer) to Kennedy, August 1962, box 18/Far East-Japan, James Thomson Papers, JFK Library. Roberts, *Sino-American Relations*, pp. 468–481.

21. Ibid.

22. Memo on Ikeda and China, Richard L. Sneider, officer in charge—Japanese Affairs, State Department, to Kennedy, June 23, 1961, box 62/CO 141, White House Central File, JFK Library. Maga, "The Politics of Non-Recognition," pp. 8–18.

23. NSC briefing papers for the Kennedy-Menzies meeting, February 22, 1961, box 111/18, POF, JFK Library.

24. Comments and testimony by Secretary of State Dean Rusk to a closed session of the Senate Foreign Relations and Armed Services Committees, February 1961, U.S. Senate, *Executive Sessions*, pp. 615–637.

25. See the introductory material to Rostow, *Stages of Economic Growth*; Rostow report: "Economic Policy (Japan)," to Kennedy, December 1961, POF/box 1236, JFK Library.

26. Kennedy's foreign affairs "theme" was largely culled from a best-seller in the fiction category, Lederer and Burdick, *The Ugly American*, pp. 163, 233. For background on the specific theme of Kennedy and economic diplomacy, see William Borden, "Defending Hegemony: American Foreign Economic Policy," in Paterson, *Kennedy's Quest For Victory*, pp. 57–85; Zeiler, *American Trade and Power*, pp. 47–72; Burner, *John F. Kennedy and a New Generation*, pp. 36–37.

27. "Observations on Proposal for a New Pacific Community and Review of April Cabiniet Sessions," J. Robert Schaetzel to George Ball, internal State Department memo and report, November 2, 1961; and Kennedy to Secretary of Defense Robert McNamara, January 31 and February 1, 1961, NSF/box 345 and Guam/box 101.

28. Kennedy to Ikeda, October 22, 1962; State Department briefing material on the visit of Prime Minister Menzies, to Kennedy, February 23, 1961; Schaetzel to Ball, November 2, 1961, POF/box 120 and 111; NSF/box 345.

29. William H. Brubeck, executive secretary to the secretary of state, to Kenneth O'Donnell, administrative assistant to the president, June 18, 1962; memo on the visit of the Australian deputy leader of the Opposition, June 18, 1962; State Department briefing papers: visit of Prime Minister Menzies, June 17–20, 1962: "Scope Paper," NSF/box 6, JFK Library.

30. Minutes of the Kennedy-Ikeda discussion, June 20–21, 1961, POF/box 120, JFK Library.

31. Subcommittee on Foreign Economic Policy, Council on Foreign Relations, *U.S. Policy Problems*, pp. 2–3. For background on the treaty debate and its impact on both the U.S. and Japan, see Packard, *Protest in Tokyo*; Kahn, *Emerging Japanese Superstate*, chapter 2; Rosovsky, *Discord in the Pacific*.

32. Report on Japanese opinion and Pacific defense issues, Donald Wilson, USIA director, to Pierre Salinger, presidential press secretary, March 11, 1961, WHCF/box 62, JFK Library.

33. Kiichi Miyazawa, "Kokusaika (International Relations): America Meets Japan in the 1960s," annual conference of the English Teachers Association of Japan, Hachinohe, Tohoku, Japan, May 9, 1989. The theme of this conference was recent U.S.-Japan relations, and Miyazawa shared his "no-nonsense" views here on the outskirts of the U.S. Misawa Air Base. He also shared more specific views with me in a postconference interview (author interview, Washington Hotel, Hachinhohe, Tohoku, Japan, May 9, 1989).

34. Edwin O. Reischauer, U.S. ambassador to Japan, to James Thomson, special assistant to the undersecretary of state, March 1961, box 18/Far East–Japan, James Thomson Papers; CIA background report "Kiichi Miyazawa," POF/box 120, JFK Library.

35. Ibid. (boxes 18 and 120). The "politics of perception" have always been important within Japan's policymaking toward America. See Destler et al., *Managing an Alliance*, pp. 89–124. See also "The Kennedy-Reischauer Offensive," in *Asahi Shimbun* (staff), *The Pacific Rivals*, pp. 219–25.

36. Miyazawa, "Kokusaika,"; Wilson to Salinger, March 11, 1961, WHCF/box 62, JFK Library.

37. Author interview with Kiichi Miyazawa, Washington Hotel, Hachinohe, Tohoku, Japan, May 9, 1989.

38. For great detail and background on the early 1960s "Ryukyus Crisis," see the report with that title in the correspondence of Col. W. A. Kelley, assistant civil administrator, United States Civil Administration of the Ryukyus (USCAR), to Lawrence O'Brien at the White House, May 12, 1961, WHCF/box 691-Ryukyu Islands, JFK Library.

39. George Kennan, career diplomat and containment thesis author, had helped create America's political and military priorities in the Ryukyus. He defends his actions in Kennan, "Japan's Security," pp. 14–28.

40. USCAR, *Joint Economic Plan*, introduction.

41. Ibid.; Kennedy to the U.S.-Japan Conference on Cultural and Educational Interchange, October 15, 1963, WHCF/box 62, JFK Library.

42. Military studies of the battle of Okinawa abound. The following work stands out from the others due to its consideration of the psychological impact of the battle on Japanese society. Simpson, *Island X*.

43. See the Defense Department's position paper "The Ryukyus Issue," in U.S. Congress, Committee on Appropriations, *Mutual Security Appropriations*.

44. Stevens, *Guam U.S.A.*, pp. 90–93.

45. Olson is quoted in Passin, *United States and Japan*, p. 73.

46. "Joint Communique issued by the president and Prime Minister Hayato Ikeda of Japan," June 22, 1961, POF/box 120, JFK Library.

47. Francis X. Hezel, "Recolonizing Islands and Decolonizing History," in Rubinstein, *Pacific History*, pp. 63–67.

48. "Basic Japanese and United States Objectives," report by James Thomson to Kennedy, August 1962, box 18/Far East–Japan, James Thomson Papers, JFK Library.

49. For a decent "civics" lesson with reference to Okinawa-U.S.-Japan relationships, see Higa, *Politics and Parties*. A strong admirer of both Kennedy and Ikeda, Higa dreams of a glorious future for both the Ryukyus and American-Japanese relations.

50. Visit of Prime Minister Ikeda—Ryukyus, June 23, 1961, POF/box 120, JFK Library.

51. The "delicate" issue of racial politics is a primary concern of Watanabe, *The Okinawa Problem*.

52. "Report and Recommendations of the Task Force Ryukyus" (a special cabinet-level mission sent to the Ryukyus to study and bring an end to the Ryukyus crisis in American-Japanese relations), to Kennedy, December 1961, POF/box 123b, JFK Library.

53. Miyazawa, "Kokusaika" address, May 9, 1989.

54. "Report and Recommendations of the Task Force Ryukyus," December 1961, POF/box 123b, JFK Library.

55. Ibid.

56. Ibid.

57. "Communication and Development: The Significance of the All Nippon Airways Decision," report by the Bureau of the Budget to Kennedy, June 28, 1961, WHCF/box 31, JFK Library.

58. The drama and significance of the Ryukyuan debate was stressed by both American and Japanese analysts of the troubled 1960s relationship between the United States and Japan. See Ministry of Foreign Affairs—Tokyo, *Okinawa: Basic Facts*; McBride, *Okinawa: Pawn*.

59. The final report and recommendations of the Task Force Ryukyus included hundreds of pages of hard facts, political strategies, and tactics, and a strong commitment to New Frontier maneuvering and diplomacy. "Report and Recommendations of the Task Force Ryukyus," December 1961, POF/box 123b, JFK Library.

60. Ibid.

61. Carl Kaysen to Seisaku Ota, chief executive, Government of the Ryukyu Islands (GRI), June 6, 1962, WHCF/box 825, JFK Library.

62. Ota to Kennedy, March 26, 1962, WHCF/box 572, JFK Library; U.S. Congress, House Committee on Foreign Affairs subcommittee, *Claims*.

63. Ibid.; Rosecrance, *The Rise of the Trading State*, pp. 118–121.

64. Donald Wilson, USIA director, to Salinger, March 6, 1961 and Reischauer to Wilson, March 30, 1961, WHCF/box 62, JFK Library.

65. Miyazawa, "Kokusaika." Reischauer considered Ikeda's economic stresses a welcome "low posture" in contrast to Japan's belligerency on defense-related issues. Reischauer, *The United States and Japan*, p. 327.

66. L. D. Battle, executive secretary to Secretary of State Rusk, to Ralph Dungan, special assistant to the president, March 22, 1961; NSC report, "The President's European Trip," June 13, 1961; Export-Import Bank of Washington to Kennedy, June 19, 1961; Allen Taylor, executive secretary, U.S.-Japan Trade Council, to Rep. John Dent, July 19, 1961; "Proposals for 1962 United States Foreign Trade and Tariff Legislation," October 4, 1961; POF/boxes 50 and 120, WHCF/box 62, box 52/Classified Subjects of Theodore Sorensen Papers and box 1 of McGeorge Bundy Papers, JFK Library.

67. Reischauer to Rusk and Rusk to Frederick P. Dutton, assistant secretary of state, Congressional Relations, October 12, 1961, WHCF/box 62, JFK Library.

68. USIA report "Major Japanese Radio-TV Network Series on `New Frontiers,'" March 6, 1962, WHCF/box 62, JFK Library.

69. Rostow report, "Economic Policy and Levels of Aid to the Ryukyus," December 1961, POF/box 1236, JFK Library.

70. Rusk to Kennedy, July 10, 1962, box 52, Theodore Sorensen Papers, JFK Library.

71. Briefing papers and transcript, Kennedy-Mikoyan meeting, November 29, 1962, box 49/Classified Cuba, Theodore Sorensen Papers, JFK Library.

72. Ibid.

73. NSC meeting (Japan Relations), January 22, 1963, and Defense Department report, "International Security Affairs—Japan," March 25, 1963, boxes 4-6/President's Views, Roger Hilsman Papers and box 294/Basic National Security Policy, JFK Library.

74. The Ikeda government's comments on finding new directions for the economy are often muted or emerge in odd places. See, for example, Japan Liberal Democratic Party, "All About the Nuclear Submarine and Genuine Peace," Capt. John Roenisk, U.S. naval attaché (Tokyo), to Robert McNamara, secretary of defense, July 8, 1963, and the lengthy report and proposal "A Presidential Trip to the Far East in Early 1964," Hilsman to Rusk, October 24, 1963, boxes 4-6/Far East Trip, Roger Hilsman Papers, JFK Library.

75. Ibid.

76. "Political Conditions in Japan," Thomson report for Kennedy, August 1962, box 18/Far East–Japan, James C. Thomson Papers, JFK Library. For background on the divisions of the Japanese left in the early 1960s, see especially Scalpino and Masumi, *Parties and Politics*, and Thayer, *How the Conservatives Rule Japan*. For a cautious but succinct U.S. government view of this period, see Reischauer, *The United States and Japan*, pp. 319–327, and "Some Thoughts on Japanese Democracy," a December 1961 treatise on U.S. response to leftist challenges in Japan, box 18/Far East–Japan, James Thomson Papers, JFK Library.

77. Kennedy to Kaifu, May 4, 1961, WHCF/box 62, JFK Library.

78. Jeffrey Kitchen, deputy assistant secretary, Politco-Military Affairs, to Rusk and McNamara, December 12, 1961, box 52/Classified Subjects, Theodore Sorensen Papers, JFK Library.

79. Ibid.; Hilsman to Bundy, October 24, 1963, boxes 4-6/Far East Trip, JFK Library.

80. "Political Conditions in Japan," Thomson report to Kennedy, August 1962, box 18/Far East–Japan, James Thomson Papers, JFK Library.

81. Quoted in *Harper's Magazine* article that Thomson sent to Kennedy with his own remarks, March 1963, box 18/Far East–Japan, James Thomson Papers, JFK Library.

82. Ibid.

83. Ikeda to Kennedy, October 25, 1962 and July 31, 1963, POF/box 120, JFK Library.

84. "Japan-United States Trade," Thomson report to Kennedy, August 1962, box 18/Far East–Japan, James Thomson Papers, JFK Library.

85. Lawrence F. O'Brien, special assistant to the president, to Rep. John Baldwin, March 8, 1961, WHCF/box 62, JFK Library.

86. Lawrence F. O'Brien to Rep. Leo W. O'Brien, and the O'Brien bill, May 4, 1961, WHCF/box 62, JFK Library.

87. Minutes, Kennedy-Ikeda meeting, June 20–21, 1961; joint communique issued by Kennedy and Ikeda, June 22, 1961; Kennedy to Henry Luce, *Time/Life*, July 10, 1961, POF/box 120 and WHCF/box 62, JFK Library.

88. For State Department and Reischauer opinions, see State Department memo "The United States–Japanese Committee," October 12, 1961, WHCF/box 62, JFK Library.

89. Dungan to McGeorge Bundy, March 20, 1961; "U.S.-Japan Trade Council Points Out Decline in Textile Imports, Opposes Quotas," U.S.-Japan Trade Council press release, May 1, 1961; Herbert Klotz, special assistant to the secretary of commerce, to Frederick G. Dutton, May 26, 1961; Edward Cliff, chief of U.S. Forest Service, to Senator Wayne Morse, December 3, 1962; box 1, McGeorge Bundy Papers, POF/box 120, and WHCF/box 62, JFK Library. For JFK's general trade/textile policy, see Zeiler, "Free Trade Politics and Diplomacy," pp. 127–142.

90. O. I. Hague, chief of U.S. delegation, Joint United States–Japan Committee on Trade and Economic Affairs, to Kennedy, and report on trade delegation meetings, October 1961–February 1962, February 27, 1962, WHCF/box 62, JFK Library.

91. "Proclamation Giving Effect to Trade Negotiations with Japan," February 1, 1963, POF/box 120, JFK Library.

92. Hilsman to Rusk, October 24, 1963, boxes 4-6/Far East Trip, Roger Hilsman Papers, JFK Library.

93. Ibid.

94. Rusk speech (Tokyo), January 28, 1964, box 18/Far East–Japan, James Thomson Papers, JFK Library.

Chapter 2: Challenged by Affluence

1. President Johnson's remarks to a group of visiting Japanese governors to the White House, May 23, 1967, box 238/Remarks, Statements of LBJ: May 23–27, 1967, Lyndon Baines Johnson Library, Austin, Texas (hereafter, LBJ Library).

2. In the years immediately following the Johnson presidency, most analysts of the Johnson White House viewed their subject through the anger and disgust associated with the Vietnam War. The passing of years and the opening of the LBJ Library has helped the power of analysis; consequently, a more sympathetic yet still hard-hitting portrait of Johnson emerges in 1990s literature. See Schulman, *Johnson and American Liberalism*, pp. 1–32; Brands, *Wages of Globalism*, pp. 3–29; Dallek, *Lone Star Rising*, pp. 346–381.

3. Dugger, *The Politician*, pp. 342–344.

4. LBJ to Robert F. Kennedy, January 14, 1964, boxes 30-32/International Meetings and Travel File, NSC Papers, LBJ Library.

5. Executive Session, Subcommittee of the Committee on Appropriations, June 21, 1960, box 360/Transcript of Executive Session, Papers of Sen. Lyndon Johnson, Committee on Appropriations, LBJ Library.

6. Ibid.

7. Ibid.

8. Author interview with Walt Rostow, July 12, 1995, LBJ Library.

9. Author interview with Walt Rostow, July 12, 1995, LBJ Library; author interview with Kiichi Miyazawa, April 29, 1989, Washington Hotel, Hachinohe, Tohoku, Japan.

10. Oral history transcript, diary of U. Alexis Johnson, U.S. ambassador to Japan, tape 15, August 1967, LBJ Library.

11. "The Trend in US-Japanese Relations," box 3/chapter 7, Classified Administrative History of the Department of State, vol. l. Amassed, and in secret, during 1968, this detailed history of LBJ-era U.S.-Japan relations remained classified until 1995. Although its narrative is weak, it is especially valuable for its charts, graphs, and on-and-off-the-record remarks of U.S. and Japanese politicians.

12. Morton Halperin, State Department policy planning staff, to Johnson, and report "Current and Future Plans" (of the policy planning staff on U.S.-Japan relations), June 14, 1967, box 1/General and Unprocessed: Morton H. Halperin, NSC Papers, LBJ Library. Like most of the material relevant to U.S.-Japan relations at the LBJ Library, this document was kept classified until mid-1995.

13. Background reports and memos to the meetings of the Joint United

States–Japan Committee on Trade and Economic Affairs (hereafter, the joint trade committee) July 1965, sent to President Johnson by the Committee on July 6, 1965, box 59/Organization for Economic Cooperation Development and joint trade committee, Confidential File, LBJ Library.

14. Ibid.

15. Transcripts, fourth meeting of the joint trade committee, July 12–14, 1965, ibid.

16. "Wool Textile Problems," memo to Johnson from the joint trade committee, July 7, 1965, box 59/joint trade committee, Confidential File, LBJ Library.

17. Joint communiques, joint trade committee, July 8, 1966 and September 15, 1967, box 3/U.S.-Japan, Classified Administrative History of the Department of State, vol. 1, LBJ Library.

18. Press briefing on U.S.-Japan relations (led by U.S. ambassador to Japan, Edwin Reischauer), January 13, 1965, and memo on the Johnson meeting with the Japanese foreign minister, Etsusaburo Shiina, July 14, 1965, box 84/Briefings: Jan. 1–15, 1965, White House Press Office files and box 152/Exchange, Statements of Lyndon Baines Johnson, LBJ Library.

19. Talking paper "Trade Matters of Particular Concern to the U.S." (in U.S.-Japan relations), joint trade committee, July 7, 1965, box 59/joint trade committee, Confidential File, LBJ Library.

20. Talking paper "Trade Matters of Particular Concern to Japan" (in Japan-U.S. relations), July 7, 1965, ibid; press conference with William Bundy, assistant secretary of state, East Asian and Pacific Affairs, and Haruki Mori, deputy vice minister, Foreign Affairs–Japan, November 15, 1967, box 87/Briefings: Nov.–Dec. 1967, White House Press Office files: Background Briefings, LBJ Library.

21. "Economic Relations" (Japan) in the State Department's classified "Administrative History," vol. 1, box 3/chapter 7, Administrative History of the Department of State, vol. 1, LBJ Library.

22. "Talking Points for the Secretary of State's Review" (Japan and U.S. protectionism), July 7, 1965, box 59/joint trade committee, Confidential File, LBJ Library.

23. Ibid.

24. White House–Diet correspondence, background material for U.S. delegation, fourth meeting, joint trade committee, July 12–14, 1965, box 59/joint trade committee, Confidential File, LBJ Library.

25. CIA background reports on Shiina and Miki for the U.S. delegation, ibid; for general background on Japanese political disputes over the United States and trade policy in the mid-1960s, see Fukui, *Party in Power*, p. 251; Quigg, "Japan in Neutral," pp. 1–33.

26. CIA background report "Takeuchi and the President," July 1965, box 59/joint trade committee, Confidential File, LBJ Library.

27. Ibid.

28. In the 1960s, one needed a scorecard to keep up with the differing and conflicting official views of the U.S.-Japan economic relationship. This was especially glaring in the Johnson era. For background, see the powerful introduction to Frank and Hirono, *How the United States and Japan See Each Other's Economy*.

29. Yanaga, *Big Business*, p. 10. Rusk to Johnson, September 12, 1967, box 59/joint trade committee, Confidential File, LBJ Library.

30. Bundy to Rostow, January 16, 1967, box 3/chapter 7, Classified Administrative History of the Department of State, vol. 1, LBJ Library.

31. Rusk to Johnson and "Scope Paper: Economic Outlook in Japan," October 13, 1965, box 59/Organization for Economic Cooperation Development, Confidential File, LBJ Library.

32. Ibid.

33. Rusk to Johnson and "Background Report: Southeast Asia Development Program and Japan," July 7, 1965, ibid.

34. See the extensive briefing report on (Japan) "Trade With Communist Countries" prepared by the joint trade committee in July 1965 and updated in September 1967, box 59/joint trade committee, Confidential File, LBJ Library.

35. Briefing Report: "Cuba and the Communist Bloc," July 1965/revised: September 1967, ibid.

36. Briefing report: "Trading Blocs," and supporting position papers "Trade Matters of Particular Concern to the U.S." and "Trade Matters of Particular Concern to Japan," July 1965/revised September 1967, ibid.

37. Rusk to Johnson, January 5, 1966; Vice President Hubert Humphrey to Johnson, January 5, 1966; and minutes, 555th NSC meeting, January 5, 1966, box 2/NSC Meetings, vol. 3, tab 37 and 56, NSC, LBJ Library.

38. See the 555th NSC meeting in the previous note and background reports "Vietnam" and "Southeast Asia Economic Development," July 1965, box 59/joint trade committee, Confidential File, LBJ Library.

39. Author interview with Kiichi Miyazawa (April 1989, Hachinohe, Japan).

40. Ibid., and Ambassador Reischauer to Press Secretary Bill Moyers, July 27, 1966, box 81/Japan, Office Files of Bill Moyers, LBJ Library.

41. Author interview with Kiichi Miyazawa (April 1989, Hachinohe, Japan), and Rusk to Johnson, September 12, 1967, box 59/joint trade committee, Confidential File, LBJ Library.

42. Scope report "Japan and Vietnam," January 5, 1966, box 2/NSC Meetings, vol. 3., tab 37 and 56, NSC, LBJ Library.

43. Ibid.

44. Talking points for secretary's review, Japan and Vietnam, July 7, 1965, and 555th NSC meeting "Peace Offensive Regarding Vietnam," January 5, 1966, box 59/joint trade committee, Confidential File, and box 2/NSC Meetings, vol. 3, tab 37 and 56, NSC, LBJ Library.

45. Author interview with Kiichi Miyazawa (April 1989, Hachinohe, Japan).

46. Brands, *Wages of Globalism*, pp. 244–245.

47. Bundy to Johnson and U.S. embassy–prepared report "Criticism of Japan by Assistant Secretary Bundy at the American Embassy," November 17, 1965, box 81/Japan, Office Files of Bill Moyers, LBJ Library.

48. Author interview with Kiichi Miyazawa (April 1989, Hachinohe, Japan). Defence Agency of Japan, *The Defence of Japan*, p. 40.

49. Rusk to Johnson, September 12, 1967, box 59/joint trade committee, Confidential File, LBJ Library.

50. CIA background report on Etsusaburo Shiina, September 1967; Reischauer to Rusk, July 22 and July 27, 1966, box 59/joint trade committee, and box 81/Japan, Office Files of Bill Moyers, LBJ Library.

51. For the Shiina/Gromyko controversy, see the entire previous note. Meanwhile, some scholars and former policymakers observe that Japan's difficult relationship with the Soviet Union was strongly influenced by the desire to deal with communist China. See Gene T. Hsiao, "The Sino-Japanese Rapprochement: A Relationship of Ambivalence," in Hsiao, *Sino-American Detente*.

52. For the Sono and Japanese press flap, see Frank Gibney of *Encyclopedia Britannica* (Japan office) to Hayes Redmon, White House Press Office, July 8, 1966 and Bundy to Johnson, November 17, 1966, box 81/Japan, Office Files of Bill Moyers, LBJ Library.

53. Bundy to Johnson, November 17, 1966, box 81/Japan, Office Files of Bill Moyers, LBJ Library.

54. 555th NSC meeting, January 5, 1966, box 2/NSC Meetings, vol. 3, tab 37 and 56, NSC, LBJ Library. For Johnson's general policy toward Asian/Pacific nations vis-à-vis America's Vietnam priority, see Blackburn, *Mercenaries*.

55. Bundy to Johnson, November 17, 1965, box 81/Japan, Office Files of Bill Moyers, LBJ Library.

56. Reischauer to Rusk, July 27, 1966, ibid.

57. See note 56 and Richard W. Petree, acting country director—Japan, State Department, to Kamesuke Oshiro, president, Association of City, Town, and Village Governments—Okinawa, December 21, 1966, box 21/ST51-3, Ryukyu, White House Central File, LBJ Library.

58. Okinawa-related policymaking, oral history transcript, tape 17, September 1968 entries, papers of U. Alexis Johnson, LBJ Library.

59. Ibid., tape 15, August 13, 1967 entry.

60. Ibid. (note 59).

61. Ibid. For further Ryukyus policy background, see Bundy and Rostow to President Johnson and report "Future of Okinawa," May 23, 1966, box 82/Ryukyus, Office Files of Bill Moyers, LBJ Library. Edwin O. Reischauer MS (Tokyo 1969?), "Trans-Pacific Relations," pp. 79–80.

62. Centre for Strategic Studies, "United States-Japanese Political Relations," p. 35.

63. Okinawa/Ryukyus policy, oral transcript, tape 15, August 13, 1967 entry, papers of U. Alexis Johnson, LBJ Library.

64. For Johnson's politics of priorities, see Geyelin, *Lyndon B. Johnson and the World*, p. 90; McMahon, *Colonialism*, pp. 10–11; Kahin, *Intervention*, pp. 201–202; Turner, *Johnson's Dual War*, pp. 116–124; Clifford, *Counsel to the President*, p. 459.

65. Bundy and Rostow to Johnson and report "Future of Okinawa," May 23, 1966, box 82/Ryukyus, Office Files of Bill Moyers, LBJ Library.

66. Press conference at the White House (on Okinawa matters) with Richard L. Sneider, director, Country Office–Japan, and George Christian, press secretary to the president, November 13, 1967, box 87/Briefings: Nov.–Dec. 1967, White House Press Office files, LBJ Library.

67. Press briefing material on "Eisaku Sato" and press conference at the White House on the Sato-Johnson meeting (with William P. Bundy, assistant secretary of state, East Asian and Pacific Affairs, and Haruki Mori, deputy vice minister, Foreign Affairs–Japan) November 17, 1967, box 87/Briefings: Nov.–Dec. 1967, White House Press Office files, Background Briefings, LBJ Library.

68. Ibid.

69. Paul C. Warnke, assistant secretary of defense, to Johnson and (lengthy) report "Reversion of Okinawa and the Bonins," August 7, 1967, box 1 (General and Unprocessed)/Morton H. Halperin, NSC, LBJ Library.

70. Author interview with Walt Rostow, July 12, 1995, LBJ Library.

71. See the introduction to Blackburn, *Mercenaries*.

72. Morton H. Halperin, director, policy planning staff, to Johnson, and memo "The Policy Planning Staff: Current and Future Plans" (Japan), June 14, 1967, and Halperin-authored report "Scenario on Negotiations with Japan on Okinawa and the Bonins," May 30, 1967, box 1 (General and Unprocessed)/Morton H. Halperin, NSC, LBJ Library.

73. U.S.-Japan relations policies, August 13, 1967, oral transcript, tape 16, papers of U. Alexis Johnson, LBJ Library.

74. Bundy and Rostow to Johnson, May 23, 1966, box 82/Ryukyus, Office Files of Bill Moyers, LBJ Library.

75. U.S.-Japan relations priorities, September 28, 1968; and Morton Halperin to Henry Kissinger, October 21, 1968; oral transcript, tape 17, papers of U. Alexis Johnson, and box 1 (General and Unprocessed)/Morton H. Halperin, NSC, LBJ Library.

76. Halperin to incoming NSC adviser Dr. Henry Kissinger, and report "Review of the International Situation" (Japan and Okinawa), January 22, 1969, box 1 (General and Unprocessed)/Morton H. Halperin, NSC, LBJ Library.

77. Author interview with Walt Rostow, July 12, 1995, at LBJ Library.

78. For the Johnson-Sato meeting, especially see Halperin to Johnson and

the lengthy, revealing report "Japan: Okinawa Reversion," December 30, 1968; press conference on Sato visit to the White House with Richard Sneider and George Christian, press secretary to the president, November 13, 1967; press conference on Sato visit to the White House with William Bundy, Haruki Mori, and Gemichi Akatani, deputy director of public affairs, Japanese Ministry of Foreign Affairs, November 15, 1967; box 1 (General and Unprocessed)/ Morton H. Halperin, NSC, and box 87/Briefings: Nov.-Dec. 1967, White House Press Office files: Background Briefings, LBJ Library.

79. Ibid. Johnson to Sato, November 14, 1967, box 253/Remarks by the President to Prime Minister Sato, Statements of LBJ, Nov. 11 1967-Nov. 18, 1967, LBJ Library.

80. Halperin to Johnson and report "Scenario on Negotiations with Japan on Okinawa and the Bonins," May 30, 1967, box 1 (General and Unprocessed)/ Morton H. Halperin, NSC, LBJ Library.

81. Author interview with Walt Rostow, July 12, 1995, at LBJ Library.

82. Halperin to Johnson and report "Japan: Okinawan Reversion," December 30, 1968, box 1 (General and Unprocessed)/Morton H. Halperin, NSC, LBJ Library.

83. Tragic incidents, September 28, 1968, oral transcript, tape 16, papers of U. Alexis Johnson, LBJ Library. Author interview with Major James Weland, U.S. Air Force Intelligence–Japan (ret.) and professor of Japanese history, Bentley College, March 12, 1996, at Waltham, Massachusetts. Weland was one of the officers involved in the F-4 incident investigation.

84. Tragic incidents, September 28, 1968, oral transcript, tape 16, papers of U. Alexis Johnson, LBJ Library.

85. Ibid., and Weland interview, March 12, 1996.

86. U.S.-Japan relations in transition, September 28, 1968, oral transcript, tape 17, papers of U. Alexis Johnson, LBJ Library.

87. Ibid.

88. Ibid.

89. Halperin to Johnson and the lengthy "Action Memo" report, "Reversion to Japan of the Ryukyus, Bonins and other Western Pacific Islands," n.d. (probably autumn 1968), box 1 (General and Unprocessed)/Morton H. Halperin, NSC, LBJ Library.

90. Ibid. For background on Japan's official and public opinion positions on the Bonins, see memo of conversation in Dr. Halperin's office between Halperin and Admiral Zenshiro Hoshina, former chairman of the LDP Security Research Council and former Diet member, and Colonel Hisatomo Matsukane, defense attaché of the Japanese embassy, October 3, 1967, box 1 (General and Unprocessed)/Morton H. Halperin, NSC, LBJ Library.

91. U.S.-Japan relations in transition, September 28, 1968, oral transcript, tape 17, papers of U. Alexis Johnson, LBJ Library.

92. Halperin to Johnson, and report "The Military Utility of Okinawa in Various Contingencies," March 24, 1967, box 1 (General and Unprocessed)/ Morton H. Halperin, NSC, LBJ Library.

93. Author interview with Walt Rostow, July 12, 1995, LBJ Library.

94. Halperin to Secretary of Defense Robert McNamara, and report "US Bases and Forces in Japan and Okinawa," November 18, 1968; Halperin to the Joint Chiefs of Staff, November 18, 1968; Halperin to Johnson, and report "Japan: Okinawan Reversion," December 30, 1968, box 1(General and Unprocessed)/Morton H. Halperin, NSC, LBJ Library.

95. "The Quantitative Restrictions Issue," in "Administrative History of the Department of State," vol. 1, 1968, box 3/chapter 7, Administrative History of the Department of State, vol. 1, chapters 7-9, LBJ Library. Author interview with Walt Rostow, July 12, 1995, at LBJ Library.

96. Ibid. (Rostow interview). Halperin to Kissinger, and report "Review of the International Situation," January 22, 1969, box 1 (General and Unprocessed)/Morton H. Halperin, NSC, LBJ Library.

97. Ibid.

Chapter 3: From Golf-Ball Diplomacy to the Ford Interlude

1. A. Lewis Burridge, president of the American Chamber of Commerce in Japan (ACCJ), to Nixon, plus ACCJ *Journal* enclosure: "Joint Japanese-American Trade Assures Far East Freedom," May 15, 1964, call no. 37/38, Pre-Presidential Papers, Richard M. Nixon Library and Birthplace, Yorba Linda, California (hereafter, NL–Yorba Linda). Nixon's presidential papers are located at the new National Archives facility near the campus of the University of Maryland–College Park. Their official reference is the "Nixon Project Papers."

2. For basic background on Nixon and Asian/Pacific interests, see Nixon, "Asia After Vietnam," *Foreign Affairs* 65, no. 2 (October 1967): iii–25; Szulc, *Illusion of Peace,* pp. 1–10; Halderman and DiMona, *Ends of Power,* pp. 1–81; Goodman, *Lost Peace,* pp. 104–111; Kissinger, *White House Years,* pp. 160–171; Nixon, *Memoirs,* pp. 557–580; Ambrose, *Nixon II,* pp. 223–241.

3. See for instance Vice President Nixon's remarks at the signing ceremony of the Mutual Cooperation and Security Treaty between the United States and Japan, January 19, 1960, call no. PPS 320.51: 147, NL–Yorba Linda.

4. Nixon to Ambassador Koichiro Asakai, December 23, 1964; Max Bishop, State Department, to Nixon, plus memo on U.S.-Japan relations, August 18, 1955; Masayuki Tani, Japanese ambassador, to Nixon, December 10, 1956; Nixon to Scott Thompson, December 1, 1958; Burridge to Nixon and ACCJ *Journal* enclosure, May 15, 1964; call no. 58: call no. PPS 320.51: 24.1; call no. PPS 320.51:66; call no. PPS 320.51:113; call no. 37/38, NL–Yorba Linda.

5. Yoshida to Nixon, November 10, 1960; Nixon to Ambassador Asakai, December 23, 1964; call no. PPS 320.51:196; call no. 58, Pre-Presidential Papers, NL-Yorba Linda.

6. Burridge to Nixon and ACCJ *Journal* article, May 15, 1964, call no. 37/38, Pre-Presidential Papers, NL-Yorba Linda.

7. Ambassador U. Alexis Johnson to Nixon, plus collection/excerpts of interviews with Nixon from the Japanese press, April 13, 1967, call no. 18, NL-Yorba Linda.

8. ACCJ *Journal*, May 15, 1964, call no. 37/38, NL-Yorba Linda.

9. Johnson to Nixon and Japanese press/interview collection, April 13, 1967, call no.18, NL-Yorba Linda.

10. State Department background/review material on the Nixon-Sato relationship for President Nixon, state visit of the prime minister of Japan, November 1969, WHCF Subject Files-Japan, box 43, Nixon Project Papers (hereafter, NPP)–College Park.

11. For Japanese "expectations" of Nixon and U.S. policy, particularly with reference to trade matters, see the very revealing first chapter of Sato, *Chrysanthemum and Eagle*.

12. Changing staff recommendations for policy or even a simple greeting to a visiting head of state, Nixon often scribbled his thoughts on paper before important diplomatic events, such as the November 19–21, 1969 visit to the White House of his old friend Prime Minister Eisaku Sato. In diplomatic history, Nixon's notes can be as revealing as the Watergate tapes in political history. See Nixon's notes to the November 1969 Sato visit, President's Personal File, box 53, NPP-College Park.

13. Nixon-NSC staff discussion on July 1973 visit of Prime Minister Kakuei Tanaka of Japan to the White House, July 31, 1973, President's Personal File, box 87, NPP-College Park.

14. Isaacson, *Kissinger*, pp. 165–179; Kissinger, *American Foreign Policy*, pp. 17–43.

15. Roo Watanaabe, Division of Language Services–State Department, to Counselor Akitane Kiuchi, December 24, 1971, and file: translations of Japanese press interviews with Dr. Kissinger; Hugh Scott, Senate Republican Leader, to Dr. Kissinger, and memo, "For the Creation of a New Era in Japan," December 8, 1971; report by Martin Anderson, Foreign Economic Policy Task Force, on the 1969 goals of U.S. foreign economic policy, WHCF-Subject Files (CO75-Japan), box 44 and 7, and Martin Anderson Papers, Task Force Subject Files/Foreign Economic Policy-1969, box 45, NPP-College Park.

16. Kissinger supported strong "executive privilege" for a strong foreign policy. Kissinger, *White House Years*, p. 65; Richard Nixon, "Radio Address on the Philosophy of Government," October 21, 1972, Nixon, *Public Papers: 1972*, p. 998–1000; Litwak, *Detente*, p. 126.

17. Peter Peterson to Anthony J. Jurich, May 24, 1971; Kissinger to Nixon,

June 7, 1971; William Rehnquist to Nixon, and attachments, August 17 and 18, 1971; Noble Melencamp to Secretary of State Rogers, September 14, 1971, WHCF, White House Staff Offices, 1971–74, box 61/ST51-3 Ryukyus, NPP-College Park. *Japan Times,* "Interview with Kiichi Miyazawa," pp. 10–11.

18. Maga, "Keeping the Peace," p. 1.

19. William Kintner, director, Foreign Policy Research Institute, to Kissinger, July 19, 1973, and enclosure: "Prescriptions for Strengthening Japanese-U.S. Relations," WHCF: Subject Files, CO75-Japan, box 44, NPP-College Park.

20. Kissinger, *World Restored,* p. 326.

21. A grateful electorate fed the Nixon administration's argument for more and not less "executive privilege" in foreign-policy making. This is a major point of the Nixon chapter in Arnold, *Managerial Presidency.*

22. U.S.-Japan Trade Strategies, memo and Report, April 1969, WHCF, Staff Member and Office Files: Hendrick S. Houthakker, Subject File: Trade, box 49, NPP-College Park.

23. Bruce Kehrli to H. R. Haldeman, October 5, 1969 and September 18, 1971, plus memo, "Blasting Foundations;" Haldeman to Buchanan, September 9, 1971; Dwight Chapin to Buchanan, April 24, 1969; See also the jottings of H. R. Haldeman on U.S.-Japan relations for July–September 1971, White House Special Files: H. R. Haldeman, August–September 1971, and Haldeman notes: July–September 1971, part 1, NPP-College Park.

24. Peter Peterson to Bob Haldeman and John Ehrlichman, August 4, 1971; Richard Allen to Peter Peterson, August 4, 1971 and transcript of secret tape of White House conversation with Wilbur Mills on the trade bill: "Your Conversation with Wilbur Mills;" Peter Peterson to Jon Huntsman and memo on "liberals turning protectionist," August 10, 1971; Fred Bergsten to Kissinger and memo, "U.S. Textile Position," October 24, 1970 and April 17, 1970 memo, "Wilbur Mills Import Quota Bill"; Peter Flanigan memos for the files, "Miyazawa and trade," October 12, 1970, and "The President's Impatience," March 15, 1970; WHCF, Subject Files: CO75-Japan, 1/1/71-6/30/71, box 43, NPP-College Park.

25. Ibid. (box 43), plus Harry Dent to Peter Peterson, August 12, 1971 also from NPP-College Park; Charles Colson to Lamar Alexander and one of six special reports on White House trade policy vs. the Democratic Congress: "Partisan Republican who is Middle-of-the-Road on Trade," November 14, 1969; Harry Dent to Bryce Harlow and memo on "Textiles," March 13, 1970; Harlow to Nixon, March 30, 1970; C. Fred Bergsten to Kissinger, and memo, "The Over-all Foreign Policy Implications of Textiles," March 30, 1970; White House Special Files, Staff Member and Office Files: Charles W. Colson, box 117; and WHCF, Subject Files, CO75-Japan, 11/18/69-6/30/71, November 18, 1969–June 30, 1971, NPP-College Park.

26. Robert Ellsworth, assistant to the president, to Nixon (with memo

from Kissinger on "textile/trade politics"), February 14, 1969; Hollings to Nixon, November 25, 1969; Nixon to Hollings, January 9, 1970; Lindsay Grant to Kissinger and memo, "Sen. Hollings," December 30, 1969; Prime Minister Sato to Kissinger, January 21, 1970; Peter Flanigan to Nixon and an extensive, exhaustive report on "Alternative Strategies on Trade Policy," July 23, 1970; WHCF, Subject Files, CO75-Japan, box 43, and White House Special Files, Staff Member and Office Files, Charles W. Colson, box 117, NPP–College Park.

27. Peter Flanigan to Treasury Secretary Maurice Stans and memo, "Okinawa and trade connections," October 24, 1969; General Haig to John Price, and memo, "Proposal Regarding Japanese Assistance for Vietnam, June 21, 1971; John Holdridge, NSC, to Haig, June 8 and 17, 1971; John Price to Kissinger, and memo, "Japanese Proposal re Vietnam," May 20, 1971; Brian Quickstad to Nixon, n.d. (probably June 1971), WHCF, Subject Files, CO75-Japan, box 43, NPP-College Park.

28. Ibid. See the previous note (Quickstad to Nixon) for further detail. The Nixon staff produced a considerable amount of paper, offering detailed memos on even the most minute matters within the policy-making process.

29. Tanaka to Nixon, August 22, 1973; NSC/State Department "Briefing for the President on Prime Minister Tanaka," September 12, 1973, WHCF, Subject Files, CO75-Japan, box 45, NPP-College Park.

30. Ibid.

31. NSC/State Department Briefing for the president on Prime Minister Tanaka (and crises in U.S.-Japan relations), September 12, 1973, WHCF, Subject Files, CO75-Japan, box 45, NPP-College Park.

32. Ibid.

33. Personal notes (handwritten) of President Nixon on the opening meeting with Prime Minister Tanaka, August 29, 1972, President's Personal File, 1972, box 79, NPP-College Park.

34. Transcripts of the Nixon-Tanaka meeting (Honolulu), August 1972, WHCF, Subject Files, CO75-Japan, box 45, NPP-College Park.

35. Ibid.

36. Anthony Jurich, State Department, to Peter M. Flanigan, July 10, 1973; Peter Flanigan to Deane Hinton and memo on U.S.-Japan trade, August 9, 1973; Maurice Stans, treasury secretary, to Frederick Dent, secretary of commerce, August 13, 1973; W. D. Eberle, special trade representative, to John Burns, governor of Hawaii, August 20, 1973; Takeshi Yasukawa, Japanese ambassador to the United States, to Nixon, September 6, 1973; Tanaka to Nixon, August 22, 1973, WHCF, Subject Files, CO75-Japan, box 45, NPP-College Park.

37. Terrence O'Donnell to Alexander Haig, and memo, "Visits by Foreign Heads of State," June 12, 1973, WHCF, Subject Files, Co75-Japan, box 44.

38. Tanaka to Nixon, August 22, 1973, WHCF, Subject Files, CO75-Japan, box 45, NPP-College Park.

39. Buchanan to John Connally, and memo, "The Need for a Fighting

President," January 20, 1972, with August 1973 updates; John Holdridge, NSC, to Alexander Haig, May 2, 1972, and memo, "USIA Poll Shows U.S. Image in Japan Slipping Among General Public," White House Special Files, H. R. Haldeman, Talking Papers, box 153, and WHCF, Subject Files, CO75-Japan, box 44, NPP-College Park.

40. "USIA poll" (see note 39).

41. William Kintner, director, Foreign Policy Research Institute, to Kissinger, and report, "Prescriptions for Strengthening Japanese-U.S. Relations," July 19, 1973, WHCF, Subject Files, CO75-Japan, box 45, NPP-College Park.

42. Colloquium on U.S.-Japan Relations, Office of the Undersecretary of State, John Irwin, n.d. (probably autumn 1973), White House Special Files, H. R. Haldeman, Talking Papers, box 153, NPP-College Park.

43. Ibid.

44. Kissinger to David Parker, May 6, 1974, and background Kissinger-authored memos on the "Buy Japan" policy, October 23, 1972, September 28 and 29, 1972, WHCF, Subject Files, CO75-Japan, box 7, NPP-College Park.

45. John Caldwell, executive secretary of the Advisory Council on Japan-U.S. Economic Relations to Special Assistant Peter Flanigan, and reports from the joint meetings of the executive committees of the Japan-U.S. Council and the Advisory Council on Japan-U.S. Economic Relations, February 9, 1974, WHCF, Subject Files, IT (International Organizations), box 9, NPP-College Park.

46. For full background on the Ford era, see Greene, *Presidency of Gerald R. Ford*. For shorter reviews of U.S. opinion and the early Ford presidency, see Makin and Hellmann, *Sharing World Leadership?* pp. 3–40; Schulzinger, *Henry Kissinger,*, pp. 163–184; Ford, *Autobiography*, pp. 35–41.

47. Edward J. Savage, NSC, to Ford, and "Briefing Book for President's Trip to the Far East," Japan chapters, Political and Economic Papers, November 1974, Papers of Edward J. Savage, box 3/Japan-President's Trip to the Far East, Gerald R. Ford Library, Ann Arbor, Michigan (hereafter, Ford Lib.).

48. Ibid.

49. Ford, *A Time to Heal*, pp. 210–211.

50. Charles H. McCall, editorial and speechwriting staff, White House, to Ford, October 17, 1974, and press articles from *Baltimore Sun* and *Washington Post* on Tanaka's political troubles, Papers of Charles H. McCall, box 18/6.27 Japan, Ford Lib.

51. Ibid.; Christopher, *The Japanese Mind*, p. 55.

52. Japan Trip Briefing Book, November 1974, Papers of Edward J. Savage, box 3/President's Trip to the Far East, 11/74-Briefing Book, Japan, Ford Lib.

53. Roy L. Ash, White House staff, to Ford and memo, "Acting Secretary Ingersoll's October 26 Memo to you," October 26, 1974; Acting Secretary of State Ingersoll to Ford, and memo, "U.S.-Japan Cultural Legislation," October

26, 1974, Papers of Patrick O'Donnell and Joseph Jenckes, Congressional Relations Office, box 6/Japanese-American Relations, Ford Lib.

54. Ibid.

55. The Ford administration, always concerned about the Watergate-like significance of the Lockheed scandal and its impact on U.S.-Japan relations, kept a close watch on Lockheed-related developments in Japan, in the U.S. Congress, and elsewhere. Indeed, the Ford Library maintains a remarkable archive of more than three thousand pages of Ford administration memos, reports, and legal wranglings on Lockheed.

56. Schmults to Ford and classified report/history, "Lockheed and Questionable Foreign Payments by U.S. Companies," March 2, 1976, Presidential Handwriting File, box 16/Task Force on Questionable Corporate Payments Abroad, Ford Lib.

57. Ibid. Ford, *A Time to Heal,* pp. 178–181.

58. "Lockheed and Questionable Foreign Payments by U.S. Companies," March 2, 1976, Presidential Handwriting File, box 16/Task Force on Questionable Payments Abroad, Ford Lib.; Welfield, *Empire in Eclipse,* pp. 322–333.

59. U.S. Embassy, Tokyo to Kissinger, and confidential report, "The Political Situation in Japan," November 7, 1975, Records of the White House Economic Affairs Office, box 189/Kissinger, Ford Lib.

60. House of Councillors-Japan to Ford with "Resolution on the Lockheed Problem," February 23, 1976, Papers of Edward J. Savage, box 3/Japan, Ford Lib.

61. Brent Scowcroft, NSC, to Ford and memo, "Charges of Lockheed Bribery," March 10, 1976, and Tom Braden, "Fostering Our Relations With Japan," *Los Angeles Times* editorial clipping of April 1, 1975, Papers of Edward J. Savage, box 3/Japan, and press clippings file from Charles H. McCall, editorial and speechwriting staff, director of research, box 18/6.27 Japan, Ford Lib.

62. Les Janka to Ron Nessen, and memo, "Nuclear Weapons in Japan," October 12, 1974, Papers of Ron Nessen, box 123/Japan, Ford Lib.

63. Norman Pearlstine, "Strained Alliance: U.S. Economic Policy, Nuclear Weapons Stir Considerable Controversy in Japan," *Wall Street Journal,* October 15, 1974, article from press clipping file; Jim Conner to Brent Scowcroft and "Report by Senator Mansfield on Trip to Japan," August 6, 1976; Mansfield to Ford, August 2, 1976; Max Friedersdorf, Congressional Relations Office: assistant to the president, legislative affairs, to Ford and memo, "Senator Mike Mansfield," August 2, 1976; NSC "Memo of Conversation between Senator Mike Mansfield and Prime Minister Takeo Miki," August 13, 1976, Papers of Charles H. McCall, box 18/6.27 Japan, and President Ford Committee Campaign Records, box 3/Countries-Japan, Ford Lib.

64. Don Oberdorfer, "Miki Enters at Trying Time for Japan," *Washington Post,* December 9, 1974, press clipping file; transcript of interview ("Issues and

Answers" television program, ABC News) of Prime Minister Miki by Bob Clark and Ted Koppell, Charles H. McCall Papers, box 18/6.27 Japan, and Ron Nessen Papers, box 66/Issues and Answers, Ford Lib. Welfield, *Empire in Eclipse*, p. 333.

65. Ambassador William Kintner to John O'Marsh, counsellor to the president, and "special report, "U.S. Policy Interests in the Asian/Pacific Area," Japan chapter, October 31, 1975, White House Central File, box 4/Asian/Pacific Area-U.S. Policy, Ford Lib.

66. William L. Seidman, assistant to the president, economic affairs, to NSC advisers, and "Memo on Pending Court Decision Affecting Imports from Japan," December 22, 1976; William E. Simon and Frederick B. Dent, Treasury Department, to Ford, and memo on Zenith Corporation, December 16, 1976; John Marsh, counsellor to the president, to Seidman, December 28, 1976; Papers of William L. Seidman, box 98/Special Trade Representative-Japanese Imports, Ford Lib.

67. Kissinger speech to the Japan Society, New York, June 18, 1975, Papers of the White House Economic Affairs Office, box 189/Kissinger, Ford Lib.

68. William Nichols, general counsel, Office of Management and Budget, to Max Friedersdorf, and memo, "Emperor Hirohito's State Visit," September 30, 1975; Patrick O'Donnell to James Lynn and James Cannon, assistants to the president, domestic affairs, and memo, "Emperor Hirohito's State Visit," September 29, 1975; John Saar, "Seal on U.S.-Japan Amity. Tokyo Sees Hirohito's Trip as National Adventure," *Washington Post*, September 30, 1975, press clipping file; Congressional Papers, O'Donnell and Jenckes, box 6/Japanese-American Relations, and Papers of Charles H. McCall, box 18/6.27 Japan, Ford Lib.

69. Schulzinger, *Henry Kissinger*, p. 2.

Chapter 4: What to Do?

1. "Mansfield and Japan," State Department background material to Mansfield appointment to Tokyo, October 1977, box 37 of White House Central File, Subject File-Japan, Jimmy Carter Library (hereafter, Carter Library).

2. Vance to Carter, "Suggested Themes for the President's Meeting with Members of the Japanese Diet," June 19, 1979; Office of the Secretary of State, "U.S. Policy Toward East Asia," June 23, 1979; Vance news conference, Q. and A. on U.S.-Japan Relations, June 22, 1979, box 19/Japan Summit, of the Gerald Rafshoon Papers, Carter Library. Vance, *Hard Choices*, p. 130.

3. State Department memo (for press release) on U.S.-Japan relations during the Carter presidency, January 29, 1980, box 14/U.S.-Japan Relations, U.S. Policy Collection, Carter Library.

4. Carter address on Human Rights, Notre Dame University, October 10,

1976, box 8/Human Rights, Speechwriters-James Fallows Papers, Carter Library. Carter, *Why Not The Best?* pp. 145–146.

5. Zbigniew Brzezinski, NSC chairman, to Rick Hertzberg and Rick Inderfurth, Speechwriters, and memo, "The World We Inherited," January 11, 1978, and attached press clipping from *Washington Post*, "Carter Sees Progress in Foreign Policy: No Easy Roads," box 30/Human Rights, Speechwriters-Subject Papers, Carter Library.

6. See the introduction to U.S. Congress, House of Representatives, *Conduct of Monetary Policy: Hearings before the Committee on Banking, Finance, and Urban Affairs*, 95th Cong., 1st Sess. (Washington, D.C., 1977).

7. U.S. Government, *Report of the Council of Economic Advisors*, p. 124. For background, see the Brookings Institution's fine, in-depth analysis, Destler et al., *Managing an Alliance*.

8. U.S. Congress, *Conduct of Monetary Policy*, p. 93.

9. Ibid.

10. State Department memo (for press release) on U.S.-Japan relations during the Carter presidency, January 29, 1980, box 14/U.S.-Japan Relations of U.S. Policy Collection, Carter Library.

11. Denison, "Interview," pp. 9–12; Pippert, *Spiritual Journey*, pp. 225–242; Rainone, "Lillian Carter Talks," pp. 51–52; Maga, *World of Jimmy Carter*, pp. 2–3.

12. Carter press conference, ambassador's residence, Tokyo, June 26, 1979, box 19/Japan Summit, Gerald Rafshoon Papers, Carter Library.

13. Memo on "Political Themes," Carter to the Democratic National Committee, January 6, 1978, box 3/Carter Administration Political Themes, Speechwriters-Subject File, Carter Library.

14. These ideas were announced in two poorly covered 1976 campaign speeches. In the first post-Vietnam presidential election, both Carter and the press kept far away from foreign-affairs-related discussions. See Carter speech at the Iowa State Fairgrounds, August 25, 1976 and Carter, "Remarks on Nuclear Policy," San Diego, September 25, 1976, box 6/Farm Policy and box 8/Nuclear Policy, Speechwriters-James Fallows Papers, Carter Library.

15. Carter address to the Foreign Policy Association, June 23, 1976, General Speeches File-Campaign '76, Carter Library.

16. Ibid.

17. Ibid.

18. "Remarks of the President at a State Dinner hosted by the Emperor," Tokyo, June 25, 1979, box 19/Japan Summit, Gerald Rafshoon Papers, Carter Library.

19. "U.S.-Japan Relations," (a State Dept. informal history of the Carter presidency's contribution), January 1980, box 14 of U.S. Policy Papers/U.S.-Japan Relationship, Carter Library.

20. Impromptu Carter interview with Ed Walsh (*Washington Post*) and

Johanna McGeary (*Time*), Meiji Shrine, Tokyo, June 25, 1979, box 19/Japan Summit, Gerald Rafshoon Papers, Carter Library.

21. Ibid.; Stu Eizenstat, Carter speechwriter, to Carter, April 19, 1977, box 31/Speechwriters-Subject File, First 100 Days and Foreign Affairs, Carter Library.

22. "Trade Between Japan and the United States: The Setting, the Current U.S. Position and U.S. Prospects," Department of the Treasury and NSC report/investigation, April 1978, box 8/Japan Study 2, in Japan Study Papers, Carter Library.

23. Ibid.; Tadashi Yamamoto, Japan-United States Economic Relations Group, to Bob Ingersoll, U.S. chairman, February 17, 1980; and the NSC-supported "A United States Industrial Policy" as told to the *Wall Street Journal*, January 12, 1981, box 8/Japan Study 2 in Japan Study Papers, and box 14/U.S.-Japan Relationship in U.S. Policy Papers, Carter Library.

24. Rick Hertzberg to Alonzo McDonald and memo, "Foreign Relations: Helmut Schmidt," December 4, 1979, box 9/Foreign Policy, Speechwriters-Subject Papers, Carter Library. Helga Haftendorn, "Germany," in May, *American Cold War Strategy*, pp. 183–184.

25. "Helmut Schmidt," December 4, 1979, box 9/Foreign Policy, Speechwriters-Subject Papers, Carter Library. Brzezinski, *Power and Principle*, pp. 290–295, 301–311, 461–464.

26. Report by W. Michael Blumenthal, secretary of the treasury, to the Los Angeles World Affairs Council, February 2, 1979, box 32/Trade of the Speechwriters-Subject File, Carter Library.

27. "U.S. Policy Toward East Asia/Japan," report and review by White House Secretary's Office, June 23, 1979, box 9/Foreign Policy, Speechwriters-Subject File, Carter Library.

28. Anthony Solomon, treasury undersecretary, "Trade Between Japan and the United States: The Setting, the Current U.S. Position, and U.S. Prospects," April 1978, box 8/Japan Study (2) of the Chronicle Files, Carter Library.

29. Jones, *Trusteeship Presidency*, pp.68–98; George, *Presidential Decision-making*, pp. 195–196.

30. For background, see Welfield, *Empire in Eclipse*, pp. 329–331.

31. For further background on the troubled Washington-Tokyo relationship and even more basic foreign-policy-making problems in the Carter years, see Hoffmann, "The Hell of Good Intentions," 29: 3–26. "Difficulties Lie Ahead in U.S.-Japan Relations"—interviews with U. Alexis Johnson, former U.S. ambassador to Japan," by Anthony Lake's State Department policy-planning staff in January 1980, box 14/U.S.-Japan Relations of the U.S. Policy Papers, Carter Library.

32. Ibid.

33. Press briefing by Cyrus Vance, (U.S.-Korea-Japan relations) secretary

of state, Hotel Shilla, Seoul, Korea, July 1, 1979, box 19/Japan Summit, Rafshoon Papers, Carter Library.

34. Impromptu Carter interview (see note 20).

35. See Lake's argumentative introduction to *The Vietnam Legacy* (1976). This book won him the appointment to head the policy-planning staff at State.

36. Stu Eizenstat, Carter speechwriter, to Carter, April 19, 1977, box 31/ Speechwriters-Subject File, First 100 Days and Foreign Affairs, Carter Library.

37. Neu to Carter, and Carter (although the signature appears to be a bad forgery by a staffer) to Neu, December 1976, box 7/Issues and Policy of the Hamilton Jordan Papers, Carter Library.

38. Muravchik, *Uncertain Crusade,*, pp. 1–7.

39. Mansfield to Carter, and Carter to Mansfield, October 25, 1977, box 37, White House Central File, Subject File-Japan, Carter Library.

40. Ibid.

41. Senate hearings testimony in USCAR, *Final Report, 1972.*

42. "Mansfield and Japan," State Department background material to Mansfield appointment to Tokyo, October 1977, box 37 of White House Central File, Subject File-Japan, Carter Library.

43. Ibid.; press conference, ambassador's residence-Tokyo, June 26, 1979, box 19/Japan Summit, Rafshoon Papers, Carter Library.

44. Jack B. Button, executive director, Japan–United States Economic Relations Group, to Robert Ingersoll, U.S. chairman, Japan–United States Economic Relations Group, January 25, 1980, box 14/U.S.-Japan Relations, of the U.S. Policy Papers, Carter Library. Button enclosed a number of press clippings that echoed the Japanese press and political community's anti-American bias dating back to the beginning of the Carter administration.

45. Ibid.

46. Ibid.

47. As always, Mansfield spoke candidly about his service as ambassador for Jimmy Carter during his lively commencement speech before the graduating class of the University of Maryland-Asian Division, New Sanno Hotel, Tokyo, May 14, 1987— author transcript. Brzezinski to Carter, April 18, 1977, and memo, "Public Understanding of Your Foreign Policy-Japan," box 3/ Political Themes, Speechwriters-Subject File, Carter Library.

48. Mansfield address, New Sanno Hotel-May 1987; National Security Council memo on Japan and nuclear policy, June 1, 1978, and similar memo from James Fallows to Carter, October 6, 1978, box 18 of the International Organizations Papers and box 10/Press Conference Briefing, Speechwriters-James Fallows Papers, Carter Library.

49. Ibid.

50. Ibid.

51. Ibid.

52. Office of the Secretary of State, memo, "Legislative Restrictions," August 16, 1977, box 10/Press Conference Briefing of Speechwriters-James Fallows Papers, Carter Library.

53. Office of the Secretary of State, memo, "Multilateral Trade Negotiations," August 15, 1978, ibid.

54. Carter, *Keeping Faith*, p. 113; "Remarks of the President in a Town Hall Meeting," Shimoda, Japan, June 27, 1979, box 19/Japan Summit, Rafshoon Papers, Carter Library.

55. Ibid. (see entire note 54).

56. "Press Briefing by Cyrus Vance," July 1, 1979, box 19/Japan Summit, Rafshoon Papers, Carter Library.

57. Memo on the Ryukyus issue, Executive Office of the President, Office of Management and Budget, January 24, 1979, box CO-4/Ryukyu, WHCF, Carter Library.

58. See the "America and the Pacific" section to Carter's lengthy campaign speech to the Foreign Policy Association, June 23, 1976, and memo on the "Trade Deficit," that includes Carter's public comments (and speechwriter-suggested updates), August 16, 1978, box 6/Foreign Policy and box 10/Press Conference Briefing of the Speechwriters-James Fallows Papers, Carter Library.

59. Carter press conference, August 16, 1978, box 10/Press Conference Briefing of the Speechwriters-James Fallows Papers, Carter Library.

60. "Background Briefing Aboard Air Force One," July 1, 1979, box 19/Japan Summit, Rafshoon Papers, Carter Library.

61. Carter and Vance interview with ROK reporter So-Whan Hyon, June 23, 1979; and George W. Ball, former undersecretary of state, to Vance, February 5, 1980, box 9/Foreign Policy of the Speechwriters-Subject Papers and box 14/U.S.-Japan Relationship of U.S. Policy Papers, Carter Library.

62. "Trade Between Japan and the United States: The Setting, the Current U.S. Position and U.S. Prospects," Department of the Treasury and NSC report/investigation, April 1978; Tadashi Yamamoto, Japan-United States Economic Relations Group, to Bob Ingersoll, U.S. Chairman, February 17, 1980; and the NSC-supported "A United States Industrial Policy" as told to the *Wall Street Journal,* January 12, 1981, box 8/Japan Study 2 in Japan Study Papers, box 14/U.S.-Japan Relationship in U.S. Policy Papers, Carter Library.

63. Ibid.

64. Author interview with Edmund Muskie, former senator and secretary of state, law office of Chadbourne and Parke, Washington, D.C., December 29, 1992.

65. Town Meeting, Shimoda, June 27, 1979, box 19/Japan Summit, Rafshoon Papers, Carter Library.

66. For the agricultural issue and Carter involvement, see "Agricultural Trade Issues," a Carter presidency review and analysis in "Report of the Japan–United States Economic Relations Group," January 1981; and remarks by W. Michael Blumenthal, secretary of the treasury, to the Los Angeles World Affairs Council, February 2, 1979, box 13/Report (Progress) of the Records of the Japan-U.S. Economic Relations Group, and box 32/Trade, Speechwriters-Subject File, Carter Library. Boyle, *Modern Japan*, pp. 381–385.

67. "Direct Investment in Japan: Why is it so Small?" Report by Jack Button, Japan-United States Economic Relations Group, sent to Mark Zimmerman, general manager of Winthrop Laboratories-Japan, October 15, 1980, box 14/U.S.-Japan Relationship, U.S. Policy Papers, Carter Library.

68. Button to James Balloun, McKinsey and Co., plus press clipping enclosures on the Suzuki government, June 12, 1980, box 14/U.S.-Japan Relationship, Carter Library.

69. For the twists and turns of the late 1970s U.S.-Japan economic relationship, see "Background on Nobuhiko Ushiba," White House Press Secretary's Office, June 25, 1979; Carter-Mansfield news conference, Tokyo, June 26, 1979; Carter-Ohira news conference, June 29, 1979; Anthony Solomon, undersecretary of the treasury, "Trade Between Japan and the United States: The Setting, the Current U.S. Position, and U.S. Prospects," April 1978; box 19/ Japan Summit, Rafshoon Papers and box 8/Japan Study (2), Chronicle Files, Carter Library.

70. "U.S. Policy Toward East Asia," report and review by White House Press Secretary's Office and attached file of *Tokyo Shimbun* and *Asahi Shimbun* newspaper reports, June 23, 1979; Carter interview with So-Whan Hyon, June 23, 1979 and Carter to Park, July 1, 1979, box 9/Foreign Policy, Speechwriters-Subject File, box 14/U.S.-Japan Relationship, U.S. Policy Papers, box 19/Japan Summit, Rafshoon Papers, Carter Library. Fallows, "Passionless Presidency," p. 36.

71. Rafshoon to Carter, June 1, 1979; Carter interview with Yuichiro Hayashi, Kyodo News Service, June 23, 1979, box 19/Japan Summit, Rafshoon Papers, Carter Library.

72. Carter/Hayashi interview.

73. Tom Thornton, NSC, to James Fallows, year-end report on human rights and the UN, December 1980, box 7/NSC, Speechwriters-Fallows Papers, Carter Library.

74. National Defense Report, 1980/81, ibid.

75. "Swing Strategy-Japan," DOD report, February 1980; "America's Strengthening of its Military Power and Japan," *Tokyo Shimbun*, February 1, 1980, p.4, box CO-4/Pacific, WHCF, Subject File, and box 14/U.S.-Japan Relationship, U.S. Policy Papers, Carter Library.

76. Mansfield confessed his frustrations with both Carter and his old

friend Ed Muskie. Author interview with Edmund Muskie, December 29, 1992; Author interview with former Japanese Prime Minister Kiichi Miyazawa, Hotel Washington, Hachinohe, Tohoku, Japan, May 14, 1989.

77. Ishihara, *Japan That Can Say No*, pp. 17–25.

Postscript

1. Paul Kennedy, "America in Decline?" p. 383.
2. Ibid., p. 391.

Sources

PRIMARY SOURCES

Unpublished Material

COLLECTIONS

John F. Kennedy Library
Boston, Massachusetts

McGeorge Bundy Papers
Roger Hilsman Papers
Arthur M. Schlesinger Jr. Papers
Theodre Sorensen Papers
James Thomson Papers
Guam Files
National Security Files (NSF)
President's Official File (POF)
U.S. Senate Files
White House Central File (WHCF)

Lyndon Baines Johnson Library
Austin, Texas

Classified Administrative History of the Department of State, 1968
Confidential File
National Security Council Papers
Office Files of Bill Moyers
Oral History Transcript: Diary of U. Alexis Johnson, U.S. Ambassador
    to Japan
Papers of Sen. Lyndon Johnson
Papers of Morton H. Halperin

Remarks and Statements of President Lyndon Baines Johnson
White House Central File (WHCF)
White House Press Office Files

Richard M. Nixon Library and Birthplace, Pre-Presidential Papers
Yorba Linda, California

Call no. 18
Call no. 37/38
Call no. 58
Call nos. PPS 320.51: 24.1; 66; 113; 147

Richard M. Nixon Presidential Project Papers, National Archives II
College Park, Maryland.

Martin Anderson Papers
President's Personal File (PPF)
White House Central File (WHCF)
White House Special Files—Charles W. Colson
White House Special Files—H. R. Haldeman

Gerald R. Ford Library
Ann Arbor, Michigan

Congressional Papers File
Papers of Charles H. McCall
Papers of Edward J. Savage
Papers of Patrick O'Donnell and Joseph Jenckes
Papers of Ron Nessen
Papers of William L. Seidman
Presidential Handwriting File
Records of the White House Economic Affairs Office
White House Central File (WHCF)

Jimmy Carter Library
Atlanta, Georgia

Chronicle Files
General Speeches File—Campaign '76
International Organizations Papers
Japan Study Papers
Hamilton Jordan Papers
Gerald Rafshoon Papers
Records of the Japan-U.S. Economic Relations Group
Speechwriters—James Fallows Papers

Speechwriters—Subject File
U.S. Policy Collection
White House Central File (WHCF)

AUTHOR INTERVIEWS

Kiichi Miyazawa
Edmund S. Muskie
Walt Rostow
James Weland

Analytical, Narrative, and Published Material

Allen, George. *Japan's Economic Recovery* (London: Macmillan, 1960).

Ambrose, Stephen. *Nixon II: The Triumph of a Politician, 1962–1972* (New York: Simon and Schuster, 1989).

Arnold, Peri E. *Making the Managerial Presidency: Comprehensive Reorganization Planning, 1905-1980* (Princeton: Princeton University Press, 1986).

Asahi Shimbun. *The Pacific Rivals: A Japanese View of Japanese-American Relations* (Tokyo: Asahi Shimbun, 1972).

Blackburn, Robert M. *Mercenaries and Lyndon Johnson's "More Flags:" The Hiring of Korean, Filipino, and Thai Soldiers in the Vietnam War* (Jefferson, N.C.: McFarland, 1994).

Boyle, John Hunter. *Modern Japan: The American Nexus* (Fort Worth, Tex.: HBJ, 1993).

Brands, H. W. *The Wages of Globalism: Lyndon Johnson and the Limits of American Power* (New York: Oxford University Press, 1995).

Brzezinski, Zbigniew. *Power and Principle: Memoirs of the National Security Advisor, 1977–1981* (New York: Farrar, Straus and Giroux, 1983).

Burner, David. *John F. Kennedy and a New Generation* (Glenview, Ill.: Scott, Foresman, 1988).

Carter, Jimmy. *Keeping Faith: Memoirs of a President* (New York: Bantam, 1982).

Carter, Jimmy. *Why Not the Best?* (Nashville: Boardman Press, 1975).

Centre for Strategic Studies, Georgetown University. *Special Report Series*, no. 7, 1968 (Washington, D.C.: Centre for Strategic Studies, 1968).

Christopher, Robert C. *The Japanese Mind* (New York: Linden Press, 1983).

Clifford, Clark. *Counsel to the President* (New York: Random House, 1991).

Dallek, Robert. *Lone Star Rising: Lyndon Johnson and his Times* (New York: Oxford University Press, 1991).

Defence Agency of Japan. *The Defence of Japan* (Tokyo: Defence Agency, 1979).

Denison, D. C. "The Interview: Jimmy Carter," *Boston Globe Magazine*, February 21, 1993, pp. 9–12.

Destler, I. M. et. al. *Managing an Alliance: The Politics of U.S.-Japanese Relations* (Washington, D.C.: Institute for International Economics, 1976).

Dugger, Ronnie J. *The Politician* (New York: Norton, 1982).

Fallows, James. "The Passionless Presidency, " *Atlantic Monthly* 233, May 1979: 36.

Fallows, James. *Looking at the Sun: The Rise of New East Asian Economic and Political Systems* (New York: Pantheon, 1994).

Ford, Gerald. *The Autobiography of Gerald R. Ford* (New York: Harper, 1979).

Ford, Gerald. *A Time to Heal: The Autobiography of Gerald R. Ford* (Norwalk, Conn.: Easton, 1987).

Frank, Isaiah and Ryokichi Hirono, eds. *How the United States and Japan See Each Other's Economy* (New York: Praeger, 1974).

Friedman, George, and Meredith LeBard. *The Coming War With Japan* (New York: St. Martin's Press, 1991).

Fukui, Haruhiro. *Party in Power: The Japanese Liberal Democrats and Policy-Making* (Canberra: National University Press, 1970).

George, Alexander. *Presidential Decisionmaking in Foreign Policy: The Effective Use of Information and Advice* (Boulder: University of Colorado Press, 1980).

Geyelin, Philip. *Lyndon B. Johnson and the World* (New York: Praeger, 1966).

Goodman, Allen E. *The Lost Peace: America's Search for a Negotiated Settlement of the Vietnam War* (Stanford: Stanford University Press, 1978).

Greene, John Robert. *The Presidency of Gerald R. Ford* (Lawrence: University Press of Kansas, 1995).

Haldeman, H. R., and Joseph DiMona. *The Ends of Power* (New York: Times Books, 1978).

Healy, David. *U.S. Expansionism: The Imperialist Urge in the 1890s* (Madison: University of Wisconsin Press, 1970).

Higa, Mikio. *Politics and Parties in Postwar Okinawa* (Vancouver: Publications Center of the University of British Columbia, 1963).

Hilsman, Roger. *To Move a Nation: The Politics of Foreign Policy in the Administration of John F. Kennedy* (New York: Doubleday, 1967).

Hoffmann, Stanley. "The Hell of Good Intentions," *Foreign Policy* 29 (winter 1977–78): 3–26.

Hsiao, Gene T. "The Sino-Japanese Rapprochement: A Relationship of Ambivalence," in Gene T. Hsiao, ed., *Sino-American Detente and Its Implications* (New York: Praeger, 1974).

Hunsberger, Warren S. *Japan and the United States in World Trade* (New York: Harper and Row, 1964).

Isaacson, Walter. *Kissinger: A Biography* (New York: Simon and Schuster, 1992).

Ishihara, Shintaro. *The Japan That Can Say No: Why Japan Will Be First Among Equals* (New York: Simon and Schuster, 1991).

Japan Times. "Interview with Kiichi Miyazawa: An elder statesman reflects on postwar and future Japan," *Japan Times Weekly International Edition*, August 28–September 3, 1995, pp. 10–11.

Jones, Charles O. *The Trusteeship Presidency* (Baton Rouge: Louisiana State University Press, 1988).

Kahin, George McT. *Intervention* (New York: Knopf, 1986).

Kahn, Herbert. *The Emerging Japanese Superstate* (Englewood Cliffs: Prentice Hall, 1970).

Kennan, George. "Japan's Security and American Policy," *Foreign Affairs*, 43 (October 1964): 14–28.

Kennedy, John F. *Public Papers of the President, 1961* (Washington, D.C.: GPO, 1961).

Kennedy, Paul. "America in Decline?" in Steven M. Gillon and Diane B. Kunz, *America During the Cold War* (Fort Worth: HBJ, 1993).

Kissinger, Henry. *American Foreign Policy: Three Essays* (New York: Norton, 1969).

Kissinger, Henry. *White House Years* (Boston: Little Brown, 1979).

Kissinger, Henry. *A World Restored* (London: Victor Gollancz, 1977).

Kranish, Michael. "Legacy of the Bush years blooming in the Clinton era," *Boston Globe*, October 23, 1994, pp. 1, 22.

Lake, Anthony. *The Vietnam Legacy: The War, American Society, and the Future of American Foreign Policy* (New York: New York University Press, 1976).

Lederer, William J., and Eugene Burdick. *The Ugly American* (New York: Norton, 1960).

Litwak, Robert. *Detente and the Nixon Doctrine: American Foreign Policy and the Pursuit of Stability, 1969–1976* (New York: Cambridge University Press, 1984).

Livingston, Jon, Joe Moore, and Felicia Oldfather, eds. *Postwar Japan: 1945 to the Present* (New York: Pantheon Books, 1973).

McBride, James H. *Okinawa: Pawn in the Pacific* (Maxwell Air Force Base, Ala.: Air War College, 1972).

McMahon, Robert J. *Colonialism and the Cold War* (Ithaca, NY: Cornell University Press, 1981).

Maga, Timothy P. "Keeping the Peace with Japan," in *Journal of Commerce* (December 14, 1992): 1.

Maga, Timothy P. *John F. Kennedy and the New Pacific Community, 1961–1963* (New York: Macmillan/St. Martin's, 1990).

Maga, Timothy P. "The Politics of Non-Recognition: The United States,

Australia, and China, 1961–1964," *Journal of Australian Studies*, no. 27 (November 1990): 8–18.

Maga, Timothy P. *The World of Jimmy Carter: U.S. Foreign Policy, 1977–1981* (West Haven, Conn.: University of New Haven Press, 1994).

Makin, John H., and Donald C. Hellman, eds. *Sharing World Leadership? A New Era for America and Japan* (Washington, D.C.: American Enterprise Institute, 1989).

May, Ernest R. ed. *American Cold War Strategy: Reinterpreting NSC 68* (New York: St. Martin's, 1993).

Ministry of Foreign Affairs—Tokyo, Public Information Bureau. *Okinawa: Some Basic Facts* (Tokyo: Ministry of Foreign Affairs, 1969).

Muravchik, Joshua. *The Uncertain Crusade: Jimmy Carter and the Dilemmas of Human Rights Policy* (Lanham, Md.: American Enterprise Institute, 1986).

Nixon, Richard M. "Asia After Vietnam," *Foreign Affairs* 65, no. 2 (October 1967): iii–25.

Nixon, Richard M. *Public Papers of the Presidents: Richard Nixon, 1972* (Washington, D.C.: GPO, 1974).

Nixon, Richard M. *RN: The Memoirs of Richard Nixon* (New York: Grosset & Dunlap, 1978).

Packard, George W. III. *Protest in Tokyo: The Security Treaty Crisis of 1960* (Princeton: Princeton University Press, 1966).

Parmet, Herbert. *Jack: The Struggles of John F. Kennedy* (New York: Dial Press, 1980).

Passin, Herbert, ed. *The United States and Japan* (Englewood Cliffs: Prentice Hall, 1966).

Paterson, Thomas G., ed. *Kennedy's Quest for Victory: American Foreign Policy, 1961–1963* (New York: Oxford University Press, 1989).

Pippert, Wesley, ed. *Spiritual Journey of Jimmy Carter* (New York: Harper, 1978).

Quigg, Philip W. "Japan in Neutral," *Foreign Affairs* 44, no. 2 (January 1966): 1–33.

Rainone, Nanette. "Lillian Carter Talks About Racism, the Kennedys, and 'Jimmy's Reign,'" *Ms.* (October 1976), pp. 51–52.

Reischauer, Edwin. *The United States and Japan* (Cambridge: Harvard University Press, 1970).

Roberts, Priscilla, ed. *Sino-American Relations Since 1900* (Hong Kong: University of Hong Kong Press, 1991).

Rosecrance, Richard. *The Rise of the Trading State: Commerce and Conquest in the Modern World* (New York: Basic Books, 1986).

Rosovsky, Henry, ed. *Discord in the Pacific* (Washington, D.C.: GPO, 1972).

Rostow, Walt W. *Stages of Economic Growth: A Non-Communist Manifesto* (New York: Cambridge University Press, 1960).

Rubinstein, Donald H., ed. *Pacific History* (Mangilao, Guam: University of Guam Press, 1992).

Rusk, Dean. "Reflections on Foreign Policy," in Kenneth Thompson, ed., *The Kennedy Presidency* (Lanham, Md.: University Press of America, 1985).

Sato, Ryuzo. *The Chrysanthemum and The Eagle* (New York: New York University Press, 1994).

Scalpino, Robert, and Junnosuke Masumi. *Parties and Politics in Contemporary Japan* (Berkeley: University of California Press, 1962).

Schulman, Bruce J. *Lyndon B. Johnson and American Liberalism* (Boston: Bedford Books of St. Martin's Press, 1995).

Schulzinger, Robert D. *Henry Kissinger, Doctor of Diplomacy* (New York: Columbia University Press, 1989).

Simpson, William P. *Island X: Okinawa* (W. Hanover, Mass.: Christopher Publishing, 1981).

Stevens, Russell. *Guam U.S.A.: Birth of a Territory* (Honolulu: Tongg, 1950).

Subcommittee on Foreign Economic Policy, Council on Foreign Relations. *U.S. Policy Problems Arising from Japanese Trade* (New York: Council on Foreign Relations, 1961).

Szulc, Tad. *The Illusion of Peace: Foreign Policy in the Nixon Years* (New York: Viking, 1978).

Thayer, Nathaniel B. *How the Conservatives Rule Japan* (Princeton: Princeton University Press, 1962).

Turner, Kathleen J. *Lyndon Johnson's Dual War* (Chicago: University of Chicago Press, 1985).

USCAR, Office of the High Commissioner. *Joint Economic Plan for the Ryuku Islands, 1961–1965* (Okinawa: USCAR, 1965).

USCAR, Office of the High Commissioner. *Final Report, May 14, 1972* (Okinawa: USCAR, 1972).

U.S. Congress, Committee on Appropriations. *Mutual Security Appropriations for 1961 and Related Agencies, Hearings Before the Subcommittee of the Committee on Appropriations, House of Representatives*, 86th Congress, 2nd Sess. (Washington, D.C.: GPO, 1960).

U.S. Congress, House of Representatives. *Conduct of Monetary Policy: Hearings before the Committee on Banking, Finance, and Urban Affairs*, 95th Congress, 1st Sess. (Washington, D.C.: GPO, 1977).

U.S. Government. *Report of the Council of Economic Advisors* (Washington, D.C.: GPO, 1978).

U.S. Congress. House Committee on Foreign Affairs, Subcommittee on the Far East and the Pacific. *Claims of Certain Inhabitants of the Ryukyus Islands and the Position of the Government of Japan*, 89th Congress, 1st Sess. (Washington, D.C.: GPO, 1965).

U.S. Senate. *Executive Sessions of the Senate Foreign Relations Committee*

Together With Joint Sessions With the Senate Armed Services Committee, vol. 12, 1961 (Washington, D.C.: GPO, 1985).

Vance, Cyrus. *Hard Choices* (New York: Simon and Schuster, 1983).

Watanabe, Akio. *The Okinawan Problem: A Chapter in Japan-U.S. Relations* (Carlton, Australia: Melbourne University Press, 1970).

Welfield, John. *An Empire in Eclipse: Japan in the Postwar American Alliance System* (London: Athlone Press, 1988).

Yanaga, Chitohsi. *Big Business in Japanese Politics* (New Haven: Yale University Press, 1968).

Zeiler, Thomas. *American Trade and Power in the 1960s* (New York: Columbia University Press, 1992).

Zeiler, Thomas W. "Free Trade Politics and Diplomacy: John F. Kennedy and Textiles," *Diplomatic History* 11, no. 2 (spring 1987): 127–142.

Index